The Encyclopedia
of
Cheap Travel

1,000 Companies, Consolidators, Agencies, and Resources

Terrance Zepke

ISBN 0-7414-0841-4

Published by:

PUBLISHING.COM

Infinity Publishing.com
519 West Lancaster Avenue
Haverford, PA 19041-1413
Info@buybooksontheweb.com
www.buybooksontheweb.com
Toll-free (877) BUY BOOK
Local Phone (610) 520-2500
Fax (610) 519-0261

Printed in the United States of America
Printed on Recycled Paper
Published April 2002

TABLE OF CONTENTS

Introduction

Savvy travelers can enjoy a five-star Mediterranean cruise, see lions and elephants up close on an African wildlife safari, leisurely float down the Danube River on a chartered barge, or delight in breathtaking scenery aboard a top-notch rail trip through the Rockies—for less than it costs to go to many popular U.S. vacation destinations.

This reference book reveals companies specializing in value-oriented vacations and also shares hundreds of money-saving tips and resources. Discover how to get rock-bottom airfares, cruises, bus and rail passes, car rentals, and accommodations, that range from rustic, log cabin hostels to magnificent castles. It has information on everything from cultural trips for mature travelers to hard-core adventures for women-only. There's even a section on how to travel free or get paid to travel, as well as a chapter filled with exceptional, travel-planning Web sites.

The information found throughout *The Encyclopedia of Cheap Travel* comes from years of research and experience. Having lived all over North America and Europe, and having traveled to every continent in the world during my career as a writer and photographer, I have made travel arrangements worldwide. I was often unhappy with the fare I was quoted by an airline representative or desk clerk. So, it became a challenge to see if I could do any better. To my surprise (and horror), eight times out of ten I found a cheaper fare by employing techniques and utilizing companies cited in this book.

What started out as my just trying to get the "most bang for the buck," expanded into helping friends and family, and then friends of friends and friends of family began asking for my help. I realized I was spending a great deal of time doing something I really enjoyed but wasn't getting paid for; so, I completed the necessary training and became a travel agent.

To ensure that I provide the best information and service to my clients, I read dozens of consumer and trade publications every month. I have conducted extensive Internet searches to keep on top of trends and fares. I have investigated hundreds of companies and thoroughly reviewed their brochures and catalogs. I have personally contacted every source listed in this book and have spoken with the manager or senior representative at most of them. I have also spent years exploring libraries and bookstores and remain disappointed in the selections, which consist mostly of destination-specific guides and travel essays. Books that have been written on the subject are limited to one aspect, such as hostels or airline consolidators. There is no single source that addresses all aspects of travel—let alone a book geared toward cost-conscious travelers.

The sum contents of this book come from more than my experience and research. Several years ago, I was asked to develop a continuing education travel program for a local college. As a result, I teach a series of classes each term. The participants, who range in age from 22–84 (although I have had a couple of 20-year-old college students looking for unusual, cheap ways to travel America during their summer vacations, and an 87-year-old man who took two of my classes), have served as informal focus groups. I listen to their travel experiences, what they are interested in, where they are going or want to go, and how much money they are willing or able to spend. The feedback I have gained from these 1,000+ travelers has heavily shaped what is included in this reference.

Additionally, I wanted to address the horror stories I have heard over the years from people about bad trips they took. When I questioned them, I discovered that most of the trips weren't bad ones, but they weren't what the travelers really wanted or thought they were getting. That is the point of the first chapter of this book, to make sure you know all your options and the correct questions to ask the right people. Chapter One also reveals the difference between regular travel agencies and rebate agencies. You should know this because using a rebate agency means getting up to 15 percent of your money back! You should know what Foreign Independent Travel (F.I.T.) means, because it's a cheap way to customize a trip. Chapter One also provides a list of agencies and organizations that monitor the travel industry and reveals some popular scams that have happened to even veteran travelers. It also explains how to make sure a trip is right for you. Just because a vacation is inexpensive, doesn't mean it's a bargain.

Even if you don't know where you want to go or how you want to get there (you just know you want to go), this book will serve you well. After studying *The Encyclopedia of Cheap Travel,* you will be armed with the knowledge to make the best decision for you. You will understand the difference between cruise lines and classifications, the discrepancy between soft-and hard-core adventures, and just what the heck an "interactive vacation" is. You'll also finally understand why most travel agents haven't heard of many of these terrific companies, and if travel agents did know about them, why they still wouldn't tell you. If you utilize the information given throughout this publication, you'll never pay full fare(or anything close to it) again. I promise!

It is my greatest hope that because of this book, you'll be able to take adventures you always dreamed about, at prices that you never dreamed were possible—even in your wildest dreams! As Samuel Johnson said, *The use of traveling is to regulate the imagination by reality, and instead of thinking how things may be, to see them as they are.* May all your travels be safe and rewarding (and may your camera never fail you)!

Every effort has been made to ensure that this reference is up-to-date, but area codes and Internet addresses seem to change more often than not these days. Even if this information has changed, it can easily be revealed by going online and entering a keyword(s) or the proper name of a company. If you know of a company listing or resource you think should be added, or a correction that needs to be made, please e-mail me: cheaptz@aol.com.

Chapter One--Planning Your Trip

Chapter One--Planning Your Trip

For my part, I travel not to go anywhere, but to go. I travel for travel's sake. The great affair is to move.
Robert Louis Stevenson, Travels with a Donkey (1878)

How To Find The Best Travel Agent Or Tour Operator For You

If you would like help planning a trip, seek the advice of a travel agent. They sell travel packages created by various types of tour operators and have many resources at their disposal. And, agents often have "insider" information, such as airline and tour operator mergers (or a heads up about a company going defunct), or new cruise ship debuts and destinations. The best part is that their service is free for consumers because travel agents are paid commissions by tour operators, cruise lines, airlines, and hotels. However, some agencies are now charging fees to issue airline tickets, so be sure to ask about policies before booking.

When selecting a travel agent, make sure she is familiar with the type of travel you are interested in because each agency typically has a specialty, such as corporate travel, cruises, European vacations, Caribbean packages, or adventure travel. If you're interested in adventure travel, an agent who primarily handles Caribbean resort stays and cruises isn't going to be much help. Don't be embarrassed to ask how many years she has been an agent and how long he or she has been with this particular agency. Once you have found someone you are comfortable with, you want to be assured that person knows what she is doing and is going to be available should any problems arise before you return from your trip.

Also, inquire as to whether the agency participates in "override incentives." Many airlines, tour companies, cruise lines, car rental agencies, and hotels offer these incentive payments, which are slightly higher commissions, to agencies that fulfill certain sales quotas. The downside is that the agent *may* steer you to these vendors as opposed to those that offer the absolute lowest fare. The upside is that agencies that are privy to these incentive plans can receive perks, such as client upgrades, 2-for-1s and other special deals. Most agents look out for the best interests of their loyal clients so they will present all options.

Additionally, find out if the agency provides information on visas, passports, and inoculations (both required *and* recommended), as well as current health and safety concerns. A good agent should be able to obtain this information or at least provide names and contact information of those who can help you. Always keep your agent's phone number with you when traveling and ask if the agency has a 24-hour toll-free number, in case of an emergency.

Another reason a travel agent is important is because she can put together a customized trip. This is called an F.I.T. or Foreign Independent Travel. An F.I.T. is used when a traveler wants an agent to do more than simply book a tour package or cruise. For example, I once took a packaged tour to India (pre travel-agent days), but I also wanted to spend a few days in Nepal at Katmandu and Royal Chitwan National Park. I found a side trip to Katmandu, but could find nothing for Chitwan. So, I asked my travel agent to put something together for me. He made some calls and discovered how to book a camp in the park and then he worked with the Katmandu tour operator to make transport arrangements. There's a small fee for the agent's extra time and attention, as well as to cover the costs of faxes and phone calls needed to make the special arrangements. Typically, this fee ranges from

$50–$100, depending on what is required. This fee may be waived at the discretion of your agent and should be, if you book much travel through the agency.

If the price is the same whether you use an agent or book directly with a tour company, why would you ever want to make all the arrangements yourself? Going through an agent gives travelers added protection. Many years ago, I booked a trip to Morocco through a travel agency. After I had paid in full, the company demanded more money, citing increased airfare. The travel agent did not feel this was acceptable and so he worked out a deal with the tour company whereby the added cost was not passed on to me. I think he also accepted a smaller commission, although being the good agent that he was, he did not share these details with his client. If I had not booked through an agency, I would have had no recourse but to pay the additional costs. Furthermore, there were some significant problems with this tour, which I related to my travel agent as soon as I got home. He wrote a letter to the tour operator stating his agency's displeasure with these events. Subsequently, the tour operator refunded part of the cost of the trip. A letter from the travel agency was far more effective than any letter I could have written.

However, there may be times when you travel with a company that doesn't offer commissions. Many of the listings in this reference are consolidators, who basically wholesale directly to consumers. In these cases, I recommend paying a small fee in lieu of a commission to your agent to book travel. This way, you have the protection of using a travel agency and the savings of using a consolidator. Typically, the fee is $50–100, but this depends on your relationship with the agent and the policies of the agency. If you are unfamiliar with consolidators and how they work, they are fully explained in Chapters Four and Five.

Ask your travel agent to notify you when she hears about good deals. Leave a list of places you want to go to on a small piece of paper, including how much you're willing to spend, so that it can be taped to a desk or computer as a daily reminder. Always tell the travel agent as much information as possible, including where you want to go, how long you want to stay, what activities you desire, and how much money you are willing to spend.

So, how do you find a good travel agent?

√ Start by asking friends, family, and coworkers if they can recommend an agent. Log on to www.travelhub.com for a list of certified travel agents and their areas of expertise. Contact the American Society of Travel Agents (see below) for a list of member agencies. Or, contact American Express Travel Services, BTI Americas/Executive BTI Travel, or Carlson Wagonlit Travel, which are the three largest travel agencies in the United States. Each handles a wide variety of U.S. and worldwide travel. Due to the quantity of business these agencies handle, they are able to offer exceptional deals. To find the nearest agency:

American Express Travel Services: 800-346-3607. www.americanexpress.com.
BTI Americas/Executive BTI Travel: 888-568-6676 or 815-397-1900.
www.executivebtitravel.com.
Carlson Wagonlit Travel: 800-728-1042 or 319-366-1042. www.carlsontravel.com.

√ If you don't mind making your own travel arrangements, you may want to consider using a rebate travel agency. Most people are unfamiliar with these kinds of agencies. They are different from traditional travel agencies because travelers work with an agent to plan the trip. Rebate agencies are for people who make all the arrangements and simply use an agent to issue the tickets. Without a travel agent identification number, you need an agency to issue the tickets.

Rebate agents usually charge a flat fee for each ticket issued and give a refund of 4–15 percent of the ticket price. Minus the fee charged for each ticket, that equals roughly 7 percent cash back. A rebate agent is similar to a consolidator, except:

Rebate agents provide discounts on *all* services from trips to car rentals. Dealing with a rebate travel agency can be a friendlier and easier experience because they will provide travel brochures, as well as a newsletter for repeat customers. Tickets can be purchased at a rebate agency using a check or credit card. Most consolidators only accept credit cards. If you use a credit card that offers cash back, you can increase your savings.

Many credit card companies now offer 1–5 percent cash back on purchases made. If your credit card company doesn't offer cash back, shop around until you find one that does, as long as its finance charges and policies are acceptable to you. It defeats the purpose to use a high interest rate credit card.

Two of the largest U.S. rebate agencies are listed below. Contact the American Society of Travel Agents to obtain a comprehensive list of rebate travel agencies.

Pennsylvania Travel rebates up to 10 percent of the ticket price. Fee is based on ticket cost. For example, a ticket that costs $4,000 has a fee of $150. After the 10 percent rebate ($400) and minus the issue fee ($150), yields $250. Savings are greater the higher the ticket price. The rebate check is sent after the agency receives its commission. If paying by check, you may deduct the rebate from the amount owed. 15 Maple Avenue, Paoli, PA 19301. 800-331-0947 or 610-251-9944. www.patravel.com.

Travel Avenue rebates 7 percent on domestic airline tickets, cruises, and vacations and tour packages, 7–12 percent on international flights, and 5 percent on car rentals. Travel Avenue offers bigger savings on domestic flights than Pennsylvania Travel because they charge a flat fee for any domestic ticket and the agency mails rebate checks *with* the tickets. 10 Riverside Plaza, Suite 1404, Chicago, IL 60606. 800-333-3335. www.travelavenue.com. or www.t100G.com.

√ You may contact one of the organizations listed below for a roster of member agencies or tour companies in your area. You may want to reconsider a company that is not a member of any of these associations. Additionally, the Web sites provide links to valuable resources.

American Bus Association (ABA) is the trade association of the intercity bus industry and represents the interests of the motorcoach industry. The organization fosters relationships between North American tour companies and motorcoach companies. ABA has roughly 3,000 members, including U.S. and Canadian motorcoach and tour operators, and 2,300 member organization representatives (travel and tour industry) in partnership with the North American motorcoach industry. Members must sign a Code of Ethics agreement and are monitored by an active ethics committee. ABA offers a list of reliable member operators in your area and a free directory listing all its members. 1100 New York Avenue, NW, Suite 1050, Washington, D.C. 20005-3934. 800-283-2877 or 202-842-1645. www.buses.org. e-mail: abainfo@buses.org.

American Society of Travel Agents (ASTA) is the biggest association of travel agencies in the United States. It will provide interested persons with a list of local member agencies. ASTA has rigid membership requirements to ensure maximum consumer protection. The association provides names and contact information of all agencies that specialize in the types of travel you desire. Its customer service department carefully tracks complaints of dissatisfied travelers. 1101 King Street, Suite 200,

Alexandria, VA 22314. 800-440-ASTA or 703-739-2782. Consumer Affairs Line: 703-739-8739. www.astanet.com.

The American Society of Travel Agents
Ten Commandments on Responsible Tourism

Whether you're traveling on business, pleasure or a bit of both, all the citizens of the world, current and future, would be grateful if you would respect the ten commandments of world travel:

1. Respect the frailty of the earth. Realize that unless all are willing to help in its preservation, unique and beautiful destinations may not be here for future generations to enjoy.

2. Leave only footprints. Take only photographs. No graffiti! No litter! Do not take away "souvenirs" from historical sites and natural areas.

3. To make your travels more meaningful, educate yourself about the geography, customs, manners, and cultures of the region you visit. Take time to listen to the people. Encourage local conservation efforts.

4. Respect the privacy and dignity of others. Inquire before photographing people.

5. Do not buy products made from endangered plants or animals, such as ivory, tortoise shell, animal skins, and feathers. Read "Know Before You Go," the U. S. Department of Customs' list of products which cannot be imported.

6. Always follow designated trails. Do not disturb animals, plants, or their natural habitats.

7. Learn about and support conservation-oriented programs and organizations working to preserve the environment.

8. Whenever possible, walk or use environmentally sound methods of transportation. Encourage drivers of public vehicles to stop engines when parked.

9. Patronize those (hotels, airlines, resorts, cruise lines, tour operators and suppliers) who advance energy and environmental conservation; water and air quality; recycling; safe management of waste and toxic materials; noise abatement, community involvement; and which provide experienced, well-trained staff dedicated to strong principles of conservation.

10. Encourage organizations to subscribe to environmental guidelines. ASTA urges organizations to adopt their own environmental codes to cover special sites and ecosystems.

Travel is a natural right of all people and is a crucial ingredient of world peace and understanding. With that right comes responsibilities. ASTA encourages the growth of peaceful tourism and environmentally responsible travel.

[Reprinted by permission of the American Society of Travel Agents (ASTA)]

Cruise Lines International Association (CLIA) monitors and promotes the cruise industry. It will answer questions (including a written quiz to determine your needs) and provide pertinent information, such as charts and descriptions of top cruise ships. 500 Fifth Avenue, Suite 1407, New York, NY 10110. 212-921-0066 or 888-Y-CRUISE. www.cruising.org.

The Ecotourism Society (TES) is an international, nonprofit organization. Its mission is to aid researchers, conservationists, and ecotour operators by setting standards and guidelines. TES also informs members of increasingly vulnerable parts of the world. Members must follow TES's standards of ecotourism. The group will provide travelers with a membership list. P.O. Box 668, Bennington, VT 05402. 802-651-9818. www.ecotourism.org. e-mail: ecomail@ecotourism.org

The National Tour Association (NTA) is a membership organization for North American tour operators. Strict requirements for membership include a minimum of three years in business, insurance coverage of $1 million annually, compliance with a strict code of ethics and monitoring by a review board. NTA can provide information as to whether a tour operator is a member and if any complaints filed have been filed against the operator. This information is free of charge. 546 E. Main Street, Lexington, KY 40508. 859-226-4444 or 800-682-8886. www.ntaonline.com.

Travel Industry Association of America (TIA) is a nonprofit association that "serves as the unifying organization for all components of U.S. travel industry." 1100 New York Avenue, NW, Suite 450, Washington, D.C. 20005-3934. 202-408-8422. www.tia.org.

The United States Consolidator's Association (USACA) monitors consolidators. Its Web site provides a list of all members, including contact information. 925 L. Street, Suite 22, Sacramento, CA 95814. 914-441-4166. www.usaca.com.

United States Tour Operators Association (USTOA) is an association of U.S. tour operators. It will provide a list of its members and advice about booking tours. 342 Madison Avenue, Suite 1522, New York, NY 10173. 212-559-6599. www.ustoa.com.

√ Check with the main office of the Better Business Bureau(BBB) to see if there are any complaints on file for the company in question. The BBB has more than 150 bureaus in the U.S. and Canada, which received more than 9,000 travel-related complaints annually. The BBB's mission is to "promote and foster the highest ethical relationship between businesses and the public...." Council of Better Business Bureaus, Inc., 4200 Wilson Blvd., Suite 800, Arlington, VA 22203-1804. 703-276-0100. The Better Business Bureau produces a helpful publication entitled "Tips on Travel Packages" (No. 24–195). The organization's Web site, www.bbb.com, provides instant access to business and consumer alerts, a member roster, resource library, dispute resolution, and help desk.

Consumer Reports Travel Letter recommends that unhappy travelers do more than write letters stating dissatisfaction. Consumer Reports advises that disgruntled travelers need to request compensation. Ask for a refund or credit on a future trip. "Suggest a reasonable dollar amount for your inconvenience, and provide documents to bolster your case, such as receipts, correspondence, or photos."

◆　　　◆　　　◆

How To Pick The Right Itinerary For Your Interests And Pocketbook

No matter how cheap a trip is, it's only a bargain if you get what you want *and* expect from it. To determine these things, you need to ask yourself several key questions. First, decide the kind of trip you're interested in taking. Do you prefer learning vacations over general sightseeing tours? Do you want some time on your own or all activities planned? Are you an independent traveler or the type of person who likes to leave all the arrangements to someone else? Have you always dreamed of adventure travel but don't know if it's for you? Do you like to see and do as much as possible or do you prefer to spend more time exploring fewer places?

In an effort to aid travelers in determining what kind of travel they are best suited to, the U.S. Tour Operators Association hired several psychologists to create this quiz.

1. a. I enjoy socializing in a large group.
    b. I like being in a small group.

2. a. I would never fall for bungee jumping or river rafting.
    b. Bungee jumping or river rafting would be exciting.

3. a. I would rather let others plan my fun activities.
    c. I like to plan fun things to do.

4. a. Sometimes I worry about my safety in public.
    c. I feel secure in most public places.

5. b. I prefer people who share my interests.
    c. I relate to many kinds of people.

6. a. I want to take it easy on my body.
    b. I enjoy a good physical challenge.

7. a. There is little I can do to deal with life's problems.
    c. I try to be resourceful when faced with problems.

8. b. In my free time I prefer to concentrate on specific hobbies.
    c. I seek out many different activities in my leisure time.

9. a. It feels better when my social events follow a plan.
    c. I like to have flexible plans for social activities.

10. b. I am willing to compromise with people.
    c. I like to have things my way.

11. a. I prefer to watch television.
    b. I like to read.

12. b. I would use a tour guide in a really exotic place.
    c. I want to explore a place on my own, even if it is strange and unusual.

13.   a. My idea of free time is to chill out and have no demands placed on me.
        b. Free time is a chance to enrich or challenge myself.

14.   b. I would like to work on a team project.
        c. I prefer to work on my own tasks.

15.   a. Good things in my life are due to luck.
        c. My own efforts bring me positive results.

<u>Scoring:</u>
Whatever letter you selected the most indicates the type of travel that is best for you.

<u>A = escorted group traveler</u>
You enjoy traveling with many people and like the comfort
of being taken care of.

<u>B = small group adventure traveler</u>
You like to go off the beaten path and to have a theme to your
vacation. You rely on experienced guides because it can be
difficult to get around on your own in these kinds of places.
You like small groups of travelers with similar interests.
Anything goes for you, from climbing Machu Picchu to
an Asian learning vacation.

<u>C = Independent Tour/Package Traveler</u>
You are open to new experiences, activities, and situations.
You like to travel on your own or with friends and family.
You like to be in charge of selecting activities, meals, and
timetables, and therefore like untour packages that provide
airfare, transfers, and accommodations but leave some
planning, such as meals and activities to you.

To further determine what's right for *you*, arm yourself with as much information as possible. Accumulate brochures and catalogs from companies that offer the type of travel you desire. To accomplish this, use the companies and Web sites listed throughout this book, look at the ads in travel magazines and in the back of those publications under "tour companies," go online, and browse the racks of two or three local agencies, including your travel agency.

Carefully scrutinize all these trips, asking yourself *How much money do I want to spend?* Eliminate all trips that exceed that amount. *How long do I want to be gone?* If you have 14 vacation days, rule out any trips that exceed two weeks. Once you have determined the type of experience you want, what you can afford, and vacation duration, ask yourself these questions:

1. What does the brochure *language* tell you? This may be the most important question you ask yourself. Watch for descriptive terms such as "challenging," "lengthy," "basic," "luxurious" or "all-inclusive." The language used in the brochure and itinerary will give you great insight into the trip.

2. Does the *itinerary* excite you? Does it go to the places you want to see and offer the things you want to do? For example, I recently saw what seemed like a fantastic trip. The brochure revealed a two-week sojourn to South Africa, including round-trip airfare, for a very low price. I excitedly read on and discovered it didn't go to some of the places I really wanted to see or offer the things I most wanted to do. As the old saying goes, "It's only a bargain if you can use it." If you're interested in

lectures, will an expert lecturer be accompanying you? If you're a bird watcher and you're planning a trip to Alaska, you would want an ornithologist or a naturalist leading your group. You would also want to find out if there will there be much bird watching, or if it's primarily a sightseeing trip. In other words, *Will you get what you want out of the trip?*

3. Does the itinerary share *specifics*? If you're going to Costa Rica and desire in-depth exploration of the rain forest, and the trip you are considering offers one half-day trip into the jungle, it's not really what you want and you should keep looking. If you have physical limitations, examine whether the walks or hikes are classified as "mildly invigorating" or cover "rugged" terrain. If going white-water rafting, you should look at how many hours the rafting trip is, what class of rapids you'll be experiencing (there's a big difference between Class I and Class III rapids!), and if beverages, lunch, or a snack is included. If it's a basic sightseeing tour, how much walking will be involved daily? The term "museum feet" refers to the heavy walking required on many tours. Could this be a problem for you? Could you have trouble keeping up with a fast-paced tour?

4. What's your *involvement?* Are you expected to help set up camp or to carry your luggage and supplies? For example, when you go white-water rafting, you will often help carry the rafts and paddles to the input area and back from the output area. If you go hiking and camping, you may have to carry a backpack or help put up tents or unload vans. Some trips are cheaper because you're less of a traveler than a participant. As such, you are required to have a turn at cooking or dishwashing detail. This is a small trade-off to more affordable travel and a good way to make new friends and have a more interactive experience, as long as you are aware of your role.

5. What is the total number of *nontravel days*? Do you want a 10-day trip with only four nontravel days? Do you want a vacation that is spent mostly on a tour bus? Some people want to see as much as possible, and for those, "Five European Cities in Seven Days" may be the perfect trip. Others may prefer "London and Paris in Seven Days."

6. What type of *accommodations* are included? Are they what you want? You may have to stay in three-star accommodations rather than five-star to get a more economical package. For some travelers, this is no big deal because they know they won't be spending much time in the room. For others, it's very important to be pampered when on vacation. Therefore, they want above-average or luxurious lodging. When cruising, the type of room is important because there's such a huge difference between an interior cabin and an outside cabin with a big window or balcony.

Also, be aware that what is considered moderate or deluxe accommodations in other countries, even in Europe, often is not so by American standards! Many of the cheaper hotels in Europe do not have private baths. Would that be a problem for you? In Europe, pensiones (a cross between a hotel and hostel) and hostels are affordable alternatives to expensive hotels, but many have curfews. Would that be a problem for you?

7. What kind of *transportation* will you be taking? How many types of transport are involved? Train? Plane? Horse? Would a small commuter plane bother you? Would you be uncomfortable riding an elephant while on safari? If you have physical limitations, get seasick, or suffer motion sickness, you may want to pay close attention to modes of transportation. A "short boat ride" may not be a pleasant experience for someone who is afraid of water or suffers motion sickness.

When I traveled to Nepal, I flew into Katmandu on a major airline. I transferred to an eight-passenger plane (with no door between the cockpit and interior so I could see the co-pilot reading the newspaper to the pilot) for the hour journey to Royal Chitwan National Park, where we landed on a grassy field. After retrieving my luggage from the pile on the grass, I was taken to a modified Land Rover. For the next hour, I bumped around the back of it until we dead-ended at a river. I was put in a canoe and taken across to the other side. Once there, I was met by a camp representative and escorted on the two-mile hike to camp. I knew what to expect (as much as one can be prepared for such an experience!) so I had worn good hiking boots, packed light, and took motion sickness medicine beforehand. Had I not been prepared, I might have been miserable and considered the trip an ordeal rather than an adventure.

8. What is the *final cost*? If a trip says "all-inclusive," that is supposed to mean transportation, lodging, meals, tour director, sightseeing fees, transfers, taxes, and most gratuities (almost all of the costs of your travel except personal expenses, such as tips, alcoholic beverages, souvenirs, and laundry) are included. Make sure everything is included because some tour operators claim a trip is "all-inclusive" but the price doesn't reflect the expense of getting to where the "all-inclusive land tour" originates.

If a trip is not "all-inclusive," make a reasonable estimate of what everything else will cost. Besides factoring in port tax or airfare,estimate personal expenses, such as tipping. Gratuities can run from $100–$500, depending on the length of trip and number of persons you tip. For example, the rule of thumb is $2–$5 per day, per person. This may include cabin stewards, waiters, drivers, porters, and guides. Multiply this by 14 days and it adds up! Make sure to take enough cash to cover these expenses. Also, if you have narrowed it down to two trips and are leaning toward one because it is cheaper, find out if the same number of meals and sightseeing fees are included. The other trip may actually be the better deal.

9. How many *people* will be in the group? Do you want to travel with a small group where you have more of a chance to get to know each other and interact or would you rather be with a big tour group? Before you opt for the smaller group, you should know that traveling with a bigger group generally equals greater savings for the traveler.

10. How many *meals* will be included and how many will you be responsible for on your own? Are options such as vegetarian, kosher, or sugar-free possible? If you have special dietary needs due to religious or medical reasons, this may be an area of concern for you. You may have to bring some food with you or make advance arrangements. Airlines offer special menus, but you must make a request at least 24 hours prior to the flight. Most cruise ships, tours, and hotels can meet all needs, if notified in advance.

11. Is the tour fully *escorted?* If so, will a representative from the U.S. tour operator who is offering the package be on the trip? This is important because often trips are subcontracted to foreign tour companies and if something is promised in your original package and not delivered, there's not much you can do about it until you get back home, and then what does it matter? Also, ask if the guide speaks *good* English. Sometimes you're promised an English-speaking guide, but the guide doesn't speak it fluently, or the accent is so heavy it's difficult to understand.

12. How many scheduled *activities* are included versus time on your own? What do you want? Some travelers prefer every minute accounted for while others like more time on their own to shop or explore(or, perish the thought—relax!). If you really want to do something that is not part of the tour package, will there opportunity to do so? Will the company help you make arrangements to fulfill your wish?

13. Are there *special things* that make the trip above average, such as a performance, farewell banquet, expert speaker, presentation, behind-the-scenes tour, or other activities that aren't offered in similar trips? Obviously, if a couple of trips are alike in cost and itinerary, look closely at these things to help decide which tour operator offers more.

14. Is there a *direct flight* or are there several airport layovers and changes? The less frequently you have to change planes and handle luggage, the better off you are. The more you change planes the greater the chances of lost luggage or missed connections. If you must change planes, check your luggage through, whenever possible. On extremely long trips, some travelers prefer to break it up by staying a night or two en route. For example, many tourists opt to visit Hawaii on their way to Asia or Australia. Some like to stay overnight in London on their way to Africa. If you have a choice whether your stopover is at the beginning or the end of a trip, it's best to have it on the front end. Usually, by

the time a trip is over, travelers are tired and ready to get home. Also, by breaking up the trip on the front end, it helps prevent jet lag.

If you connect through a city you would like to visit, ask the agent about a "stopover" when you are permitted to stay briefly in a connecting city rather than just make a connection. A *nonstop* flight does not stop; a *direct* flight stops, but you will not have to change planes. However, a *connecting* flight means you will stop and change planes. A *through* flight means that passengers have to change planes and airlines.

15. Does the trip allow enough *time* for your body to adjust to the time difference? This is important because it can reduce the chances of jet lag or other travel-related problems. The more time your body is permitted to get used to its new surroundings, the better it will respond to the hardships of traveling and the disruption of your normal routine. If a tour arrives in the morning, it's best to have a "free morning" (no planned activities) as opposed to starting out on a tour soon after arrival. If you arrive in the evening, take a stroll or brisk walk, eat a good meal without alcoholic beverages, and be sure to take a bath or shower instead of going straight to bed. This is advisable even if you are tired.

16. How many *years* has the tour operator been in business? If the tour operator has been in business 10 or 20 years and no complaints have been registered against them with any of the before-mentioned organizations, chances are they are a reliable and reputable company. If this is the first year or so the operator has been in business, be sure to ask for references from satisfied customers. Also, verify that the operator belongs to one of the agencies that regulate the travel industry.

17. How *long* has the tour operator been doing this particular trip? If a company has been going to Europe for over 20 years, chances are they know the "ins and outs" and problems should be minimal. If it is the first time they are offering the particular trip, it could go either way. I've been on new trips where a tour operator was anxious to please and went the extra mile and the trip couldn't have been better. I've also had the other extreme with all kinds of problems.

18. Are the *amenities* offered acceptable to you? If you envision staying in a lodge that has a fireplace, hot tub, bar, and big, beautiful, post-and-beam dining room, and the brochure says "rustic cabins with dining hall," it's probably not for you! The same thing with cruise ships. There is no comparison between the amenities offered on a budget cruise line and those on a deluxe cruise line. There's also no comparing the activities offered on a megaship with those provided on small ships.

19. If one of the packages seems comparable to what the other companies are offering, but the price is much less (assuming all companies are legitimate), check what time of *year* the cheaper trip is. You don't want to go to India during its summer season when it's 110° in the shade, or to Borneo during its monsoon season. Is it a bargain because it's a bad time to travel? Just because it's the low season doesn't mean it's a bad time to travel, so be sure to ask about weather and if all places of interest will be open.

20. Lastly, will the tour operator provide you with *references* of satisfied customers, preferably of recent travelers? If the tour operator has a policy against giving out the names of its customers, check to see if it has any complaints filed against it. Be sure to get answers to Questions 11, 16, and 17.

I recommend purchasing trip cancellation insurance. The policy typically covers trip cancellations, lost baggage, and emergency air evacuations, which can cost upwards of $10,000. Sometimes the insurance is included with the cost of the trip. But if not, it is worth the money ($100 per person, on average). Ask your travel agent or tour operator.

Many travelers who have had trouble collecting on a policy will say trip cancellation insurance is not worth the paper it's written on, but that is not true if you carefully read and understand the terms of the policy. These policies are very explicit in their pay-off terms. For example, if the policy does not reimburse if the cancellation is work-related, don't go with that policy if you have the kind of job that might cause you to cancel the trip. NEVER pay for a policy you have not seen in writing.

Don't Get Ripped Off By Travel Scams

Have you ever gotten one of those postcards saying you have won a free vacation to Florida or the Caribbean? All you have to do to claim your prize is to call an 800 number. If you've ever done that, you found out "...all you have to do is pay a low surcharge of two hundred dollars." These are not free vacations!

You also have to watch out for "prizes" like "Congratulations! You have won one free round-trip ticket and lodging for two," and all you have to do to claim your prize is to buy the second airline ticket (or purchase something else) from them. This is a popular scam because you are required to buy one full-fare airline ticket, or worse still, you buy an airline ticket and never see your "prize."

What about those postcards or faxes you receive that guarantee cheap travel to Orlando or the Bahamas? They must be booked immediately and are good for travel up to one year from date of purchase. These open-ended trips are not usually good deals at all. When you decide to go (if you can get through on the 800 number and not get a continuous busy signal), you may discover that the dates you desire are not available or that the company is no longer in business. It's almost impossible for a company to uphold a promise to thousands of people that whatever date they ultimately choose will be available. Multiply this by hundreds of companies making the same offer to thousands of people, and with all of them utilizing the same ships and lodging. Travel scams bring unscrupulous agents and operators over 12 billion dollars every year. Watch out for telemarketing tour operators, especially if they use high pressure tactics, such as the offer is only good if you accept during the phone call, and give a credit card number to cover the small "surcharge."

Watch out for trips offered at too low a price. If other companies are offering comparable packages at a much higher cost, be leery about how one company can offer something similar at such a cheap price, even if they claim some super discount awarded just to them or a special close-out sale.

Online auctions have become a good place for scams. To avoid getting ripped off on the Internet, ask that your payment be held in an Internet escrow account until the trip documents and tickets arrive. Tradeable/i-Esgrow will provide this service for a fee. (650-598-3800, www.I-Escrow.com.). Be sure to get all promises in writing and try to verify flights and such prior to making a commitment. For more help, try the Better Business Bureau (703-276-0100, www.bbb.org) or the National Fraud Information Center (800-876-7060, www.fraud.org/ifw.htm).

Travelers are often tricked into buying stolen tickets. The Airlines Reporting Corporation (ARC) has revealed that they are often unable to recover unused blank tickets from travel agencies that have gone defunct. With more than 33,000 travel agencies in the U.S., it's difficult for ARC to keep up with every one of the companies that closes down or goes bankrupt. When that happens, employees sometimes walk away with pockets full of blank tickets they sell to unsuspecting travelers. Additionally, break-ins and burglaries at travel agencies are becoming more common. Unfortunately, the victim who has paid for the ticket in good faith is the one arrested at the airport and the stolen ticket is confiscated.

On handwritten tickets, be aware of any erasures or alterations. For computer-generated tickets, make sure all fonts match. If you see more than one style of font, that could mean the ticket has been changed. Make sure the travel agency's plate validation is properly located on the upper right hand corner, right below the ticket number, and above the airline's plate validation.

Never pay for any airline ticket with cash or check if you areunfamiliar with the company. Use a credit card. If a company says they only accept cash or check or push you to pay with cash or check—don't!Some companies offer discounts for paying with cash or check instead of a credit card. If you want the discount, check references and find out if any complaints have been filed against the company. If the company says it belongs to an organization, such as NTA or USTOA, verify this. Again, if they don't belong to any trade associations, be wary.

My advice is to ask specific questions, such as how long a company has been in business and to which travel organizations they belong. Do they belong to the BBB, ASTA or NTA? Find out if there will be add-on costs later, such as transfers and taxes. These are called "hidden costs." Get the names of the hotels, restaurants, and whatever else they claim is included in your package. Contact these places yourself if you are suspicious. Find out exact dates and times. Don't let tour operators tell you that information will be sent after you have paid. Find out about cancellation and refund policies. Get all information in writing before you agree to buy. A legitimate company will have no problem with this. Get a street address for the company offering the trip. Verify they exist. Many illegitimate companies set up post office boxes long enough to collect checks and then close them out and abscond with the money.

Don't give out a credit card number until you have verified the company is legitimate. Don't let the operator talk you into sending a check or money order by overnight mail. Using a credit card gives you the right to dispute fraudulent charges under the Fair Credit Billing Act. The deadline for disputing a credit card is 60 days, so if you're told the vacation doesn't take place for three months, but you must pay now, be wary! However, many legitimate companies do ask for payment at least 60 days prior to departure, especially to developing countries and for adventure travel so the company can be assured of enough travelers to go ahead and line up the overseas land operators and guides they use. If you are required to pay more than 60 days before departure, or need to do so to obtain an "early bird" discount, verify the company's reputation by checking with ASTA, NTA, BBB, and so forth. Ask for references.

If no one is able to answer all your questions or they tell you the information will be sent after you have paid for the trip, don't do it. If in doubt, say no! For more information, contact the Federal Trade Commission at 877-382-4357, 202-326-2222, or www.ftc.gov.

◆   ◆   ◆

Chapter Two--How To Get The Best Deals From Tour Operators

Chapter Two--How To Get The Best Deals From Tour Operators

How hard to realize that every camp of men or beast has this glorious starry firmament for a roof! In such places standing alone on the mountaintop it is easy to realize that whatever special nests we make--leaves and moss like the marmots and birds, or tents or piled stone--we all dwell in a house of one room--the world with the firmament for its roof--and are sailing the celestial spaces without leaving any track.
John Muir, 1930, John of the Mountains

What No One Tells You

Some tours will always cost more than others because of the destination or activities involved. Trips to remote or undeveloped places are more expensive because there are fewer transportation and lodging options. Travelers will pay more to go to resorts and faraway destinations. Obviously, airline tickets cost more to go from New York to Cairo, Egypt than to go from New York to London, England. Certain types of travel, such as interactive and adventure travel, are more expensive than general sightseeing tours because of the activities involved and the highly skilled leaders needed to guide or instruct groups participating in these activities. However, most types of travel can be achieved at reasonable rates if you know where and how to look for the best deals.

√ Start by carefully reviewing *all* travel brochures and catalogs that pertain to your interests, even those that seem expensive. I have discovered that while a company may appear to offer trips that are out of your acceptable price range, its brochure or catalog usually contains at least one or two trips that are actually quite affordable. If you don't take the time to look at each trip and what the cost includes, you may miss out on one of these good deals.

Be sure to comparison shop. At first glance, a trip may seem too expensive, but you may find that after looking at what other companies are charging for a similar trip, the price looks better! In the end, what you pay is determined by how much you *can* pay and how *badly* you want to go on a particular trip.

√ Traveling during the off-season or shoulder (low)-season costs considerably less than traveling during high season. Trips usually cost *40– 70 percent less* during these times than in peak season. Fewer people travel in low-or off-seasons, so vendors (tour operators, hotels, tourist attractions, etc.) lower their prices to entice travelers. Conversely, in the high season, the demand is so great they raise prices.

Off season is usually September 15 through December 15, excluding Thanksgiving. Shoulder (low) season is January 5 until Easter (March or April), and high season runs from Easter(March or April) until mid-September. High-season rates also apply mid-December until early January, due to the holidays. Bear in mind that for some destinations, such as Antarctica or Alaska, travel is only possible in their summer, so seasonal savings are not applicable. Although people traveling at the beginning or end of the season will obtain the lowest fares. Some operators offer exceptional "deals" when the weather is (or might be) unpleasant or downright bad, such as during the rainy season. Alaskan Inside Passage cruises operate mid-May to early September but the weather is most predictable (meaning sunny and as warm as it gets) July to mid-August. I've been to Scandinavia at the very beginning of tourism season and would highly recommend it. While it gets about 10 or 15 degrees warmer three weeks later, it also becomes more crowded and significantly more expensive. Considering that it never gets warm enough for shorts and sundresses at any time of year in this part of the world, I find it a reasonable trade-off. Ask about weather conditions and then decide what's right for you.

√ Going with a group, such as nonprofit organizations, churches, zoos, trade, or alumni associations, is a way to travel for less money because group rates are always cheaper than those offered to individual travelers. The organization sponsors the trips, which are actually operated by an established tour company. The sponsor gets a percentage of money from the tour operator for each person booked. There are other advantages to group travel, besides the reduced rate. First, departure is guaranteed. Also, there are usually some extras thrown in, such as a welcome banquet or behind-the-scenes tour. Most importantly, if there are problems, the tour company will do their best to make it right or make it up to travelers because they really want to continue to do business with the group.

√ Airline e-mailers are discussed in Chapter Four, but I would like to emphasize again that they are an excellent way to save money on airfares and vacation packages. Most airlines provide a free weekly electronic newsletter advertising special fares. To sign up, go to each airline's Web site (one-time process), click on the registration or "sign me up now" button and enter your e-mail address. You may just as easily unsubscribe at any time.

These specials vary from domestic weekend getaways, with Friday or Saturday departures and Monday or Tuesday returns, to extended overseas stays. Some of the deals expire within a week or two, while others are good for several months. The deals vary from air and hotel packages to all-inclusive vacation packages. For example, last year American Airlines extended a five day European air and hotel package, which included continental breakfasts, transfers, and a couple of sightseeing vouchers, for less than $500 per person(pp). Northwest Airlines advertised a Hong Kong special that included air, five nights hotel, transfers, half-day sightseeing tours, hotel taxes and service charges, for less than $800pp. Delta sent an e-mailer a few months ago promoting an off-season special to Venice, Italy. Travelers received round-trip air from New York to Venice, water taxi transfer from airport to hotel, five nights in a four-star hotel, and breakfast daily, for just over $900pp. Single travelers could enjoy the same package by paying a nominal supplement.

Airlines aren't the only ones that notify travelers of promotions and specials via the Internet. Most publications, such as *Travel and Leisure* and *Travel Holiday*, send periodic e-mailers announcing Hot Deals. Additionally, tour operators and travel agencies use e-mail to apprise travelers of last-minute deals and unadvertised specials. Request these e- mailers whenever possible. If you don't want your online mailbox flooded with junk mail, sign up with your favorite airlines and travel companies *only* and request that your contact information not be passed on to others. There's usually a box you can X at the bottom of the electronic request form if you do not want your name given to other companies.

√ Ask to be put on direct mail lists to learn about special promotions. This is another option or an alternative if you don't have e-mail or don't want to give out your online address. Furthermore, if you are afraid you might be tempted by a good deal, you can throw the mail in the trash without even opening it! Recently, Austrian Airlines mailed out brochures showcasing its latest promotion, a Vienna getaway. For less than $700, travelers received round-trip air from New York to Vienna, a local city sightseeing tour, three nights accommodations, continental breakfasts daily, and one dinner. Swissair offered a similar package to Zurich for roughly the same price. Tour operators often send special "incentives" to people on their mailing lists, such as $100pp discounts, free travel insurance, or notification of an unadvertised special.

√ Always ask about discounts. Fares are often reduced for members of certain organizations, such as AAA, CAA, or AARP. Many companies grant year-round discounts to adults 50 or older and youths who are 17 or younger. Rates are almost always discounted for the third or fourth person (adult or child) staying in a room or cabin. Companies frequently provide discounts for first-time travelers to entice them or to reward frequent travelers. Sometimes, discounts are not listed in a brochure for various reasons so always ask before booking. Prices can often be adjusted by a company representative. It depends on company policy and the willingness of the representative. That's why it pays to be nice and also to ask if there is any way you can get a better rate than what is listed. I once had a rep give me the off-season rate, even though it wasn't off season, because the trip wasn't full and she was in a good mood (and authorized to modify cost).

√ Ask about payment. Those who pay well in advance of the payment due date usually receive an early bird discount. Sometimes, a company will offer a small price break if you pay with a check or money order, as opposed to a credit card. For example, SmarTours reduces their rates $100pp if you pay by check or money order. Even if the pricing information does not mention early bird or cash incentives, be sure to ask. I know I sound like a broken record, but I can't emphasize how important it is to inquire about these things.

√ Booking a trip on behalf of yourself and a group of friends or family, entitles you to 50–100 percent off the fare. If you gather a group of 8–12, you will almost certainly travel free. Some companies offer reduced rates for the person who brings in 3–4 travelers. It all depends on the company and its policies. Additionally, if a trip is not full or it is low- season, tour operators tend to be more generous. Ask the company representative or negotiate directly with the manager.

√ Consider using a consolidator. Consolidators buy many tickets from tour operators, cruise lines, hotels, and airlines. Buying in volume typically entitles them to the very best fares that these vendors can give. Therefore, consolidators usually have the lowest fares. See "consolidators" in Chapters Four, Five, and Six for more information on how these discounters work, as well as a list of companies and their addresses.

√ Join a travel club or subscribe to a travel newsletter. These are good places to learn about discounted travel. Both cost money, either through subscriptions or membership, but they are worthwhile investments. Newsletters are head and shoulders above the information found in most magazines because they are not restricted to "advertising feature themes." A couple of exceptional newsletters are *Consumer Reports Travel Letter* and *Travel Smart*. Information and addresses on these(and other) publications and clubs can be found in Chapter Eight: Travel Clubs and Helpful Resources at the end of every chapter.

√ Unadvertised specials are often posted on tour company Web sites. Additionally, great deals and special promotions worldwide can be found on www.TourDeals.com. The last time I accessed this site I found some exceptional deals offered by many of the companies listed in this reference, including cruises and all-inclusive resort stays. There was even an additional 10 percent discount offered.

◆   ◆   ◆

TOURS, TOURS, TOURS: General, Escorted Sightseeing; Learning, Active, and Interactive; Solo Travelers; Women-Only; Tours geared to Mature Travelers; and Specialty Travel: Adventure and Ecotravel

Here you'll read about tour operators who provide worldwide vacations for budget-minded travelers. The chapter is broken down into six categories: general sightseeing (escorted); learning, active, and interactive; solo travelers (not to be confused with independent travel, discussed in Chapter Three); women-only, mature travelers, and adventure travel. Specific itineraries and prices have not been included because they change periodically.

There are thousands of tour operators, so this list is not meant to be conclusive. It's a good representation of *long-established, reputable* companies that *I have dealt with or am at least familiar with their management*, that offer *affordable* vacations and adventures. In the travel industry, a company's reputation is paramount because once you pay a deposit you agree to all the company's terms and conditions, which usually allows many loopholes or safeguards on behalf of the company.

For example, did you know that departure is not always guaranteed? A trip can be canceled just days or hours before it is to take place. And, if a company cancels a trip, it can keep some of your money, depending on the reason for cancellation. Additionally, a company can claim increased airfare or accommodation costs and demand more money—even after you have paid in full. Read Chapter One- Planning Your Trip before choosing a company or booking any kind of travel.

Some of the same listings may be found in more than one category of this chapter because some operators offer a variety of travel options, such as learning trips *and* women-only adventures. Additionally, tour operators that are owned by the same company have been grouped together.

General, Escorted Sightseeing

Ambassador Tours offers discounted land and cruise vacations, with emphasis on cruises. 717 Market Street, San Francisco, CA 94103. U.S. and Canada: 800-989-9000. Outside U.S. and Canada: 415-357-9876. www.ambassadortours.com. e-mail: ambtours@ambassadortours.com

Brendan Tours offers many value tours, cruises, and independent travel deals worldwide. They have very reasonable single supplements, usually between $100–200. Brendan frequently extends specials. 15137 Califa Street, Van Nuys, CA 91411. 818-785-9696. www.brendantours.com. e-mail: info@brendantours.com

Carlson Wagonlit offers many worldwide budget vacations. Early bookers and people over 55 are entitled to a discount. Get together a group of 8 and receive 50 percent off or get together a group of 16 and travel free. 222 Second Street SE, Cedar Rapids, IA 52401. www.carsontravel.com. Carlson Leisure Group, 12755 State Hwy. 55, Plymouth, MN 55441. www.carlsonwagon.com.

Central Holidays has incredible worldwide cruises, escorted tours, and independent adventures at bargain prices. They are best known for their Mediterranean trips. 120 Sylvan Avenue, Englewood Cliffs, NJ 07632. 800-935-5000 or 800-611-1138 or www.centralholidays.com. e-mail: bookonline@centralh.com

China Focus offers 10-night tours to several Chinese cities, including Beijing and Shanghai, for approximately $1,000pp. Price includes round-trip airfare from the West Coast (U.S.), internal transport (air, bus, or train), three or four-star hotels, all sightseeing fees, guide, and most meals. 870 Market Street, Suite 1215, San Francisco, CA 94102. 800-868-7244, 888-688-1898 or 415-788-8660. www.chinafocustravel.com. e-mail: info@chinafocus.com

CIE Tours provides one of the most economical ways to see the United States, Canada, Ireland, and Britain. The company has tours ranging from 5–15 days, as well as good independent traveler packages. Significant discounts often available for low season travel, early booking, and for those 55 or older. A couple of my favorite itineraries are "Irish Heritage" and "Alaska Spectacular", which includes a train ride into Denali National Park, a dogsled ride, gondola ride, cruise, visits to Kenai Peninsula, Seward, Alyeska Resort, and much more. 100 Hanover Avenue, P.O. Box 501, Cedar Knolls, NJ 07927-0501. 800-CIE-TOUR, 800-243-8687 or 973-292-3438. www.cietours.com. e-mail: helpdesk@cietours.com

Collette Tours offers affordable tours and independent travel throughout the U.S. and worldwide, especially Europe. In addition to its sightseeing tours, the company provides Discovery Vacations and Exotic Adventures. 162 Middle Street, Pawtucket, RI 02860. 800-340-5158 or 888-424-0712. www.collettevacations.com

Contiki is the world's biggest travel company for 18–35 year olds. Contiki operates budget vacations to Europe, Africa, Mexico, Canada, Australia, New Zealand, and the U.S. Book early and save 2.5 percent on the land tour portion of any trip that lasts at least seven days. Contiki offers savings for mid-week departures (Monday, Tuesday, or Wednesday) and quadruple-occupancy rooms. 2300 E. Katella Avenue, #450, Anaheim, CA 92806. In U.S. and Canada: 888-CONTIKI. www.contiki.com. e-mail: contiki@contiki.com.

Discover Travel offers deep discount escorted and self-drive packages to Australia and New Zealand. 2192 Dupont Drive, Suite 116, Irvine, CA 92612-1322. 800-576-7770 or 888-TAHITI-1 or 949-833-1139. e-mail: info@discovertravel.net

Eastern Tours Consolidated/Morris Travel specializes in travel to Russia and Eastern Europe. Adventurous travelers will delight in the blini-caviar-vodka feast that is part of the Russian Winter Festival Tour to St. Petersburg and Moscow package. Great prices on tours and untour packages. 10 E. 39th Street, Suite 906, New York, NY 10016. 800-339-6967 or 212-683-8930. www.traveltorussia.com. e-mail: travelnow@traveltorussia.com.

EC Tours, Inc. offers train trips, river cruises, and tours to Spain, France, Italy, Portugal, Morocco, Great Britain, and Turkey. Participants stay in exotic lodging, such as palaces, chateaux, and prehistoric caves (!). 12500 Riverside Drive, Suite 210, Valley Village, CA 91607-3423. 800-388-0877. www.ectours.com e-mail: ectours@aol.com.

Far & Wide offers worldwide river cruises, escorted sightseeing, cultural, educational, religious tours, and independent traveler packages. Their best deals are to Europe. 80 S. W. 8th Street, Suite 2601, Miami, FL 33130. 800-206-8898, 800-511-1194 or 305-908-7543. www.farandwide.com.

France Vacations has offered tours and untours throughout France and England for more than a decade. Their Web site reveals great deals in its Specials, Top Deals, and Featured Destinations sections. Their all-inclusive Getaway Specials include a week in Paris, the French Riviera, Painting in Provence, Waterways of France, and Discover Provencal Cooking. The company also offers Fly and Drive packages, as well as budget hotels in France, London, and Brussels for independent travelers. They even book Venice Orient Express rail trips. 800-332-5332. www.francevacations.net. e-mail: reservations@francevacations.net

Gate1 offers low-cost cruises and all-inclusive worldwide tours, including photo tours and untours. Best deals are to Italy, China, and Spain. 101 Limekiln Pike, Glenside, PA 19038. 800-682-3333, 888-88-Gate1 or 215-572-7676. www.gate1travelcom. e-mail: info@gate1travel.com.

General Tours/ TBI Tours provides affordable tours, cruises, and independent travel packages to worldwide destinations. 53 Summer Street, Keene, New Hampshire 03431. 800-221-2216. www.generaltours.com. e-mail: info@generaltours.com

Globus & Cosmos is a worldwide independent travel and escorted travel tour operator, offering both first class and budget travel. They offer approximately 110 budget tours to six continents. Discounts of 10 percent available for those 18 and under on land portion. Minimum age accepted is eight years old. 5301 S. Federal Circle, Littleton, CO 80123. 800-338-7092. www.globusandcosmos.com.

Go Ahead Vacations offers discounted tours and cruises throughout Europe, as well as to Egypt, Israel, Kenya, Australia and New Zealand, China, Panama, and Costa Rica. If you have previously traveled on a Go Ahead vacation or bring five friends, you'll receive a substantial discount. Bring 10 people and travel free, plus earn a cash bonus. Apply to be a group leader and travel free(see Web site). Go Ahead offers several 7–10-day vacations, such as to Paris or London, for less than $1,000pp, including air from New York. One Education Street, Cambridge, MA 02141. 800-590-1170. www.goaheadvacations.com. e-mail: goahead@ef.com.

Homeric Tours provide low-cost Greek Island cruises, escorted tours, charters, and independent tours. 55 E. 59th Street, New York, NY 10022. 800-223-5570 or 212-753-1100. www.homerictours.com. e-mail: homeric@aol.com.

Paul Laifer Tours offers several value-oriented vacations to Eastern Europe. Ten day trips to Budapest, Prague, and Vienna often cost less than $1,000pp (including air from Newark, hotels, breakfast daily, transfers, and sightseeing tours in all cities). 106 Laifer Tours, 106 Parsippany Road, Parsippany, NJ 07054. 800-346-6314 or 973-887-1188. www.laifertours.com. e-mail: travel@laifertours.com.

Menatours USA operates tours to Egypt. 181 Boulevard, Suite 2D, Hasbrouck Heights, NJ 07604. 800-386-8885. www.menatours.com. e-mail: mena@menatours.com.

MTL Vacations has been providing deeply discounted vacation deals to Canada since 1991. I'm talking many packages are less than $350! 375 Riverside Avenue, Medford, MA 02155 800-MONTREAL or 800-666-8732. www.mtlvacations.com e-mail: info@yescanada.com.

Nordique/ Norvista Tours provide bargain tours and independent trips to many Northern European cities, such as Helsinki, Prague, Budapest, Vienna, and Warsaw. For those willing to travel during the winter, prices are exceptional. 11099 S. LaCienega, Suite 210, Los Angeles, CA 90045. 800-995-7997 or 310-645-4400. www.nordiquetours.com.

Oussaden Tours takes travelers to Morocco. 10 East 39th Street, Suite 1000 (10th floor), New York, NY 10016. 800-206-5049 or 212-685-4654. www.morocco-oussaden-tours.com.

Pacha Tours specializes in affordable travel to Turkey. 1560 Broadway, New York, NY 10036. 800-722-4288 or 212-764-4080. www.pachatours.com. e-mail: info@pachatours.com.

Pacific Delight Tours are "North America's #1 operator of deluxe tours to China, the Orient, and Southeast Asia for nearly 30 years." The company offers great rates and is a member of USTOA and ASTA. 205 East 42nd Street, Suite 1908, New York, NY 10017-5706. 800-221-7179 or 212-818-1718.

Petrabax offers very good deals on escorted tours and untours to London and Spain, especially November through March. 800-634-1188. www.petrabax.com. e-mail: info@petrabax.com

Pleasant Hawaiian Holidays takes travelers on to Honolulu, Maui, Kauai, Hawaii, and Molokai, as well as the Orient, Mexico and Tahiti. Discounts and upgrades available for mature travelers. 2404 Townsgate Road, P.O. Box 5020, Westlake Village, CA 91359-5020. 800-242-9244. www.pleasant.net.

♦ FYI: Some Hawaiians speak a dialect they call "pidgin," but linguists call it "Hawaiian creole." It is a mixture of Hawaiian, Japanese, Chinese, and English languages. Common greeting is howzit (How are you?).
The wettest spot in the world is Mt. Waialeale, Hawaii, with an average annual rainfall of 460 inches. The driest spot is Atacama Desert, Chile, with barely enough rainfall to be measurable.

Russian National Group (Russian National Tourist Office) offers bargain-priced cruises and escorted and independent tours of Russia by land, river cruise, or Trans Siberian Train. Discounts available to student travelers. They can arrange Visas for independent travelers. Many parts of Russia have high crime rates and getting around can be difficult because English is not widely spoken and public transport is minimal. Also, drink purified or bottled water in many places, such as St. Petersburg. 130 West 42nd Street, Suite 412, New York, NY 10036. 877-221-7120 or 212-575-3431. www.russia-travel.com. e-mail: info@russia-travel.com.

Russian Travel Bureau (subsidiary of Orbitair International Ltd.) provides affordable travel to Eastern Europe. 225 E. 44th Street, New York, NY 10017. 800-847-1800 or 212-986-1500. www.russiantravelbureau.com. e-mail: russtvl.com.

Sceptre Tours offers value vacations to Ireland. 9 South Long Beach Road, Rockville Centre, New York 11570. 800-221-0924 or 516-255-9800. www.sceptretours.com.

SmarTours extends discounted travel from the Orient to Egypt. All tour prices include air, transfers, guides, first class hotels, ground transportation, and some sightseeing. Single supplements are usually $150–$199. 501 Fifth Avenue, Suite 812, New York, NY 10017. 800-337-7773. www.smartours.net.

Sunbeam Tours offers escorted tours to Europe, Asia, South Pacific and Canada. 3631 S. Harbor Blvd., Suite 225, Santa Ana, CA 92704. 800-955-1818 or 714-434-1810. www.sunbeamtours.com.

Thomson Family Adventures offers family-oriented expeditions around-the-world. Their best trips are to Turkey, Indonesia, Costa Rica, and Tanzania. 14 Mount Auburn Street, Watertown, MA 02472. 800-262-6255 or 617-923-2004. www.familyadventures.com. e-mail: info@familyadventures.com.

TourCrafters Inc. has been offering bargain trips throughout much of Europe since 1980. 28085 North Ashley Circle, Unit 202, Libertyville, IL 60048. 800-ITALY95 (482-5995) or 847-816-6510. www.tourcrafters.com. e-mail: info@tourcrafters.com.

Tour International provides small group and active tours, as well as independent travel packages, to Russia and Eastern Europe. 3105 Eastlake Avenue, Seattle, WA 98102. 877-394-0572 or 206-498-3066. www.tourinternational.com. e-mail: info@tourinternational.com.

Troy Tours has extremely affordable escorted and independent trips to Turkey and Italy, especially November through March. 6151 W. Century Blvd., Suite 1114, Los Angeles, CA 90045. 800-748-6878. www.troytours.com. e-mail: troytours@mindspring.com.

Valtur provides all-inclusive tours and resort stays in Italy, Morocco, and Caribbean. No single supplement charged and discounts available for children. Great packages for singles, couples, families, and mature travelers. 877-582-2284 or 619-297-4100. www.clubvaltur.com. e-mail: vacation@clubholidays.com.

Value World Tours offers an assortment of bargain tours and untours to Eastern Europe and worldwide river cruises. 17220 Newhope Street, #230 Fountain Valley, CA 92708. 800-795-1633 or 714-556-8258. e-mail: mail@vstours.com.

YMT Vacations has guaranteed weekly departures on scheduled airlines from most U.S. cities to many resort locations, including Hawaii and Mexico. Packages are usually all-inclusive. Get together a group of nine and travel free. Become a group leader to travel free and receive cash incentives. 8831 Aviation Blvd., Inglewood, CA 90301. 800-922-9000 or 800-888-8204 or 310-649-3820. www.GoYMT.com. e-mail: comments@ymtvacations.com.

♦ FYI: When work on the Crazy Horse Monument in South Dakota is finished, it will be the largest sculpture on Earth. The Sioux Chief, Crazy Horse, who is perched on his stallion, is so big that it's higher than the Washington Monument, and the four presidential heads that comprise Mount Rushmore (located just 17 miles away) could be stacked inside the warrior's head. A five-room house would fit in each of the horse's nostrils. Crazy Horse's outstretched left arm will be almost as long as a football field and will point to nearby Sioux burial grounds.

♦ ♦ ♦

Learning, Active, and Interactive
Travelers interested in participatory trips geared to learning and discovery, with more lectures and programs than general sightseeing tours provide, this section presents some interesting options. It includes both active and interactive trips because vacations are often a combination of learning, activities, and interactive experiences. The listings found here have been carefully selected so as to provide the most affordable and diverse activities—from art and cultural immersion programs to scuba-diving vacations.

Most colleges and universities offer weekend and week-long learning opportunities. For example, Cornell University has adult study programs for wines, antiquing, and painting, as well as travel and learn programs. Check with schools in your area to see what they offer. The Senior Summer School's "Education Vacation" programs take place at campuses across the U.S. and fees include dorm rooms, classes, some meals, and activities. Participants are picked up at the airport in all cities (except Los Angeles and New York City). 800-847-2466. www.seniorsummerschool.com. There are also organizations that provide volunteer vacations and work/study/travel abroad programs. Names and contact information for many good organizations can be found in Chapter Eight.

There are some companies that provide exceptional deals on all-inclusive resort stays. They have been put in this section because participants can be as active as they like. Most resorts offer myriad activities, including diving, swimming, parasailing, and nature walks. These kinds of vacations can be appreciated by any type of traveler, from swinging singles to families.

AHI International is for ages 25–45 who are looking for all-inclusive tours, untours, cruises, and educational programs in Europe, such as a one-week educational program in Scotland or a week-long London escape. 6400 Shafer Court, Rosemont, IL 60018. 800-323-7373. www.ahitravel.com.

American Adventures & Road Runner offers small group adventures throughout North America. Lodging includes hotels, hostels, and/or camping and transport vehicles are air-conditioned "maxiwagons." No single supplements. P.O. Box 1155, Gardena, CA 90249. 800-873-5872 or 310-324-3447. www.americanadventures.com. e-mail: amadiax@aol.com.

American Wilderness Experience (AWE) specializes in small group travel adventure and says it is "America's premier purveyor of domestic and international back country adventure and Old West dude ranch vacations." They offer skiing trips, sailing excursions, and dude ranch vacations geared to singles, families, women-only, independent, and mature travelers. Discounted rates are often available for solo travelers. 2820-A Wilderness Place, Boulder, CO 80301. 800-444-0099 or 303-444-2622. www.gorp.com/awe. e-mail: awedave@aol.com.

      GORP's Web site is a also a great source for all outdoor activities, outdoor tour companies and outfitters, books, maps, and gear. It even offers a Hot Deals section. Or call 877-440-GORP.

Apple Vacations has great deals to the Caribbean, Bahamas, Bermuda, Mexico, Hawaii, Costa Rica, and Las Vegas. Its specialty is all-inclusive beach vacations. The average cost is less than $900pp (with even cheaper fares in low-and off-seasons or with mid-week departures) and that price includes a week's lodging at a resort, airfare, all meals, and activities/sports. It can offer bargains because it contracts with more than 500 hotels in nearly 50 destinations and flies from 25 U.S. cities on both charter and commercial flights. Some cruises are also offered. Its Web site is impressive and browsers should be sure to check out "Sizzlin' Specials." Apple vacations must be booked through a travel agent. 800-569-0988. www.applevacations.com.

Atelier Bez is a photography workshop in the South of France. It's located in the hills of the Parc Naturel du Haut Langeudoc, off the beaten path and unspoiled by progress. Inspiration includes fields of sunflowers, rolling hills, forests, gorges, rivers and lakes, nearby medieval Cathar sites, vineyards, and Mediterranean coast. Participants do not have to speak French. The summer workshop combines an exploration of France, including photo festivals, with a focus on photography. Painters and writers are welcome. The studios and accommodations are the former village dance hall and cinema. The darkroom is equipped to professional standards and the lighting studio doubles as a painting studio. Cost ranges from $500–$900 and includes tuition, darkroom chemistry/lab fee, meals (croissant breakfasts, picnic lunches, and regional wines and specialties prepared by a chef for dinner), bed and breakfast in shared rooms with private baths, and field trips. In France, contact Mabel Odessey, Atelier Le Bez, Le Bez, 81260 Brassac France; Telephone and fax: 05-63-74-56-22. e-mail: artlebez@aol.com. In the U.S., contact Kevin Martini-Fuller, P.O. Box 2156, St. Louis, MO. 63158. 314-457-1008. e-mail: KevinMF@mindspring.com.

Authentic 1870's Cattle Drives allow participants to "come and experience the Colorado High Country. Go back in time, spend a week in the 1870's." Modern working cowboy experiences also available. P.O. Box 69, Manassa, CO 81141. 719-843-5026. www.lxbar.com. e-mail: lxbar.rmi.

Backroads offers gourmet tours, deluxe camping, and active trips that emphasize watersports, bicycling, and walking tours. These can be enjoyed by the beginner, as well as advanced. Special interest trips for singles, students, families, and mature travelers. Catalogs clearly indicate activities and length, such as "kayaking half day" or "easy walking, 2–4 miles/day." Most trips take place in California, Rockies, Hawaii, Ireland, and Italy. Singles-oriented trips include Europe, Latin America, Canada, and U.S. While singles are encouraged in these dedicated trips, there is still a supplement for those who wish to have private accommodations. Discounts available for those 65 or older who are first-time travelers with Backroads. 801 Cedar Street, Berkeley, CA 94710. 800-GO-ACTIVE(462-2848)510-527-1555. www.backroads.com. e-mail:goactive@backroads.com.

Bar H Dude & Guest Ranch (Clarendon, TX) is an authentic working ranch that has one of the lowest rates in America. Guests can participate by helping move cattle or herding, or just relax by fishing, swimming, horseback riding, playing games, and reading. Low single supplement. 888-987-2457. Book through Hidden Trails and receive 5 percent discount. Hidden Trails also books other U.S. and worldwide guest ranches, riding tours, bison and cattle drives, and covered wagon train adventures. 888-9-TRAILS. www.hiddentrails.com.

Beaches offers all-inclusive resort vacations for singles, couples, and families, to exotic destinations, such as Turks and Caicos, Jamaica, Bahamas, St. Lucia, and Antigua. Departure cities are usually Miami, New York, or Chicago. 4950 SW 72nd Avenue, Miami, FL 33155. 888-BEACHES or 305-284-1300. In Canada: 416-223-0028. www.beaches.com. e-mail: info@beaches.com.

Breakaway Adventures specializes in self-guided and escorted bicycling and walking trips worldwide, such as Provence, Tuscany, Morocco, and Nepal. The company also offers mountain climbs. Each trip is geared differently; participants can set the pace. Itineraries clearly detail a trip's physical requirements, such as easy, moderate, or challenging. 1312 18th Street, Washington, DC 20036. 800-567-6286 or 202-293-2974. www.breakaway-adventures.com. e-mail: brkaway@clark.net.

CampAlaska Tours is the way the pristine wilderness of Alaska was meant to be explored and enjoyed. The Alaska-based company devotes itself exclusively to travel within Alaska, so guides are both knowledgeable and enthusiastic about the places and experiences. P.O. Box 872247, Waailla, Alaska 99687. 800-376-9438 or 907-376-9438. www.campalaska.com. e-mail: campak@alaska.net.

CBT Tours specializes in hiking and biking tours in Europe. 2506 N. Clark Street, #150, Chicago, IL 60614. 800-736-2453 or 312-475-0625. www.cbttours.com. e-mail: adventure@cbttours.com.

Club Med offers all-inclusive resort vacations in the U.S. and around the world. Price includes lodging, watersports, and land activities (including instruction), all meals with beer or wine for lunch and dinner, night time entertainment. Specialty programs include singles, single parents, families, couples, adventure, faraway, and Forever Young (55 or older). Half the guests are 24–44 years old. Roommates are assigned or a 20–40 percent single supplement is assessed. Each Club Med resort specializes in a different program so be sure to ask about resorts that meet your needs. Rates are typically less than $1,000 per week. 800-CLUBMED or 888-932-2582. For groups: 800-453-2582. www.clubmed.com. e-mail: info@clubmed.com.

Contiki is the world's biggest travel company for 18–35 year olds. They operate budget vacations to Europe, Africa, Mexico, Canada, Australia, New Zealand, and the U.S. Book early and save 2.5 percent on the land tour portion of any trip that lasts at least seven days. Contiki offers savings for mid-week departures (Monday, Tuesday, or Wednesday) and quadruple-occupancy rooms. 2300 E. Katella Avenue, #450, Anaheim, CA 92806. In U.S. and Canada: 888-CONTIKI. www.contiki.com. e-mail: contiki@contiki.com.

Council On International Educational Exchange(CIEE) is a nonprofit group that develops and administers international study, work, travel, and voluntary service programs worldwide, including educational home stays. Council Travel is a division that provides travel resources for students, teachers, and budget travelers. Council also offers discounted airfares, including around-the-world fares(See chapter on Airlines for more information). 205 East 42nd Street, New York, NY 10017-5706; 888-COUNCIL, 800-2COUNCIL or 212-661-1414. e-mail: info@ciee.org For detailed information on working, studying, and volunteering abroad, go to www.ciee.org. A complete travel resource for students and budget travelers, www.counciltravel.com.

Cross-Culture is a company "for travelers rather than tourists." They take small groups on budget-conscious cultural and learning adventures. 52 High Point Drive, Amherst, MA 01002-1224. 413-256-6303.

Disney Institute has programs for every age, from young children to older adults. Participants can work with Disney's world-renowned horticulturists through the Disney Institute Teaching Garden and Great Outdoors Programs. Make nature-inspired gifts, create a container garden, build a topiary, plan a garden party, take a canoe adventure on the Walt Disney World Waterways, and climb a 30-foot wall. Learn how to put together incredible brunches, barbecues or gourmet meals at the Disney Institute Culinary Arts program. Other possibilities include the Disney Institute of Television and Film, Disney Institute Animation and Story Arts, and Disney Institute Photo programs. Disney Institute, P.O. Box 10333, Lake Buena Vista, Florida 32830-0333. 800-496-6337. www.disneyinstitute.com.

Earthwise Journeys offer many specialty trips worldwide, including art and nature, ecotravel, outdoor adventure, cultural exploration, women-only, and volunteer vacations. P.O. Box 16177, Portland, OR 97292. 800-344-5309 or 503-736-3364. www.earthwisejourneys.com.

Eduvacations combines language study with other activities, such as painting, cooking, learning about French wines, photography, sailing, diving, bicycling, walking, and horseback riding in the U.S., France, Italy, Spain, and Latin America. Discounts are often offered for those who pay in full well in advance. All skill levels are welcome in the drawing, watercolor, painting, and tapestry programs. Taught in English and French in an old Mediterranean village in southern France that is famous for its jazz festival, opera, and bullfighting, conditions are ideal for creative inspiration. Work is usually done outside, but a studio is available. Students have private rooms in the artist's restored 15th-century house. Tennis courts, public pool, rivers, Camargue area beaches, and the Cevennes Mountains are all nearby. If you prefer, take French lessons and French Cooking classes in Chateau de Matel in Roanne. This program combines learning French in the morning with cooking demonstrations in the afternoon. Accommodations are in a countryside chateau, near the wine areas of Beaujolais and Burgundy. Optional activities include golf, horseback riding, bicycling, and tennis. 1431 21st. Street NW, Suite 302, Washington, DC 20036. 202-857-8384. www.eduvacations.com.

Escapes Unlimited has been in business for more than 20 years. Founded by a former social worker, each trip focuses on learning about and gaining a better insight into other cultures tourists rarely visit. Destinations include Asia (such as Mongolia, Borneo, and Vietnam) and the Americas. Web site browsers are privy to super specials, such as Peru: Lost City of the Incas, Hidden Thailand, and Bali Paradise Package—all at or less than $999pp, including air. 17842 Irvine Blvd., Tustin, CA 92780. 800-243-7227. www.escapesltd.com. e-mail: info@escapesltd.com.

France Vacations has offered tours and untours throughout France and England for more than a decade. Their Web site reveals great deals in its Specials, Top Deals, and Featured Destinations sections. Their all-inclusive Getaway Specials include a week in Paris, the French Riviera, Painting in Provence, Waterways of France, and Discover Provencal Cooking. The company also offers Fly and

Drive packages, as well as budget hotels in France, London, and Brussels for independent travelers. They even book Venice Orient Express rail trips. 800-332-5332. www.francevacations.net. e-mail: reservations@francevacations.net.

Hidden Trails provides a wide variety of riding adventures in North America and many other parts of the world. Participants can choose from lodge rides, guest ranches, working ranches, cattle drives, camping rides, horse drives, pack trips, wagon trains, and riding clinics. In addition to the reasonable rates normally offered, specials are frequently advertised on its Web site. 202-380 West 1st Ave., Vancouver, BC Canada V5Y 3T7. 888-9-TRAILS(987-2457) or 604-323-1141. www.hiddentrails .com. e-mail: res2001@hiddentrails.com.

Holiday Expeditions has been offering outdoor trips that feature mountain biking, kayaking, and white-water rafting, for more than 35 years. They also have special programs, such as Women's Yoga, Ghost Boats, and Kayak School. 544 East 3900 South, Salt Lake City, Utah 84107. 800-624-6323 or 801-266-2087. www.bikeraft.com. e-mail: holiday@bikeraft.com.

John Newcombe's Tennis Ranch has 28 tennis courts and lots of other activities on site or close by, such as golf, swimming, horseback riding, and river rafting. Choose between two clinics a day or one clinic in the morning with the afternoon free to pursue other activities. P.O. Box 310469, New Braunfels, TX 78131-0469. 800-444-6204 or 830-625-9105.

Kelly's On The Bay is one of the best bargain companies offering scuba diving adventures at Key Largo, Florida. Year-round packages start at less than $300pp for three nights lodging and four dives at the Key Largo National Maritime Sanctuary. 10422 Overseas Hwy., Key Largo, FL 33037. 800-226-0415 or 305-451-1622. www.kellysonthebay.com. e-mail: info@aquanuts.com.

Language Immersion Institute offers language-learning vacations in Mexico, France, Italy, Costa Rica, and Spain. Classes can be in the mornings or afternoons, leaving the rest of the day for sightseeing. The College at New Paltz, State University of New York, New Paltz, NY 12561. 845-257-3500. www.new.paltz.edu/lii.

Le Cordon Bleu offers affordable five-day cooking courses at its London and Paris schools. Learn to make succulent soufflés, petits fours, French sauces and pastries, and more. Students are given a list of nearby apartments and hotels they may rent, as well as sightseeing and city information. 800-457-CHEF. www.cordonbleu.net. e-mail: info@cordonbleu.net.

Lingua Service Worldwide, established 1988, is for those interested in Vacation 'N Learn language and culture courses. Lingua has programs for all ages, interests, and budgets in many countries, such as China, Venezuela, Israel, Austria, Netherlands, Russia, Greece, Spain, Italy, France, and Germany. Participants may opt to combine a study course with golfing, skiing, cooking, or studying art. Accommodations include apartments, hotels, dormitories, and home stays. For example, in Spain participants learn Spanish and get free cooking and dance lessons. Participants also have a chance to visit small towns nearby, and tour wineries, as well as see horse shows and take part in informal meetings and parties for language practice and socializing. Optional activities include golfing, swimming, and horseback riding (lessons available). At least one school per country has programs for older travelers. These programs cost less and go at a more leisurely at pace. 75 Prospect Street, Suite 4, Huntington, NY 11743. 800-394-LEARN(5327) or 631-424-0777. www.itctravel.com. e-mail: itctravel@worldnet.att.net.

Mountain Fit Health And Fitness Adventures offers hiking holidays in America, Canada, Scotland, and France. In addition to hiking, other activities can usually be arranged, such as white-water rafting and horseback riding. Those who have taken at least one trip with the company or who pay in full 90 days before departure receive discounts. Travelers receive a discount for every referral who signs up for a trip. Additional savings are available for those who take two vacations in the same year. Several "Women's Week" trips offered. P.O. Box 6188, Bozeman, MT 59771. 800-926-5700 or 406-585-3506. www.mountainfit.com. e-mail: hike@mountainfit.com.

National Audubon Society--Audubon Ecology Camps And Workshops offer youths and adults a chance to study nature by participating in one of their many programs, which range from family adventures to natural history trips. 700 Broadway, New York, NY 10003. 212-979-3067. www.audubon.org. e-mail: aew@audubon.org.

National Trust Study Tours provide study tours and cruises featuring art, architecture, and preservation in the U.S. and around the world. Trips vary from year to year. Former trips include Eurasia and the Black Sea, In the Footsteps of Lincoln, and Lost Cities of History. Most trips are not for the budget-conscious but there are a few reasonably-priced ones. 1785 Massachusetts Avenue, NW, Washington, D.C. 20036. 800-944-6847 or 202-588-6000. www.nthp.org. e-mail: tours@nthp.org.

Original Golf School is an excellent and affordable way for golf enthusiasts to vacation and improve their game. Schools are held at these resorts: Snow Resort, VT; Crystal River, FL; Sugarloaf, ME; and Ocean City, MD. 800-240-2555. www.thegolfschool.com. e-mail: info@thegolfschool.com.

Outward Bound USA was established in 1961 and since then roughly 500,000 people have participated in their programs. For those looking for more than a vacation, Outward Bound has many programs "to help you go beyond your self-imposed physical and mental limitations." While physically challenging, they can be enjoyed by just about anyone in reasonable health. Route 9D, R2, Box 280, Garrison, NY 10524-9757. 888-88-BOUND or 914-424-4000. www.outwardbound.org.

Port Yacht Charters has both small and large power and sail yachts, for the "economy-minded to luxurious." Sailing adventures take place in the Caribbean, Mediterranean, and the Pacific Ocean (including Alaska). There is no set itinerary or meal plan because every trip is custom-tailored. Make your plans directly with Port Charles Charters, 9 Belleview Avenue, Port Washington, NY 11050. 800-213-0465. Outside the U.S: 516-886-0998. www.portyachtcharters.com. You may also book through a travel agent or call the U.S. Virgin Islands Department of Tourism (800-372-USVI) to make reservations.

Roadtrips offers hockey, basketball, football, golf, baseball, and auto racing vacations. Packages range from cheap to very expensive. 800-191 Lombard Avenue, Winnipeg, Manitoba Canada R3B OX1. 800-465-1765 or 204-957-1241. www.roadtrips.com. e-mail: info@roadtrips.com.

Sheri Griffith Expeditions provides all-inclusive rafting vacations. They raft only on nationally recognized and protected rivers through national parks, national monuments, and proposed wild and scenic rivers. The trips vary in the skill levels so any age and physical condition can be accommodated. Special trips are held annually for families, women-only, and singles. Customized trips are available upon request. Sheri Griffith says their Westcater Canyon/Colorado River trip "is the best short white-water trip in the West and a favorite of National Geographic." It involves two days of camping, hiking, and rafting using oar rafts(or paddleboats by request) and inflatable kayaks for the small rapids. Meals are guaranteed to satisfy even the most voracious appetites. They are "moveable feasts," such as fresh honeydew, blueberry pancakes with warm maple syrup, fresh baked spice cake with berries and cream, hors d'oeuvres, and grilled steak. Tents are equipped with deluxe mattress pads, and porta potties. P.O. Box 1324, Moab, UT 84532. 800-332-2439 or 435-259-8229. www.GriffithExp.com. e-mail: classriver@aol.com.

Sierra Club was founded in 1901 by John Muir. He helped lead the first Sierra Club Outing to Yosemite National Park. Formerly a nonprofit organization, Sierra Club dropped that status a couple of years ago so it could become more involved in political issues concerning the environment. Sierra Club now offers over 300 wilderness trips through their Sierra Club National Outings Program. It affords active travelers a chance to experience America and the world through a wide variety of options including backpacking, canoeing, bicycling, snow-shoeing, sailing, and more. Sierra Club has trips specifically designed for any and all interests and age levels, such as singles-only, women-only, seniors, photography buffs, teens, and vegetarians. Additionally, Sierra Club has lodges and huts available for rent in Yosemite National Park and other great places in the U.S. and Canada. 85 Second Street, Second Floor, San Francisco, CA 94105-3441. 415-977-5522. www.sierraclub.org/outings. e-mail: national.outings@sierraclub.org.

Smithsonian Institution's Study Tours & Seminars are designed to "reflect the vision, interests, and concerns of the Smithsonian Institute." It accomplishes this by giving participants a chance to learn about a wide range of topics including art, history, and science. They offer trips to 250 destinations through programs, such as Smithsonian Study Voyages, International Seminars, and Smithsonian Odyssey Tours. The Odyssey Tours, which Smithsonian classified is "Extraordinary Travel, Everyday Prices," are the best deals. 1100 Jefferson Drive SW, Suite 3077, MRC 702, Washington, DC 20560. 202-357-4700. www.si.edu/tsa/sst.

Southwest Ed-Ventures is a program run by Four Corners School of Outdoor Education and promises "Adventure with a Mission for People of All Ages." Many exciting, learning adventures are offered, from traversing the Grand Canyon to researching ancient cultures. Cultural or art studies and archaeological explorations are offered for individuals, families, and women-only. Customized trips can be arranged. College credit is available for all programs or tax deductions are available on some ed-ventures. These are popular trips and spaces fill fast. P.O. Box 1029, Monticello, Utah 84535. 800-525-4456 or 435-587-2156. www.sw-adventures.org or www.fourcornersschool.org. e-mail: fcs@sanjuan.net.

Space Camp And Aviation Challenge Camps are open to both children and adults, year-round. Programs start at $700 (for kids), per week, excluding airfare. Cost is slightly higher for adults. Camps are held in Alabama, California, and Florida. Camps fill quickly in the summer and during holidays. Group rates, scholarships, and sibling discounts available. 800-637-7223. www.spacecamp.com.

Superclubs(active)/Breezes(active)/Grand Lido(luxury)/ Hedonism(wicked) is similar in concept to Club Med, but slightly more upscale. Therefore, cost is a little higher than Club Med. Some facilities, such as Hedonism resorts, are more geared to the those 18–35 with a "wild and crazy-anything goes" mentality, so be sure to ask what age or type of traveler a resort caters to before booking. Specials frequently offered, including no supplements, to single travelers. 877-GO-SUPER(467-8737). www.superclubs.com. e-mail: info@superclubs.com.

Tauck World Discovery offers 59 North American adventures, including family vacations, weekend learning trips, and resort getaways. 276 Post Road West, Westport, CT 06880. 800-788-7885. www.tauck.com. email: info@tauck.com.

The Underwater Explorers Society (UNEXSO) is the world's largest dive resort. *Skin Diver* Magazine states "It is the most sophisticated and best equipped dive facility in the world." Founded in 1965, UNEXSO is located on Grand Bahamas Island, which is surrounded by shallow (15 ft.) to deep (80 ft.) ocean reefs. Participants can learn or refine scuba diving skills at one of the training pools and in class. There is a restaurant, full-service dive and repair center, and boutique, as well as a photo-video center where underwater cameras can be rented. Whether you're into snorkeling or diving or just interested in marine life, this is the place for you. UNEXSO promises "an exciting array of packages for every level of diver and every budget." Their Shark Feeder Program, which lets participants feed sharks (requires special training), is proof of that! P.O. Box 22878, Ft. Lauderdale, Florida 33335. 800-992-DIVE(3483) or 954-351-9889. Bahamas Address: Box F42433, Freeport, Grand Bahama Island, The Bahamas. 242-373-1244.

NOTE: For information on 100+ diving resorts and liveaboards worldwide offering "unbelievably priced dive travel packages," call 800-594-6826. www.worldive-tours.com.

Vacation Express offers nearly three dozen charters every week departing from most major gateways. Destinations include Cancun, Cozumel, Aruba, Dominican Republic, Jamaica, and Costa Rica. Check out the "Hot Deals" portion of its Web sites for outstanding specials. Prices are less than $1,000pp (all-inclusive at big resorts with unlimited drinks, entertainment, recreation, three meals daily, and more) from May through September. 800-309-4717 or 800-486-9777 or 800-848-8047 or 404-315-4848. www.vacationexpress.com. e-mail: sales@vacationexpress.com.

Valtur provides all-inclusive tours and resort stays in Italy, Morocco, and Caribbean. No single supplement charged and discounts available for children. Great packages for singles, couples, families, and mature travelers. 877-582-2284 or 619-297-4100. www.clubvaltur.com. e-mail: vacation@ clubholidays.com.

Wandering Wheels is a nonprofit organization that offers a variety of trips for adults who are interested in mixing Bible study with bicycling. They have taken more than 3,000 riders on long-distance cycling trips through Canada, Netherlands, and USA. P.O. Box 207, Upland, IN 46989. 765-998-7490. www.wanderingwheels.org.

Wayfarers offer 16 different European Walking Tours in the British Isles, France, Italy, and Switzerland. Participants are typically Americans and Canadians, mid-30s to late-50s. Walks vary from very gentle walking with an average of four miles daily to 10 miles daily average over rugged terrain. Walking starts around 9 a.m. and ends by 5 p.m., with stops and meandering along the way. Drinks and snacks are included. A van will take those who are tired, or just don't feel like walking, on to the next hotel. Participants may choose from four different types of walking trips: adventure walks, culture walks, classic walks, or expedition walks. Most of the tours are not for the budget-minded, but Wayfarers does offer a few affordable walking trips. 172 Bellevue Avenue, Newport, RI 02840-3582. 800-249-4620 or 401-849-5087. www.thewayfarers.com.

Wilderness Inquiry provides many different outdoor adventures, such as a seven-day canoe trip that follows the trail of explorers, Lewis & Clark. 612-676-9400. www.wildernessinquiry.org.

YMT Vacations has guaranteed weekly departures on scheduled airlines from most U.S. cities to many resort locations, including Hawaii and Mexico. Packages are usually all-inclusive. Get together a group of nine and travel free. Become a group leader to travel free and receive cash incentives. 8831 Aviation Blvd., Inglewood, CA 90301. 800-922-9000 or 800-888-8204 or 310-649-3820. www.GoYMT.com. e-mail: comments@ymtvacations.com.

TIP: America's Most Affordable Weight Loss Spas

Regency House Natural Health Spa (in Hallandale, Florida, est. 1984). Vegetarian cuisine, calorie-controlled, exercise (depending on how much you want to do) ranges from yoga, meditation, stretching classes, aerobics, morning walks, gym workouts, and more. 800-454-0003. www.regencyhealthspa.com.

Lido Spa Hotel & Health Resort (near South Beach, Miami Beach, Florida). Lido caters to an older crowd, but aquatic exercise in the saltwater and freshwater pools, vegetarian and nonvegetarian cuisine, and tai chi appeals to all ages. Tipping expected. 800-327-8363. www.lidospa.com.

Deerfield Spa (Pocono Mountains, East Stroudsburg, Pennsylvania). Guests can choose from aquatic karate, belly dancing, tae kwon do, and kickboxing. And, best of all, there's no tipping! 800-852-4494. www.deerfieldspa.com.

The Oaks at Ojai (Ojai, California). In the mountains of California, this spa offers the perfect combination of gourmet cuisine and sixteen daily health classes, such as mountain biking, yoga, and morning strolls, as part of your weekly fee. 800-753-6257. www.oaksspa.com.

Red Mountain Resort & Spa (Ivins, Utah). The scenery is spectacular, but that's no surprise considering the resort is located 3,000 feet above sea level and boasts a mild year-round climate. Activities include snowshoeing, backcountry hiking, horseback riding, overnight camping, plus fitness classes. 800-407-3002. www.redmountainspa.com.

The Seventh-Day Adventists run a couple of low-cost wellness resorts. Poland Spring Health Institute is in Maine (207-998-2894) and Black Hills Health & Education Center in South Dakota (800-658-5433). Prices start at $500pp, per week, and include lodging, vegetarian meals, medical lectures, classes, personal fitness training, massage, whirlpools, and more. No religious discussions.

◆   ◆   ◆

Solo Travelers

Congratulations for taking the initiative to travel on your own! As part of the travel series I teach, I offer a class for solo travelers. Many of the participants are men and women whose spouse or friends do not want to take the kinds of vacations they are interested in— yet they charge on and have exciting and rewarding experiences. Traveling on your own provides more opportunities to make friends you wouldn't have met otherwise because it "forces" you to be more interactive.

Unfortunately, it is difficult to find trips that do not charge an additional fee for single accommodations. The reason is obvious: two people equals two paying guests. If a seven day trip to say, Mexico, costs $1,200pp, that comes to a total of $2,400 for two (double occupancy). However, if you put just one person in a room, that is only $1,200. A supplement helps offset the revenue loss. That's why single supplements often seem high. Supplements vary, according to companies and whether it is a land tour or cruise, which usually have the highest single supplements.

However, many companies offer minimal or no single supplements on certain trips, as well as travel companion programs. Also, if a suitable roommate cannot be found, you will most likely get your own room at no extra cost. Always ask about these things when requesting information.

American Adventures & Road Runner offers small group adventures throughout North America. Lodging includes hotels, hostels, and/or camping and transport vehicles are air-conditioned "maxiwagons." No single supplements. P.O. Box 1155, Gardena, CA 90249. 800-873-5872 or 310-324-3447. www.americanadventures.com. e-mail: amadiax@aol.com.

American Wilderness Experience (AWE) specializes in small group travel adventure and says it is "America's premier purveyor of domestic and international back country adventure and Old West dude ranch vacations." They offer skiing trips, sailing excursions, and dude ranch vacations geared to singles, families, women-only, independent, and mature, travelers. Discounted rates for are often available for solo travelers. 2820-A Wilderness Place, Boulder, CO 80301. 800-444-0099 or 303-444-2622. www.gorp.com/awe. e-mail: awedave@aol.com.

GORP's Web site is a also a great source for all outdoor activities, outdoor tour companies and outfitters, books, maps, and gear. It even offers a Hot Deals section. Or, call 877-440-GORP.

Atelier Bez is a photography workshop in the South of France. It is located in the hills of the Parc Naturel du Haut Langeudoc, off the beaten path and unspoiled by progress. Inspiration includes fields of sunflowers, rolling hills, forests, gorges, rivers and lakes, nearby medieval Cathar sites, vineyards, and Mediterranean coast. Participants do not have to speak French. The summer workshop combines an exploration of France, including photo festivals, with a focus on photography. although painters and writers are welcome. The studios and accommodations are the former village dance hall and cinema. The darkroom is equipped to professional standards and the lighting studio doubles as a painting studio. Cost ranges from $500–$900 and includes tuition, darkroom chemistry/lab fee, meals (croissant breakfasts, picnic lunches, and regional wines and specialties prepared by a chef for dinner), bed and breakfast in shared rooms with private baths, and field trips. Single supplements are just $50! In France, contact Mabel Odessey, Atelier Le Bez, Le Bez, 81260 Brassac France; Telephone and fax: 05-63-74-56-22. e-mail: artlebez@aol.com. In the U.S., contact Kevin Martini-Fuller, P.O. Box 2156, St. Louis, MO. 63158. 314-457-1008. e-mail: KevinMF@mindspring.com.

Backroads offers gourmet tours, deluxe camping, and active trips that emphasize watersports, bicycling and walking tours. These can be enjoyed by the beginner, as well as advanced. Special interest trips for singles, students, families, and mature travelers. Catalogs clearly indicate activities and length, such as "kayaking half day" or "easy walking, 2-4 miles/day." Most trips take place in California, Rockies, Hawaii, Ireland, and Italy. Singles-oriented trips include Europe, Latin America, Canada, and U.S. While singles are encouraged in these dedicated trips, there is still a supplement for those who wish to have private accommodations. Discounts available for those 65 or older who are first-time travelers with Backroads. 801 Cedar Street, Berkeley, CA 94710. 800-GO-ACTIVE(462-2848) or 510-527-1555. www.backroads.com. e-mail:goactive@backroads.com.

Bar H Dude & Guest Ranch (Clarendon, TX) is an authentic working ranch that has one of the lowest rates in America. Guests can participate by helping move cattle or herding, or just relax by fishing, swimming, horseback riding, playing games, and reading. Low single supplement. 888-987-2457. Book through Hidden Trails and receive 5 percent discount. Hidden Trails also books other U.S. and worldwide guest ranches, riding tours, bison and cattle drives, and covered wagon train adventures. 888-9-TRAILS. www.hiddentrails.com.

The Barge Lady offers European canal and river cruise tours. Many trips start at less than $1,000pp. On several of their barge trips in England, France, and Ireland, single cabins are available with no single supplement. Barge lady has been highly recommended by many prestigious publications, including *Gourmet Magazine*, *Town and Country*, and *New York Times*. What makes the cruises exceptional is the gourmet cuisine, lovely, air-conditioned cabins, and many public areas (so passengers can meet fellow passengers or simply find a quiet spot to read and enjoy the view). 101 W. Grand Avenue, Suite 200, Chicago, IL 60610. 800-880-0071 or 312-245-0952. www.bargelady.com. e-mail: carol@bargelady.com.

Beaches offers all-inclusive resort vacations for singles, couples, and families, to exotic destinations, such as Turks and Caicos, Jamaica, Bahamas, St. Lucia, and Antigua. Departure cities are usually Miami, New York, or Chicago. 4950 SW 72nd Avenue, Miami, FL 33155. 888-BEACHES or 305-284-1300. In Canada: 416-223-0028. www.beaches.com. e-mail: info@beaches.com.

Club Med offers all-inclusive resort vacations in the U.S. and around-the-world. Price includes lodging, watersports and land activities(including instruction), all meals with beer or wine for lunch and dinner, night time entertainment. Specialty programs include singles, single parents, families, couples, adventure, faraway, and Forever Young (55 or older). Half the guests are 24–44 years old. Roommates are assigned or a 20-40 percent single supplement is assessed. Each Club Med resort specializes in a different program so be sure to ask about resorts that meet your needs. Rates are typically less than $1,000 per week. 800-CLUBMED or 888-932-2582. For groups: 800-453-2582. www.clubmed.com. e-mail: info@clubmed.com.

Contiki is the world's biggest travel company for 18–35 year olds. They operate budget vacations to Europe, Africa, Mexico, Canada, Australia, New Zealand, and the U.S. Book early and save 2.5 percent on the land tour portion of any trip that last at least seven days. Contiki offers savings for mid-week departures (Monday, Tuesday, or Wednesday) and quadruple-occupancy rooms. 2300 E. Katella Avenue, #450, Anaheim, CA 92806. In U.S. and Canada: 888-CONTIKI. www.contiki.com. e-mail: contiki@contiki.com.

Grand Circle Travel is a leading tour operator for people 50 or older. It was established in 1958 by the same woman who founded AARP. Since that time, more than 600,000 travelers have been all over the world with GCT on land tours and cruises. It offers lower prices than most companies do for single travelers and a roommate service is provided for those willing to share a room or cabin. GCT often has 2-for-1s on many cruises. 347 Congress Street, Boston, MA 02210. 800-955-1034 or 800-321-2835. www.gct.com.

Sheri Griffith Expeditions provides all-inclusive rafting vacations. You raft only on nationally recognized and protected rivers through national parks, national monuments, and proposed wild and scenic rivers. The trips vary in the skill levels so any age and physical condition can be accommodated. Special trips are held annually for families, women-only, and singles. Customized trips are available upon request. Sheri Griffith says their Westcater Canyon/Colorado River trip "is the best short white-water trip in the West and a favorite of National Geographic." It involves two days of camping, hiking, and rafting using oar rafts(or paddleboats by request) and inflatable kayaks for the small rapids. Meals are guaranteed to satisfy even the most voracious appetites. They are "moveable feasts," such as fresh honeydew, blueberry pancakes with warm maple syrup, fresh baked spice cake with berries and cream, hors d'oeuvres, and grilled steak. Tents are equipped with deluxe mattress pads, and porta potties. P.O. Box 1324, Moab, UT 84532. 800-332-2439 or 435-259-8229. www.GriffithExp.com. e-mail: classriver@aol.com

O Solo Mio Singles Tours specializes in trips for single travelers, including trips for Ages 35 and younger. The company, established in 1991, offers 25 domestic and international singles-only trips every year. "Our main objective is travel, therefore we have excursions for many different interests and group sizes...these trips will combine all the advantages of a friendly organized group, as well as leave you with plenty of spare time to explore on your own or with new-found friends." Low group airfare is available. They also offer a subscription newsletter that details trips and provides other useful information. Cost is subtracted from the price of your first trip so it is free for participants. O Solo Mio gives interested travelers a free sample issue. 636 Los Altos Rancho, Los Altos, CA 94034. 800-959-8568 or 650-917-0817. www.osolomio.com. e-mail: osolomioat@aol.com.

Preferred Adventures, Ltd. offers worldwide tours and adventure-oriented vacations. Some trips are discounted for mature travelers and the company president told me "single supplements are usually negotiable." One West Water Street, Suite #300, St. Paul, MN 55107. 800-840-8687 or 651-222-8131. e-mail: paltours@aol.com.

Saga Land And Cruise Tours is another big tour operator for travelers 50 and older. They provide cruises and tours to just about everywhere in the world. If traveling on your own, Saga will pair you up with a traveling companion. Single rooms or cabins are available without paying a surcharge on some of their trips and cruises. 222 Berkeley Street, Boston, MA. 02116. 800-952-9590 or 800-343-0273. www.sagaholidays.com.

SmarTours extends discounted travel from the Orient to Egypt. All tour prices include air, transfers, guides, first class hotels, ground transportation, and some sightseeing. Single supplements are usually $150-$199. 501 Fifth Avenue, Suite 812, New York, NY 10017. 800-337-7773. www.smartours.net.

Solo Flights And Mature Tours has been offering singles-only trips for over 25 years to Alaska, Britain, Greece, Canada, Italy, and Costa Rica. 10 Greenwood Lane, Westport, CT 06880. 800-266-1566 or 203-256-1235.

Suddenly Single Tours offers domestic and international trips for singles looking to make new friends. Single rooms are available without paying a supplement. Trips vary from year to year. 161 Dreiser Loop, New York, NY 10475. 718-379-8800.

Superclubs(active)/Breezes(active)/Grand Lido(luxury)/ Hedonism(wicked) is similar in concept to Club Med, but slightly more upscale. Therefore, cost is a little higher than Club Med. Some facilities, such as Hedonism resorts, are more geared to the those 18–35 with a "wild and crazy-anything goes" mentality, so be sure to ask what age or type of traveler a resort caters to before booking. Specials frequently offered, including no supplements, to single travelers. 877-GO-SUPER (467-8737). www.superclubs.com. e-mail: info@superclubs.com.

Untours offers some untours to Europe each year with no single supplements. For example, it offers a package to Venice that includes airfare from the states, apartment stay in Venice for 2-4 weeks, Italian Rail FlexiPass, and airport greeting and orientation. P.O. Box 405, Media, PA 19063. 888-UNTOUR1(868-6871). www.untours.com.

UTc(United Touring Company) is one of the most well-established tour operators in Africa (53 years in business as of 2000) and offer some of the cheapest single supplements for African travel that I have ever seen. They offer both packages and customized safaris. Recently, they began offering trips to Arabia. One Bala Plaza, Suite 414, Bala Cynwyd, PA 19004. 800-223-6486 or 610-617-3300. www.unitedtour.com. e-mail: utcusa@unitedtour.com.

Valtur provides all-inclusive tours and resort stays in Italy, Morocco, and Caribbean. No single supplement charged and discounts available for children. Great packages for singles, couples, families, and mature travelers. 877-582-2284 or 619-297-4100. www.clubvaltur.com. e-mail: vacation@ clubholidays.com.

TIP: When contacting tour companies, be sure to specify that you are interested in their singles-oriented trips or cruises. I recommend contacting any of the companies mentioned in this reference that you are interested in traveling with, even if special deals for singles are not indicated. A singles-only trip may have recently been added or they may work out something that is not listed in their brochure (such as waiving the single supplement). Men traveling on their own usually get their own rooms or cabins because there aren't as many men traveling unaccompanied as women.

Cruises, especially those aboard large cruise ships, can be difficult for those traveling by themselves, unless it is a singles-oriented cruise. Royal Caribbean and Carnival offer several singles-only cruises at very reasonable rates. Royal Caribbean and Norwegian have a guaranteed singles rate, subject to availability. Most cruise lines will try to match you with a roommate. Some upscale cruise lines, such as Crystal and Cunard, have gentlemen hosts for solo cruisers. The hosts are single, older gentlemen who do not get romantically involved with the passengers but simply make sure they have a good time by dancing with them or talking to them over dinner.

For more information on singles cruises and resources, see Chapter Five: Cruises. American Dream Cruises has information regarding cruises for singles. 800-805-0053. Encore Singles also specializes in singles-only cruises. 888-269-7656. www.encoresingles.net.

Wayfarers offer 16 different European Walking Tours in the British Isles, France, Italy, and Switzerland. Participants are typically Americans and Canadians, mid-30s to late-50s. Walks vary from very gentle walking with an average of four miles daily to 10 miles daily average over rugged terrain. Walking starts around 9 a.m. and ends by 5 p.m., with stops and meandering along the way. Drinks and snacks are included. A van will take those who are tired, or just don't feel like walking, on to the next hotel. Participants may choose from four different types of walking trips: adventure walks, culture walks, classic walks, or expedition walks. Most of their tours are not for the budget-minded, but Wayfarers does offer a few affordable walking trips. 172 Bellevue Avenue, Newport, RI 02840-3582. 800-249-4620 or 401-849-5087. www.thewayfarers.com.

Windjammer Sailing Cruises offer singles-only sailing trips. They promise "an even mixture of fun-loving males and females and a sailing adventure you'll never forget!" Singles rates(for those who insist on private accommodations) are 175 percent of the double occupancy rate. Otherwise, participants will be paired up with suitable room mates. Prices start at less than $1,000 per week on singles-only cruises. Windjammer's famous single sailings have been featured in many publications and on The Travel Channel. More information is available on Windjammer in Chapter Five: Cruises. P.O. Box 190, Miami Beach, FL 33119-0120. 800-327-2601. www.windjammer.com.

<u>Women-Only</u>

Adventure Associates offers both co-ed and women-only adventure trips. P.O. Box 16304, Seattle, WA 98116. 888-532-8352. www.adventureassociates.net. e-mail: advntrass@aol.com.

Adventure Women (formerly Rainbow Adventures) specializes in active adventure holidays worldwide for women over 30. Trips are rated easy, moderate, or high energy so you can be sure to pick what's right for you. The company began offering a new level of adventure trips a couple of years ago, "Women Born to be Wild." It is for women who "seek thrilling wilderness challenges and out of the ordinary experiences in places beyond the realm of traditional travel." No single supplements are assigned because all rooms or cabins are double occupancy. A suitable roommate will be arranged for those traveling on their own. 15033 Kelly Canyon Road, Bozeman, MT 59715. 800-804-8686 or 406-587-3883. www.adventurewomen.com. e-mail: info@adventurewomen.com.

Adventures in Good Company offers a wide variety of women-only trips, all led by former Woodswomen guides. 5506 Trading Post Trail, Afton, MN 55001. (toll free) 877-439-4042 or 651-998-0120. www.gorp.com/goadventure.

Annette's Adventures provide several intriguing women-only Hawaiian vacations, as well as links to other resources for women travelers. 45-403 Koa Kahiko Street. Kaneohe, Hawaii 96744. 808-235-5431. www.annettesadventures.com. e-mail: annettesadventures@juno.com.

Earthwise Journeys offer many specialty trips worldwide, including art and nature, ecotravel, outdoor adventure, cultural exploration, women-only, and volunteer vacations. P.O. Box 16177, Portland, OR 97292. 800-344-5309 or 503-736-3364. www.earthwisejourneys.com.

Explorations In Travel provides active women over 40 unusual travel experiences by taking them off-the-beaten track. They offer trips to Europe, Latin America, and several other worldwide destinations. Explorations also offers year-round volunteer programs with placements for small groups and individuals, as well as teachers and their students. Examples of these unique cultural adventures include working on organic farms in New Zealand, ecotourist projects in Belize, and organizing recreational and fundraising events for homeless children in Costa Rica. 1922 River Road, Guilford, VT 05301. 802-257-0152. www.exploretravel.com. e-mail: women@exploretravel.com

Merry Widows Dance Cruises are presented by AAA Travel Agency and Auto Club South. AAA created Merry Widow Cruises in 1977 for single, widowed, or divorced women ages 50–90. These unusual trips combine travel with dance. The cruises go to exotic ports of call, such as the South Pacific, Mediterranean, Europe, South America, Caribbean, Canada, Alaska, the Orient, and more, as well as U.S. destinations, such as Sea Island, Georgia. Professional male dance teachers are aboard every cruise with one professional dance host per every four women passengers. Rotating dance cards and dinner table assignments enable participants to meet and enjoy the company of many different people. P.O.Box 31087, Tampa, FL 33622. 813-289-5923. Or, contact your local AAA Travel Agency.

Mountain Fit Health And Fitness Adventures offers hiking holidays in America, Canada, Scotland, and France. In addition to hiking, other activities can usually be arranged, such as white-water rafting and horseback riding. Those who have taken at least one trip with the company or who pay in full 90 days before departure receive discounts. Travelers receive a discount for every referral who signs up for a trip. Additional savings are available for those who take two vacations in the same year. Several "Women's Week" trips offered. Single supplements average $300 on most trips. P.O. Box 6188, Bozeman, MT 59771. 800-926-5700 or 406-585-3506. www.mountainfit.com. e-mail: hike@ mountainfit.com.

ReQuest Adventures provide all kinds of travel, such as Food and Wine Tours; Art, History, and Sightseeing Tours; Walking Tours; Barge Cruises; and a couple of annual women-only offerings. Their budget-priced 'Ladies on the Loose in Paris' trip has been praised by participants and travel writers alike. P.O. Box 531, Corte Madera, CA 94976. 415-389-1892. www.requestadv.com.

SacredPlay Nature Tours takes women on expeditions into the high desert of southern Arizona. 800-411-2367. www.sacredplay.com. e-mail: info@sacreplay.

Travel In Style offers affordable tours and cruises to Greece, Jordan, Morocco, Japan, Israel, Syria, and Tunisia. Their women-only cultural exploration of the customs and lifestyles of Turkish women is one of the most popular trips they offer. Participants meet local artisans, prepare traditional Turkish meals, and much more. Turkey trips depart the first Friday of every month. 1255 Post Street, Suite 506, San Francisco, CA 94109. 888-466-8242 or 415-440-1124. www.travelinstyle.com.

Wild Chickadee Adventures offers several active ecoadventures for women of all ages. 1169 Croft Road, Quesnel, B.C., V2J SR5. (toll-free) 866-991-0130 or 250-747-2199. www.chickadeeadventures .com. e-mail: chickadeeadventures@yahoo.com.

Wild Women Expeditions offers a myriad of outdoor adventures, ranging from canoeing to dogsledding. P.O. Box 145, Station B, Sudbury, Ontario, Canada P3E4N5. 705-866-1260. www.wildwomenexp.com. e-mail: beth@wildwomenexp.com.

Women Traveling Together takes small groups of women over 40 on worldwide trips. They offer 20 cruises and trips to southwestern United States, Australia, New Zealand, and England. Trips range from weekend getaways to extended holidays. Group size averages 12 and age range is 40–65. Guaranteed share program on rooms. For those wanting their own rooms, single supplements start at $300. There's a fee to join and receive information on trips because it's a small organization. Membership Correspondence: 300 Crestview Lane, Suite 200, Spartanburg, SC 29301. 800-795-7135 or 410-956-5250. www.women-traveling.com.

Women's Nature Adventures/Wild Heart Journeys of Discovery offers nature, photography, and 'outdoor skills' vacations in the U.S. and Canada. P.O. Box 313, North Pomfret, VT 05053. 802-457-9367. www.nature-adventures.com. e-mail: wildheart@valley.net.

◆ FYI: The southernmost city in the world is Ushuaia, Argentina. The northernmost town is NY-Alesund, Spitsbergen, Norway.

◆　　◆　　◆

Mature Travelers
Club Med offers all-inclusive resort vacations in the U.S. and around-the-world. Price includes lodging, watersports and land activities(including instruction), all meals with beer or wine for lunch and dinner, night time entertainment. Specialty programs include singles, single parents, families,

couples, adventure, faraway, and Forever Young (55 or older). This program also entitles older travelers to a discount at several resorts that offer golf, shopping, tennis, and more. Rates are typically less than $1,000 per week. 800-CLUBMED or 888-932-2582. For groups: 800-453-2582. www.clubmed.com. e-mail: info@clubmed.com.

Elderhostel is "a preeminent provider of high quality, affordable educational opportunities for older adults." Anyone 55 years of age or older is eligible and a spouse or adult companion may accompany an eligible participant, even if that person is not 55. Elderhostel is the biggest and most diverse organization catering to mature travelers. It offers hundreds of distinctive domestic and international travel and learn opportunities, varying in physical demands and costs. Participants are assured of meeting their vacation needs because Elderhostel offers everything from a Study and Cruise Program in Greece to Camping in Mexico—even homestay programs and spiritually oriented trips. Prices are always all-inclusive, which includes round-trip international airfare, classes, field trips, excursions, cultural events, room and board, transfers, staff, insurance, and gratuities. There are no hidden costs or additional arrangements to be made. 11 Avenue de Lafayette, Boston, MA 02111. 877-426-8056. www.elderhostel.org.

Eldertreks provides more than 28 soft, exotic adventures for those over 50 to worldwide destinations. Trips vary greatly, from searching for dinosaur bones in the Gobi, to tracking lemurs in Madagascar. Prices are just as varied with some trips being much more affordable than others. 597 Markham Street, Toronto, ON M6G 2L7, Canada. 416-588-5000 or 800-741-7956. www.eldertreks.com. e-mail: eldertreks@eldertreks.com.

Golden Age Travellers is actually a club that offers a wide array of ever-changing adventures for people 50 or older. Pier 27, the Embarcadero, San Francisco, CA 94111. 800-258-8880. www.gatclub.com.

Grand Circle Travel (GCT) is a leading tour operator for those 50 or older. It was established in 1958 by the same woman who founded AARP. Since that time, more than 600,000 travelers have been all over the world with GCT on land tours and cruises. It offers lower prices than most companies do for single travelers and a roommate service is provided for those willing to share a room or cabin. GCT often has 2-for-1s on many cruises. 347 Congress Street, Boston, MA 02210. 800-955-1034 or 800-321-2835. www.gct.com.

Interhostel is an "International Educational Travel Experience for Adults Over 50." Programs take place in the U.S. and overseas. They also offer Family Hostel programs, which are reasonably priced. Their U.S. programs are better deals than their international programs. Interhostal, University of New Hampshire, 6 Harrison Avenue, Durham, NH 03824-3529. 800-733-9753 or 603-862-1147. www.learn.unh.edu. e-mail: learn.dce@unh.edu.

Lingua Service Worldwide, established 1988, is for those interested in Vacation 'N Learn language and culture courses. Lingua has programs for all ages, interests, and budgets in many countries, such as China, Venezuela, Israel, Austria, Netherlands, Russia, Greece, Spain, Italy, France, and Germany. Participants may opt to combine a study course with golfing, skiing, cooking, or studying art. Accommodations include apartments, hotels, dormitories, and home stays. For example, in Spain participants learn Spanish and get free cooking and dance lessons. Participants also have a chance to visit small towns nearby, and tour wineries, as well as see horse shows and take part in informal meetings and parties for language practice and socializing. Optional activities include golfing, swimming, and horseback riding (lessons available). At least one school per country has programs for older travelers that cost less and go at a more leisurely at pace. 75 Prospect Street, Suite 4, Huntington, NY 11743. 800-394-LEARN(5327) or 631-424-0777. www.itctravel.com. e-mail: itctravel@worldnet .att.net.

Mayflower Tours provides deluxe escorted holidays within the continental U.S., as well as Alaska, Hawaii, Mexico, and Canada, for those 55 and older. They have a Guaranteed Share Program, which means if you are interested in a roommate and they are unable to find you a suitable roommate, you will not have to pay a single supplement. The best prices are on specials and last minute deals. 1225 Warren Avenue, P.O. Box 490, Downers Grove, IL 60515. 800-323-7604.

Merry Widows Dance Cruises are presented by AAA Travel Agency and Auto Club South. AAA created Merry Widow Cruises in 1977 for single, widowed, or divorced women ages 50–90. These unusual trips combine travel with dance. The cruises go to exotic ports of call, such as the South Pacific, Mediterranean, Europe, South America, Caribbean, Canada, Alaska, the Orient, and more, as well as U.S. destinations, such as Sea Island, Georgia. Professional male dance teachers are aboard every cruise with one professional dance host per every four women passengers. Rotating dance cards and dinner table assignments enable participants to meet and enjoy the company of many different people. P.O. Box 31087, Tampa, FL 33622. 813-289-5923. Or, contact your local AAA Travel Agency or the national office at 888-222-7869. www.aaa.com.

Preferred Adventures, Ltd. offers worldwide tours and adventure-oriented vacations. Some trips are discounted for mature travelers and the company president told me "single supplements are usually negotiable." One West Water Street, Suite #300, St. Paul, MN 55107. 800-840-8687 or 651-222-8131. e-mail: paltours@aol.com.

Saga Land And Cruise Tours is another big tour operator for travelers 50 and older. They provide cruises and tours to just about everywhere in the world. If traveling on your own, Saga will pair you up with a traveling companion. Single rooms or cabins are available without paying a surcharge on some of their trips and cruises. 222 Berkeley Street, Boston, MA 02116. 800-952-9590 or 800-343-0273.

Senior Escorted Tours is "designed with senior travelers in mind but trips are open to all age groups." They offer both U.S. and European vacations. 223 N. Main Street, Box 400, Cape May Court House, NJ 08210. 800-222-1254 or 609-465-4011.

Senior World Tours offers "active travel for mature adults," ranging from snowmobiling tours of Jackson Hole, Wyoming to summer pack trips through the Grand Teton National Park. Also offers some non-senior trips, as well as women-only tours. Senior World Tours, a subsidiary of ZIM Hi-Country Tours, 2205 N. River Road, Fremont, OH 43420-9483. 888-355-1686 or 419-355-1686. e-mail: Zimhico@nwohio.com.

Solo Flights And Mature Tours has been offering singles-only trips, tours, and group bookings with other tour companies, for over twenty-five years to Alaska, Britain, Greece, Canada, Italy, and Costa Rica. 10 Greenwood Lane, Westport, CT 06880. 800-266-1566 or 203-256-1235.

Trafalgar's Autumn Years Tours are for people 55 and older who are interested in trips through the United States, Canada, Europe, and Great Britain. They offer deluxe and first class tours, as well as a Cost Saver program. They say they are "Europe's Premier Escorted Budget Tours." Special discounts are given for groups of three or five traveling together, children, early bookings, multiple tour bookings, and repeat travelers. Trafalgar also offers Club 21-35, which provides exciting European tours specially for ages 21-35. 11 E. 26th Street, Suite 1300, New York, NY 10010. 800-854-0103. www.trafalgartours.com.

Walking The World is for travelers over 50 "...who still have or want to rekindle your personal sense of adventure." They have offered North American and European vacations for more than 15 years. Currently, there are 30 hiking and horseback riding trips offered. P.O. Box 1186, Fort Collins, CO 80522. 800-340-9255. www.walkingtheworld.com. e-mail: walktworld@aol.com.

◆ FYI: Adventure travel is now a $250 billion a year industry. Over 685 travel agencies currently specialize in it. For more information on adventure travel, log on to www.away.com

---

◆   ◆   ◆

Specialty Travel: Adventure and Ecotravel

This section examines specialty land tours. Any kind of experience you are seeking can be found through most of the companies listed here. This section is not divided, such as women-only, or mature travelers because these companies basically treat all travelers the same—as fellow adventurers. Most of these experiences are self-explanatory, with the exception of ecotravel. If you are unfamiliar with ecotravel, it's defined by three criteria. Participants take extra care to learn about and respect the local culture. This is manifested in appropriate dress, behavior, and so forth. Travelers follow established guidelines, such as no littering, staying on trails, and keeping a safe distance from and not interfering with wildlife. The ecotravel motto is *"Leave nothing behind but footprints."* Ecotravel operators and travelers seek and support local business, such as eating at local restaurants. The Ecotourism Society is an international, nonprofit organization with a mission "to aid researchers, conservationists, and ecotour operators by setting standards and guidelines and informing them of increasingly vulnerable parts of the world so as to protect the ecology worldwide." They provide travelers with a complete up-to-date membership list of ecotour operators. P.O. Box 755, Bennington, VT 05402. 802-651-9818. www.ecotourism.org. e-mail: ecomail@ecotourism.org.

Adventure travel usually costs more than other types of travel. As mentioned earlier, this is because of the remote destinations and types of activities included. As with all listings in this reference, I have only included companies that have been in business for a long time, maintained a good reputation, and provide the most "bang" for the buck. Most companies offer land-only packages with optional add-on airfares. I recommend combining land-only tours with the cheap airfare strategies found in Chapter Four: Airlines. Compare prices to see if you came up with a cheaper fare than what the tour operator offers.

2Afrika offers incredible adventures throughout Africa at exceptional prices. Be sure to check out Web site for latest specials. 444 Washington Blvd., Suite 3144, Jersey City, NJ 07310. 877-200-5610 or 201-533-1075. www.2afrika.com. e-mail: info@2afrika.com.

Above The Clouds Trekking provides travelers in-depth exploration, through walking and trekking adventures in Nepal, Madagascar, Europe, and the Americas. The founder of the company spent five years living in Nepal and speaks Nepali fluently, as well as eight other languages. P.O. Box 398, Worcester, MA 01602-0398. 800-233-4499 or 508-799-4499. www.gorp.com/abvclds.htm. e-mail: sconlon@world.std.com.

Adventurebus–Adventure Planet is a cheap and fun way "to explore the planet." Trips range from Mexico to India. 34560 Ave B. Yucaipa, CA 92399. 888-73-PLANET (737-5263) or 909-797-7366 (outside the U.S.). www.adventurebus.com. e-mail: info@adventureplanet.com.

Adventure Center (has something for everyone no matter where or how you are interested in traveling, such as wildlife safaris, cultural tours, sailing adventures, jungle exploration, trekking expeditions, and wilderness experiences. 5540 TMT College Avenue, Oakland, CA 94618. 800-227-8747. www.adventurecenter.com.

Adventures Abroad, established in 1988, provide in-depth holidays for small groups, all ages welcome. More than 400 worldwide trips, including destinations that are not normally offered by tour operators, such as Iran, Albania, Czech Republic, Yucatan, Nicaragua, Yemen, and Vietnam. 1123 Fir Avenue, Blaine, WA 98230. 800-665-3998 or 604-303-1099. www.adventures-abroad.com. e-mail: info@adventures-abroad.com.

Adventure Collection is "six of the highest quality adventure travel companies in a cooperative organization dedicated to providing consumers with comprehensive and reliable adventure travel information and furthering the preservation and enhancement of the cultures and environments that we visit." Companies include Backroads, Canadian Mountain Holidays, Geographic Expeditions, Mountain Travel Sobek, O.A.R.S., and Special Expeditions. Tour operators remain independent, but have united for this venture. These are not budget operators but if you heed the advice given at the beginning of this chapter, you will save money when using them. 866-GO-BEYOND. www.AdventureCollection.com.

Adventure Specialists combine "adventure, historical background and a healthy dose of awesome scenery" in their trips to Colorado, Peru, Mexico, and Spain. Bear Basin Ranch, Westcliffe, Colorado 81252. 719-783-2519. Winter phone number: 719630-7687. www.gorp.com/adventure. e-mail: adventur@rmii.com.

African Travel, Inc. provides travelers opportunities to see any part of Africa they desire. Best deals are their 2-for-1 safaris. Travelers stay in first class safari lodges and are led by expert local guides. All participants are guaranteed window seats and modern game-watching vehicles. The Safari Building, 1100 East Broadway, Glendale, CA 91205. 818-507-7893 or 800-421-8907 or 800-444-2874. www.africantravelinc.com. e-mail: ati@africantravelinc.com.

Big Five Tours And Expeditions is a soft adventure/ecotourism company with tours to all continents except Antarctica. Its biggest selection of trips are to Africa. 1551 SE Palm Court, Stuart, Florida 34994. 800-244-3483 or 561-287-7995. www.bigfive.com e-mail: bigfive@bigfive.com.

Ecovoyager links travelers to South American adventures, including the Galapagos Islands, through their "distinctive, ecological, soft adventures." Adventures include a variety of activities, such as hiking, horseback riding, fishing, birding, scuba diving, rafting, and photography outings. One of their best deals is a 7d Amazon Rain Forest Adventure, which departs every Saturday. P.O. Box 432144, Miami, FL 33243-2144. 800-326-7088 or 617-769-0676. www.ecovoyager.com. e-mail: info@ ecovoyager.com.

TIP: If you're willing to go to the North Pole in the winter when temperatures average in the 20's during the daytime, you'll get a steal of a deal. A one week Northern Lights package to Finland usually cost less than $1,500pp, including air from New York, tours, and activities, such as snowmobiling, dogsledding, and reindeer sleigh rides. For more information, contact Norvista (800-677-6454).

Every December through March, Icelandair (800-223-5500) offers unbeatable deals. Departs from several U.S. cities and includes two nights in a three-star hotel in the capital city, Reykjavik, Iceland, all breakfasts, and transfers, for about $300pp. Optional activities include horseback riding on magnificent Viking horses, city tour, snowmobiling safaris, Blue Lagoon outing (a must!), thermal pools, spa treatments, and more. Icelandair offers the same package in fall for a slightly higher fare. The city is lit up and decorated for Christmas in December, but the best time to see the Northern Lights and go snowmobiling is in January.

Exodus Worldwide Adventure Holidays offers trekking, walking, biking, watersports, wildlife safaris, expedition cruises, adventure sports, mountain climbing adventures. 760 North Bedford Road, Suite 246, Bedford Hills, NY 10507. 800-692-5495 or 914-666-4417. www.exodustravels.co.uk. e-mail: sales@exodustravel.co.uk.

G.A.P. Adventures specializes in small group trips to South America, Central America, and Mexico, but they also have trips within the U.S., Asia, and Europe. G.A.P. utilizes "local transportation, visits local haunts, and books family-run hotels" to give travelers the best cultural immersion. They also have an excellent visa and vaccination guide in the back of their catalog. 266 Dupont Street, Toronto, Ontario M5R 1V7, 800-465-5600 or 416-922-8899. www.gap.ca. e-mail: adventure@gap.ca. In the U.S. contact Himalayan Travel, 110 Prospect Street, Stamford, CT 06901. 800-225-2380 or 203-359-3711. e-mail: worldadv@netaxis.com.

Grand Expeditions is not one company but a partnership between seven adventure travel companies: Adventure Network International, Country Walkers, International Expeditions, Park East Tours, TCS Expeditions, TRAVCOA, and Voyages International. Most of these companies are not included in this reference because they are not for the budget-conscious. However, special rates are occasionally extended through this cooperative Web site. www.grandex.com.

International Wildlife Adventures does as the name implies--takes participants on wildlife adventures around-the-world, with programs such as Summer in Churchill by Tundra Buggy (Polar Bear expeditions), Discover Belize, Springtime in the Smokies, Galapagos Islands, and Wildlife of Japan. P.O. Box 1410, Vashon Island, WA 98070. 800-593-8881. www.wildlifeadventures.com. e-mail: info@wildlifeadventures.com.

♦ FYI: Swim Free with the Sharks! At California's Santa Catalina Island, pregnant leopard sharks arrive every summer. They have very small teeth suitable only for eating marine life. Swimming is free but restricted to certain times. For more information, call 310-510-0811.

National Audubon Society--Audubon Ecology Camps and Workshops offer both youth and adults a chance to study nature by participating in one of their many programs, which range from family adventure to natural history programs. 700 Broadway, New York, NY 10003; 212-979-3067. Or, 613

Riversville Road, Greenwich, CT 06831. 203-869-2017. www.aubudon.org. e-mail: aew@audubon. org.

Natural Habitat Adventures is an international tour company which offers a variety of travel options to Africa, Costa Rica, Galapagos, Antarctica, and many other nature lover destinations. Choose from nature trips, expedition voyages, photo-adventures, wildlife safaris, and special birding expeditions. Group size is usually eight people. Singles are encouraged. As of December 2001, Natural Habitats offers trips where no other tourists have gone before--space! Six travelers, plus crew, depart on a "journey previously reserved exclusively for government astronauts...made possible by special technology developed by expert team of top U.S. aerospace professional." If you've always dreamed of being an astronaut, here's your chance to walk in John Glenn's space boots. After five days of astronaut training and flight preparation at the space institute, you board the Space Cruiser and travel 100 kilometers above sea level. You'll experience space gravity and view of earth. The cost is $98,000pp.

Note: The Antarctic trip is offered by Natural Habitat's sister company, **Planet Expeditions**. 2945 Center Green Court, Boulder, CO 80301. 800-543-8917 or 303-449-3711. e-mail: andrear@ naturalhabitat.com.

Outland Adventure offers land or sea adventures through a wide variety of options, such as cultural safaris and van-kayak-hike-bike tours. P.O. Box 16343, Seattle, WA 98116. 206-932-7012. e-mail: outlandadv@serioussports.com .

Overseas Adventure Travel (OAT) provides small group, affordable adventure travel. OAT offers a substantial early payment discount and a frequent traveler credit, which is good for discounted travel up to four years later. Travel free if you bring 10 or more friends or family. Get 50 percent off the published fare if you round up a group of eight. 625 Mt. Auburn Street, Cambridge, MA 02138. 800-955-1925 or 800-221-0814. www.oat.com

Park East Tours offers travel opportunities worldwide, from Asia to Antarctica, but its best sojourns are to Africa. Some trips are better buys than offers, such as their 13d Grand Safari to Kenya. Highlights include: welcome dinner and show, complimentary bottled water and use of binoculars throughout trip, deluxe accommodations including a stay at the Mt. Kenya Safari Club, English speaking guide and drivers, naturalist, discussion with park ranger in the Maasi Mara, game drives, stay at private ranch, boat ride to Chimp Sanctuary, all park entrance fees, taxes, transfers, and insurance. Optional balloon rides, fishing junket to Lake Victoria, and visit to Giraffe Manor or National Museum, possible. 1841 Broadway, New York, NY 10023. 800-223-6078 or 212-765-4870. www.parkeast.com. e-mail: nass@parkeast.com.

Special Interest Tours takes travelers all over Africa and surrounding islands, or through the jungles of Central and South America. They also offer custom designed itineraries. 10220 North 27th Street, Phoenix, AZ 85028. 800-525-6772 or 602-493-3665.

TIP: If going on safari, consider taking a thrilling balloon trip!

My experience hot-air ballooning over the Northern Serengetti...
We signed our liability waivers and headed out to the jeep. It was only 5 a.m., so it was completely dark outside. As we were strapped and zipped into the jeep, we could see nothing and our only indication of activity was the muffled Swahili being exchanged between drivers. The jeep's motor cut into the stillness and we hurled down into the Rift Valley. It crossed my mind that the ride felt similar to Disney World's Space Mountain, which is a pitch black roller coaster ride. When we reached our destination, we watched as the men finished blowing up the spectacular balloon and listened as our pilot explained take-off and landing positions.

It was something to watch as the pilot maneuvered the tanks over our heads. We flew at altitudes of 500–800 feet over the plains, spotting gerenuks standing on their hind feet eating young leaves off trees, hyena families playing, and elands chasing each other while gnus and topis cleared out of the way. After landing, we sat down to a breakfast of mouth-watering crepes, spicy omelets, and champagne, as ostriches and impalas strutted by as if we weren't there. It was one of the best experiences of my life.

Most of the companies offering African safaris also provide optional hot-air balloon adventures. Rates are $300–$400pp.

Trek Adventures/AmeriCan Adventures specializes in small group, soft adventure tours involving camping and hotel stays in the U.S., Canada, and Mexico. They offer 25 trips using trained and certified trek leaders, specially equipped luxury vans, and optional activities, such as jet-skiing, mountain biking, and horseback riding. Specials, early booking discounts, and Hot Discounts(Web site) are all good ways to save money. P.O. Box 2955 Rohnert Park, CA 94927. 800-88-8735 or 707-577-8735. www.trekadventures.com. e-mail: info@adventureaccess.com.

Utc (United Touring Company) is one of the most well-established tour operators in Africa (53 years in business as of 2000) and offer some of the cheapest single supplements for African travel that I have ever seen. They offer both packages and customized Safaris. Recently, they began offering trips to Arabia. One Bala Plaza, Suite 414, Bala Cynwyd, PA 19004. 800-223-6486 or 610-617-3300. www.unitedtour.com. e-mail: utcusa@unitedtour.com.

Wildland Adventures give active and enthusiastic travelers the chance to experience nature and cultural diversity from Turkey to the Andes Mountains. 3516 NE 155th, Seattle, WA 98155. 800-345-4453 or 206-365-0686. www.wildland.com. e-mail: info@wildland.com.

◆　　◆　　◆

Helpful Resources
Learning, Active, and Interactive
Colorado Dude Ranch & Guest Ranch Association sends out a free directory listing all dude and guest ranches throughout Colorado. Although summer rates can be a little high, low winter rates allow participants a chance to enjoy snow-related activities and scenery. The association also provides employment information for member dude ranches. Positions include kitchen help, job wrangling,

general ranch work, or entertaining guests. 2120 Granby, CO 80446. 907-887-3128. www.coloradoranch.com. e-mail: fun@coloradoranch.com.

The Dude Ranchers' Association has a directory that lists and describes 109 "inspected and approved" member ranches, ranging from rustic to luxurious, in Arizona, Arkansas, California, Colorado, Idaho, Nevada, Oregon, South Dakota, Texas, Wyoming, and British Columbia. P.O. Box F-471, LaPorte, CO 80535. 970-223-8440. www.duderanch.org. e-mail: duderanches@compuserve.com.

TIP: Some very affordable and intriguing dude, guest, and working ranches include Sweet Grass Ranch, Montana (listed on the National Register of Historic Places. 406-537-4477. www. sweetgrassranch.com. Baker's Bar M Dude Ranch, Oregon (log ranch house that served as stagecoach stop during Civil War. 888-824-3381. www.barmranch.com. Lozier's Box "R" Ranch, Wyoming (1,600 acre working ranch sixty miles from Jackson Hole. 800-822-8466. www.boxr.com. La Garita Creek Ranch, Colorado(organized children's programs. 888-838-3833. www.lagarita.com. Diamond D Ranch, Idaho (centerpiece of 300-acre ranch is 110-year old hunting lodge, lake, and group of cabins. 800-222-1269. www.westerntravel.com/cm. Homeplace Ranch, Alberta, Canada (homesteaded in 1912. 403-931-3245. www.canadaranches.com/homeplace.

The Institute Of International Education has information on overseas adult study programs. 809 U.N. Plaza, New York, NY 10017. 212-984-5413.

On The Go publishes many useful travel publications and its Web site provides pertinent travel news and tips. P.O. Box 91033, Columbus, Ohio 43209. www.onthegopublishing.com.

River Travel Center is "your source for rafting and sea kayak trips throughout the U.S. West and around the world." The center represents more than 100 outfitters. 15 Riverside Drive, P.O. Box 6, Point Arena, CA 95468. 800-882-RAFT(7238) or 707-882-2258.

Travel Smart newsletter informs readers of "insider" deals on fares and destinations. The monthly publication promises subscribers they will "travel better for less." They will send a free sample issue, upon request. Dobbs Ferry, NY 10522. 800-FARE-OFF or 914-693-8300. www.travelsmartnews.com. e-mail: travelsmartnews@aol.com.

Solo Travelers
Contact the **American Society Of Travel Agents** for a list of agencies that specialize in travel planning for singles. 1101 King Street, Suite 200, Alexandria, VA 22314. 703-739-2782 or 703-739-8739. www.astanet.com.

Connecting: Solo Travel Network offers both a paper and Internet newsletter, which are published six times a year. They have been operating for more than a dozen years and have 1,500–2,000 members. Their newsletters and Web site reveal tours and cruises that do not charge single supplements and answer FAQs, as well as offer tips for solo travelers. 689 Park Road, Unit 6, Gibsons BC V0N 1V7 Canada. 800-557-1757 or 604-886-9099. www.cstn.org. e-mail: info@cstn.org.

Travel Chums is a free service for those who don't want to travel alone. Initial contact is anonymous. More than 4,000 members have joined since it was founded in 2001. Members may place ads, contact other members, and obtain valuable advice and tips. www.travelchums.com. e-mail: info@travelchums .com.

TravelCompanions.com is a bi-monthly newsletter that discusses different aspects of travel and topics of interest to single travelers. It was rated as "one of the best general travel newsletters in the U.S." by *Newsday* in a year-end review. One-year newsletter subscription has been $48 for the last several years or $6 for a sample issue. It also provides a service, Travel Companion Exchange (TCE), which pairs suitable travelers. TCE is currently one of the biggest singles travel services. VIP Membership is available for single travelers interested in making new friends or a getting a travel companion. By filling out an in-depth profile page, TCE can match you with the most suitable travel companion(same sex or opposite sex, according to you). The profile allows TCE to find like-minded and suitable travel partners. There are special introductory rates for new members.

Additionally, TCE also a hosting exchange for singles who don't have a lot of time or money to travel but prefer not to dine alone or find their way in a strange city. Participation in this program is by visiting and hosting each other. Stay in the home of the host and he or she shows you their city and its sights. Box 833, Amityville, NY 11701. 800-392-1256 or 631-454-0880.

Travel Companions International provides escorts for those who do not want to, or are not able to, travel alone. 304-697-8304.

Travel Companion Network is a resource for those seeking a suitable travel companion or information. www.travel-companion.net.

Travel In Twos (a subsidiary of ATC Travel) is an association that offers members travel-mate matching, a quarterly newsletter with information about single-oriented trips, and other travel opportunities. c/o ShawGuides, Inc., P. O. Box 231295, New York, NY 10023. 212-787-2621.

Travelmate will pair up single travelers. Provide a description of your travel plans and Travelmate gives you a list of persons that match your request. It is a service for singles who cannot find friends who have the time, money, or inclination to travel with them. 18 Cavendish Road, Bournemouth BR1 1RF England. Telephone and fax number: 44 0202 558314.

Vacation Partners is an Internet company that, for a fee, matches single travelers with compatible single travelers, after participants answer a 200 questionnaire. The comprehensive questionnaire is then entered into the 1000+ travelers database and four potential travel partners are selected. 800-810-8075. www.vacationpartners.com.

TIP: According to spa experts, top spas for making friends are Cal-A-Vie (CA), Golden Door (CA), The Greenhouse (TX), Lake Austin Spa Resort (TX), The Lodge at Skylonda (CA), and The Oaks at Ojai (CA). Good spas for romance are Canyon Ranch (AZ), Echo Valley Ranch Resort (B.C., Canada), Harbour Village Beach Resort (Bonaire), Rancho La Puerta (Mexico), Red Mountain Resort and Spa (UT), The Spa at Doral (FL), and Wyndham Peaks Resort & Golden Door Spa (CO). For more information, contact Spafinder at www.spafinder.com.

International Federation Of Women's Travel Organizations (IFWTO) will provide names and addresses of worldwide travel groups that are just for women. IFWTO was founded in 1969 when eight travel clubs merged to form one resource for female travelers. The organization currently has more than 5,000 members in 25 countries. 7432 Caminito Carlotta, San Diego, CA 92120. www.ifwto.org.

More Women Travel-Adventures And Advice From More Than 60 Countries, edited by Natania Jansz and Miranda Davis. Published by Rough Guides.

Solo Woman Traveler (G1) is a useful planner for women traveling on their own, $5. Transitions Abroad, P.O. Box 1300, Amherst, MA 01004-1300. 800-293-0373.

Travel Alone & Love It,-A Flight Attendant's Guide To Solo Travel, by Sharon B. Wingler. Published by Chicago Spectrum Press. This book is full of practical advice and plenty of anecdotes. www.travelaloneandloveit.com.

Women's Travel Club is a great resource for women travelers. Members can find out about trips, share experiences and information, and more. You must pay dues and be a member for three months or more before taking a trip or else pay a surcharge. The club specializes in cultural trips to Costa Rica, China, Mexico's Copper Canyon, France, Italy, and the U.S. 21401 NE 38th Avenue, Aventura, FL 33180. 800-480-4448. www.womenstravelclub.com. e-mail: womantrip@aol.com.

Women Welcome Women is a 70-country travel hospitality organization with more than 3,000 members. Members host other members. They also receive a membership list and periodic newsletters. c/o Betty Sobel, U.S. Rep., 10 Greenwood Lane, Westport, CT 06880. 203-259-7832.

These **Web sites** disclose women-only trips, offer advice, and provide resources:
> www.maiden-voyages.com.
> www.journeywoman.com. (including free online travel magazine)
> www.adventuredivas.com.
> www.citywomen.com. (guides for many major U.S. cities)

Mature Travelers
American Association Of Retired Persons (AARP) has a Travel Service division that offers all kinds of discounts and resources for its members. Anyone 50 and older can join. Membership is around $10 a year and entitles members to reduced rates at numerous nationwide hotels, car rental agencies, etc. 601 E. Street, NW, Washington, D.C. 20049. 202-434-2277.

Golden Age Travellers is actually a club that offers a wide array of ever-changing adventures for those 50 or older. Pier 27, the Embarcadero, San Francisco, CA 94111. 800-258-8880. www.gatclub.com.

The Mature Traveler is a monthly newsletter with "travel bonanzas for 49ers-Plus." It is packed with helpful features such as "How to Get Paid to Visit Yellowstone," "Limit Your Time in dangerous Quito," and "Air Jamaica posts new Senior Discounts." New subscribers get a free copy of *The Mature*

Traveler's Book of Deals. P.O. Box 1543, Wildomar, CA 92595. 909-461-9598. e-mail: MatureTrav@aol.com.

Senior Travel Tips, published eight times a year, discusses destinations, packages, itineraries, and is targeted at the western senior market (group travel planners, clubs and organizations, and tour operators). Offers tours and cruises in western U.S. and Canada, as well as some other U.S. regions and overseas. 5281 Scotts Valley Drive, Scotts Valley, CA 95066. 408-438-6085. e-mail: seniortraveltips.com

101 Tips For Mature Travelers is a free booklet for travelers. Grand Circle Travel, 347 Congress Street, Boston, MA 02210. 800-248-3737 or 800-221-2610.

Travel Tips For Mature Citizens (#8970) is a free publication produced by the U.S. Government Printing Office, Washington, D.C. 20402.

Adventure Travel

Adventure Travel Society provides tips and advice, as well as information on adventure travel operators. 719-530-0171. www.adventuretravel.com.

Adventurous Traveler Bookstore says it's "The world's most complete source of outdoor travel books and maps." With 4,000+ books, videos, maps, and CD-Roms in stock, it is a great resource for travelers. P.O. Box 577, Hinesburg, VT 05461. 800-282-3963 or 802-860-6776(overseas) for a free paper catalog which includes rare and out-of-print books. www.adventurousTraveler.com. e-mail: info@adventuroustraveler.com.

GoNomad is a good resource for adventure, alternative, independent, women-only, tours, family trips, and lodging. It also accepts freelance articles and photos. P.O. Box 44, E. Arlington, VT 05252. 802-375-1114. www.GoNOMAD.com. e-mail: info@gomad.com.

Rascals In Paradise (a Division of Adventure Express Travel) is a worldwide family adventure travel specialist. Rascals offers a chance to travel with your children or grandchildren and still have time to yourself. Enjoy romantic candlelit dinners with your spouse while the kids eat earlier with other kids. Optional activities include windsurfing, snorkeling, golf, bicycling, sailing, playgrounds, etc. Some destinations offer special rates for single parents. Customized trips can be arranged. 2107 Van Ness Avenue, Suite 403, San Francisco, CA 94109. 800-U-RASCAL or 415-978-9800. www. RascalsinParadise.com. e-mail: trips@RascalsinParadise.com.

South America Explorer Club is a wonderful source for soft adventures and travel information in South America or Central America. The nonprofit membership organization has a quarterly magazine filled with travel essays and tours. Periodically, SAEC offers their own tours. It also has a catalog of books and maps with pertinent topics to travelers interested in Central or South America. 126 Indian Creek Road, Ithaca, NY 14850. 800-274-0568 or 607-277-0488. www.samexplo.org. e-mail: explorer @samexplo.org.

These **Web sites** disclose adventure trips and companies, offer advice, and provide resources, including free electronic newsletters:

www.AdventureSeek.com
www.Away.com
www.GORP.com

♦ FYI: The highest point on earth is Mt. Everest at 29,028 feet. The lowest point is the Dead Sea (Israel-Jordan border) at 1,300 feet below sea level.

♦　　♦　　♦

Chapter Three-How To Get The Best Deals On Independent Travel

Chapter Three-How To Get The Best Deals On Independent Travel

The day shall not be up so soon as I,
To try the fair adventure of tomorrow.
Shakespeare

The best thing about independent travel is that travelers can go "off the beaten track" and spend as much time as they like at places of interest, but this type of travel isn't for everyone. It's best suited to those who are comfortable being on their own and making their own arrangements, as well as being willing and able to address problems that might arise, such as overbooked accommodations or delayed flights. As is the case with any kind of travel, you should always be careful, patient, and flexible.

The best advice I can give is to arm yourself with as much information as possible. If you're driving, be sure to have a detailed, current map. You may have to take an alternate route, due to heavy traffic or road construction. Or, you may discover a place along the way that is worth a slight detour. Know some things about your destination. What will the weather be like? You don't want to drag around too much luggage, so you need to know how to pack. Do you need train passes or ferry reservations? If so, how far in advance do you need to make them? If there's a show or concert you would like to see, should you buy advance tickets to ensure a seat? Will all the historic sites or attractions you plan to visit be open during your stay? If a museum you wish to visit is closed on Mondays, you don't want that to be the day you have allotted to visit.

For those who like to "fly by the seat of your pants" and feel that too much planning interferes with that mentality, beware that too much spontaneity can be hazardous to travelers. The happiest traveler is one who has a game plan (a rough outline will do!) and is able to modify it when problems arise.

This chapter is made up of three parts: what every independent traveler should know; untours; and where and how to get good deals on transportation. Additionally, there's a Helpful Resources section at the end of this chapter that lists planning guides and safety information. I highly recommend utilizing these resources. You should always check with the State Department to find out if there is any reason why travel might not be advisable, such as a natural disaster or unstable government. The latter is especially true in the Middle East and developing countries such as Africa and Central or Latin America.

What No One Tells You

There are some wonderful resources to assist the independent traveler, which can be found throughout this chapter. Most of the sections in this reference contain information that is pertinent to independent travel, particularly those on airlines, accommodations, and travel-planning Web sites. Additionally, there are useful FYIs (okay, some are just interesting trivia I couldn't stop myself from inserting!) and TIPS highlighted throughout this publication.

√ Airline Packages are a lifesaver for independent travelers. Most airlines, big and small, domestic or international, offer air and accommodations packages. Rates are hard to beat, especially in the low and off seasons. For example, KLM Airlines (800-800-1504) usually offers a great deal to Amsterdam every year from November 1-March 31. Typically, travelers receive round-trip airfare from New York, two nights lodging, breakfast daily, and a tour or two, for less than $600pp. Virgin

Atlantic Airways (888-937-8474) usually offers London Jaunt packages in the fall and spring. For approximately $700pp (half that fare in the winter or add $200pp in the summer), travelers receive airfare from the East Coast, three nights in moderate to deluxe hotels (centrally located), airport transfers, and breakfast daily, with add-on theater tickets or day trip excursions available. Northwest WorldVacations (800-800-1504) frequently offers a five night fall Hong Kong air and hotel package for approximately $700pp. United (800-328-6877) offers a similar deal to Bangkok. See Chapter Four for more information, including toll-free phone numbers and Web sites. Call and request to be added to direct mail lists or go to their Web sites and register for free e-mailers detailing specials. www.aol.com/directories/airlines.html.

√ Airline Passes are another bargain offered by most airlines. Most major airlines offer passes, which are much cheaper than tickets. For example, Cathay Pacific Airlines (800-233-2742 or 800-228-4297) offers an All Asia Airpass that has remained close to $1,000 for the past few years. It includes one round-trip flight from New York to Hong Kong, plus *unlimited* flights to 17 cities, such as Tokyo and Singapore, for up to 30 days. British Airways offers a Europe Airpass, which is good for travel to 100 European cities. Cost has remained around $90, with a minimum purchase of three tickets required. See Chapter Four for more information on passes and other airfare programs.

√ American Automobile Association (AAA) is a federation of 113 travel clubs that offer travel planning advice; car and accommodation discounts; free maps, camping guides, U.S. tour books; car rental discounts; and much more. One of the biggest advantages of membership, besides the 24-hour emergency road service, is AAA's travel agency. AAA will make train, hotel, airline, cruise, tour, and car rental reservations. Additionally, members receive no-fee American Express Travelers cheques. Basic membership starts at $50 a year. AAA's online TourBook® offers over 27,000 accommodations, 12,000 restaurants, and many places of interest in North America. At www.aaa.com, travelers can see photos of all listings, make car, air, and hotel reservations, and find tour and cruise vacations. Call the national office at 888-222-7869, find your local AAA office by looking in a telephone directory, or access their Web site for information, www.aaa.com.

√ The American Association of Retired Persons (AARP) is an excellent travel-planning source. Members may utilize its extensive Travel Service Department for a multitude of independent travel resources. Annual dues are $10 a year and membership is open to anyone over the age of 50. 601 E. Street NW, Washington, DC 20049. 800-424-3410. www.AARP.com. e-mail member@aarp.org. The Web site has a Discounts page that lists companies (airlines, cruise lines, hotels, tour operators, etc.) providing reduced rates for AARP members.

√ Rick Steves, an expert on independent travel throughout Europe and author of 21 guidebooks on the subject, offers a free quarterly travel newsletter and his Web site includes numerous travel ideas, sample itineraries, transportation information, packing tips, and much more. www.ricksteves.com

√ Buy a pass that bundles admission to various attractions. These passes can really save you money. For example, a CityPass includes admission to many area attractions and transportation. They can be purchased for use in New York, Boston, Chicago, Seattle, Hollywood, San Francisco, and Philadelphia. The card cost around $30 for adults and is greatly discounted for seniors, children, and groups, so it is an excellent value. In Philadelphia, for example, cardholders are entitled to admission to the Philadelphia Museum of Art, Philadelphia Zoo, New Jersey State Aquarium, Independence Seaport Museum, and Franklin Institute Science Museum. In New York, CityPass includes admission to the Empire State Building, Guggenheim Museum, Museum of Natural History, Museum of Modern Art, and Intrepid Sea Air Space Museum. Passes can be bought through a travel agent or directly. 888-330-5008. www.citypass.net. e-mail: info@citypass.net. In addition to being able to buy passes online, browsers will also find maps, details of each attraction, and more.

Both DisneyWorld and DisneyLand now offer a FASTPASS, which is a free service that lets visitors make reservations to attractions. It won't save you money, but it will save you time. At certain turnstiles located near busy attractions, you can validate your ticket for a one-hour period. During that time span, you may enter the attraction through a special entrance—no waiting! The rub is you have to go at the designated time, not a requested time. And, only one attraction at a time can be reserved. 714-781-4565.

The London Pass allows reduced or free admission to sixty museums, attractions, tours, trains, buses, and entertainment, throughout the city, such as the London Aquarium and St. Paul's Cathedral. Pass holders enter without waiting in line. They also receive a guidebook, commission free currency exchange, and more. Multi-day passes are available (011-44-181-588-8817. www.londonpass.com.

Note: Do not confuse this with the London Visitor Travelcard (800-274-8724), which is good for 3–7 days unrestricted use on London's buses and subway. London Theatre & More is a tour operator that sells discounted tickets to London tourist attractions, plays and musicals, as well as airfare and accommodations. 800-683-0799. Or, contact the British Tourist Authority at 212-986-2266. www.visitbritain.com.

Always check with the tourism bureau where you are going to see what is offered. Also, you may wish to consider joining the local zoo or science center so that your family can visit all state zoos, aquariums, and museums around the country that reciprocate, free of charge.

√ Eurocamps are affordable "self-catering family holidays" throughout Europe. Eurocamp has won many prestigious awards, including Guardian & Observer Travel Award and Tommy Award for most parent-friendly family holiday. Amenities and activities vary according to location. For example, La Sirene, in the South of France, has a large tropical pool complex, scuba diving lessons, windsurfing, tennis, miniature golf, bicycles, table tennis, badminton, game room, play area, kids' club, disco, bar, pizzeria, restaurant, laundry facility, and more, including a free shuttle bus to the beach. Day trips can be arranged at most camps. Specials and discounts are frequently offered. Eurocamp Travel Unlimited, Hartford Manor, Greenbank Lane, Northwich, Cheshire CWB IHW, England. Telephone: 01606 787878. www.eurocamp.co.uk. e-mail: enquiries@eurocamp.co.uk.

√ Check with Tourism Bureaus or colleges and universities where you will be traveling about renting dorm rooms. When available, these are usually very affordable and centrally located. For example, several schools in London have dorm rooms available to tourists from mid-June until late September and during Easter break, for a very low price. Rooms are basic, but linen is supplied and private bathrooms are available in many rooms. For example, Ramsey Hall at University of London has rooms with breakfast included. e-mail: ramsay.hall@ucl.ac.uk. Walter Sickert Hall at City University is very nice and includes tea/coffee makers in-room and many single rooms, with continental basket breakfast brought to your room. www.city.ac.uk/ems. e-mail: i.gibbard@city.ac.uk. King's College offers lodging at four of its dorms, some have kitchens with microwave, stove, toaster, and kettle. e-mail: vac.bureau@kcl.ac.uk.

To Tip or Not to Tip...

In the U.S., patrons are expected to add 15-20 percent of the bill as a tip. In Europe, 10-15 percent, known as a "service charge(tipping)," is usually added to the bill before it is given to the customer. If the service was exceptional and you would like to leave a little something extra, 5–10 percent is suggested. Tipping is discouraged in certain countries, especially Iceland and Spain.

In Asia, a surcharge is often added to your bill. If not, 5 percent is recommended. In the Americas: Central, Latin America, and South America, tipping is often included in the bill. If not, leave 15 percent. Don't tip taxi drivers unless they help you with your luggage. However, in resort areas of Brazil and Argentina, drivers expect 10 percent. If in doubt or if you would like to add a little something extra, give your server or driver 5–10 percent.

In Australia, New Zealand, and other parts of the South Pacific, tips to servers, tour guides, and taxi drivers, aren't expected outside of big cities, such as Sydney, Melbourne, Christchurch, and Queenstown. Tipping is discouraged in Fiji and Tahiti, but sometimes you'll find tip boxes at the front desk where patrons can drop envelopes, if so inclined.

In the Caribbean, 15 percent is the rule of thumb, except in all-inclusive resorts where it's part of the package you purchased, so none is required. In Africa, wages are low and tips are expected. Depending on service, 5–15 percent is a good amount. Safaris are like cruises, as far as tipping is concerned. Be prepared to pay gratuities to the guides, drivers, and porters.

Make sure to read the fine print of your tour contract or check your bill to see if service charges have been added before you start passing out tips. Additionally, ask the manager or your guide to learn more about what is expected. And lastly, remember that a tip is earned. If you did not get good service, do not feel compelled to tip if it is optional.

√ Line up tickets to shows you really want to see before departure. For tickets to shows all over the United States, call Ticketmaster (800-755-4000, www.ticketmaster.com). While tickets are not discounted, you will be guaranteed admission to a show you have your heart set on seeing. Don't think you are the only one with the bright idea to see Seigfred & Roy or Madonna! The Web site also provides contact information for local ticket centers.

√ Utilize all the free trip planning resources that are available on the Internet and through tourism bureaus. For example, some Web sites permit printing out free customized maps, including door-to-door instructions. Online research also permits finding out the best restaurants, attractions, hours of operation, and much more (even free mini-guidebooks can be compiled or are all ready to download and print). The National Park Service's Web site, www.nps.gov/parks.html, includes more than 400 national parks, including highlights information, admission charges, special kids programs, and more. The best thing is that browsers may search by state or three special interest categories: specialty(glaciers, endangered species, Civil War, etc.), activities (snowmobiling, fishing, camping, etc.), or type (seashore, historic site, lakeshore, etc.). Get official guidebooks and welcome packets from tourism bureaus. In addition to general planning information, coupons and discount cards are often included. See Chapter Eight for numerous travel-planning Web sites.

National Geographic offers a CD-ROM Trip Planner. It's not free, but it does reveal more than 70,000 points of interest in the United States and Canada. It provides photo tips, customized maps, and walking tours. For example, if you're planning to travel from North Carolina to Arizona, the trip planner will produce a customized map, which includes the kinds of things you are interested in seeing and doing, as well as pertinent directions. It's available at most computer stores and office supply centers, such as CompUSA, OfficeDepot, and Best Buy. Or, call National Geographic. 800-881-9919. Outside the U.S. and Canada: 916-939-1004. e-mail: ngi@ngs.org.

√ Seek the extraordinary. The reason you are traveling independently is to enjoy unusual encounters and experiences, so be sure you look for them. For example, Adventure on a Shoestring offers really cheap tours that explore off-the-beaten path New York by showing you real neighborhoods, such as SoHo, Astoria, Roosevelt Island, and Little Odessa. The guide shares history and stories of growing up in New York and tours may include visits to neighborhood bakeries, a stop at a Greek tavern, or wine-tasting. 212-265-2663. Additionally, visit the New York City Family Guide online at www.FocusonNYC.com and discover some different ways to experience New York, such as an escorted bicycle tour of Central Park and seaplane adventure or helicopter flight tour of the city. Check www.nycvisit.com or call 800-NYCVISIT for more information on ticket kiosks for museums, tours, and Broadway shows. Don't waste your time standing in long lines with other frustrated tourists! Kiosks are at most tourist locations, such as Empire State Building and World Trade Center.

City Search has valuable information on all major cities in the United States, www.citysearch.com. Always check with the tourism bureau where you'll be visiting or look in the phone book and welcome center or tourism office for small tour companies or unique experiences. The best tours come from long-time local residents who take interested visitors on an "insiders tour." They will share firsthand experiences, folklore, and history. I live near a historic beach community and there are several companies that offer tours of the area, but one of the best sightseeing excursions is conducted by a gentleman who has lived there his entire life and has a gift for storytelling. He has a trolley tour that is both informative and entertaining because he shares anecdotes, hurricane experiences, folklore, ghost tales, and general stories of what the town used to be like when he was growing up. He doesn't have a set schedule nor does he advertise. You have to ask around or get lucky to catch his tour. Remember, the Chamber of Commerce will only tell you about member companies. If you have trouble finding a guide, check with the staff at a local museum or library to see if they can recommend someone.

◆   ◆   ◆

Untours

These are packages that include airline tickets, hotel vouchers, and train passes or car rental vouchers. Not only do these packages simplify things for the independent traveler, but they are much more affordable than purchasing airline tickets, lodging, and transportation separately.

Additionally, most tour operators offer at least one or two trips geared to independent travelers. These are usually found in the very back of a brochure or catalog (see Chapter Two: Tours for a listing of tour operators). Many escorted tours allow enough free time to satisfy independent spirits while guaranteeing transport and admission to key historic sites and attractions. In certain parts of the world, such as Morocco or Kenya, at least partially escorted tours are the smartest choice. Because of the high crime rate, it's just not safe to be a tourist on your own in the medina at Fez or in center city of Nairobi. Another option for those opposed to group travel is to utilize companies that handle small groups only (average 12–16 people), such as Overseas Adventure Travel (OAT) or G.A.P. Adventures. And remember, any tour operator will customize a trip to suit your needs, but you will pay more for that privilege.

AATKings offers independent "explore Australia, New Zealand, and Fiji packages for the average to super-adventurous traveler." At first glance, some of offerings may not seem particularly cheap, but they are actually very reasonable if you understand what you're getting. For example, their two-week Australian Highlights takes travelers to every major sight in Australia and includes many incredible highlights. Most tours take travelers to the Great Barrier Reef and a couple of major cities, usually Sydney and Melbourne. You'll find that if the untours do offer these same highlights, the price is double or triple what AATKings charges. Their packages exclude airfare so you can use an air consolidator or buy an air pass (see Chapter Four) to receive even greater savings. 9430 Topanga Canyon Blvd., Suite 207, Chatsworth, CA 913199. 800-353-4525. In Canada, 3284 Yonge Street, Suite 201, Toronto, Ontario M4N 3M7. 800-353-4525 or 416-486-4240. Outside North America: 818-700-2732. www.aatkings.com. e-mail:reservations@aatkings.com.

AHI International is for travelers ages 25–45 who are looking for European untours. Un-Group Tours, such as their 5n Austrian Alps package, include low airfares, centrally located accommodations, breakfast daily, and airport/hotel transfers. AHI also offers nifty extras on these trips, such as transportation and a guide, to local ski resorts, for just a few dollars a day. The company also offers all-inclusive tours, educational programs, and cruises, such as a one-week educational program in Scotland or a week-long London Escape. 6400 Shafer Court, Rosemont, IL 60018. 800-323-7373. www.ahitravel.com. See Budget Escapes on their Web site for the best deals.

ATS Tours offers self-discovery travel packages to the South Pacific, including Australia, New Zealand, Tahiti, and Fiji. The best deals on their week-long explorer packages, which include airfare from Los Angeles, hotel, and car rentals. 2381 Rosecrans Avenue, Suite 325, El Segundo, CA 90245. 800-423-2880 or 310-643-0044. www.atstours.com. e-mail: info@atstours.com.

◆ FYI: It is 2,435 miles from Seattle, Washington, to Anchorage, Alaska.

Brendan Tours offers many value tours, cruises, and independent travel deals worldwide. They have very reasonable single supplements, usually between $100–200. Brendan frequently extends specials. 15137 Califa Street, Van Nuys, CA 91411. 818-785-9696. www.brendantours.com. e-mail: info@brendantours.com..

Carlson Wagonlit has many independent vacations in Great Britain and Ireland. One of their best deals is Go-As-You-Please Britain or Ireland, which includes a self-drive car and unlimited mileage, pick up and drop off in London, Glasgow, or Edinburgh, accommodations at first class hotels, bed & breakfasts, or mansions and manors, maps, full daily breakfasts, service charges and taxes, and Privilege Pass (a guide to 200+ visitor attractions and discount vouchers). Early bookers and those over 55 are entitled to a discount. Get together a group of eight and receive 50 percent off or get together a group of 16 and travel free. 222 Second Street SE, Cedar Rapids, IA 52401. www.carsontravel.com or Carlson Leisure Group, 12755 State Hwy. 55, Plymouth, MN 55441. www.carlsonwagon.com.

Central Holidays has incredible worldwide cruises, escorted tours, and independent adventures at bargain prices. They are best known for their Mediterranean trips. 120 Sylvan Avenue, Englewood Cliffs, NJ 07632. 800-935-5000 or 800-611-1138. www.centralholidays.com. e-mail: bookonline@ centralh.com.

CIT Tours provide many exciting possibilities for independent travelers, ranging from semi-escorted to completely independent exploration of Italy, France, and Great Britain. Travelers may opt to put together their own Italian holiday by utilizing some of CIT's three night stay options in cities, such as Sorrento, Sicily, Venice, Florence, and Tuscany. These packages include hotels, taxes and service charges, airport or train transfer, breakfast daily, and half-day sightseeing tour. Optional tours and additional nights are offered at bargain prices to those participating in any of CIT's independent "city stays." 15 West 44th Street, New York, NY 10036. 800-CIT-TOUR (248-8687). www.cit-tours.com. e-mail: info@city-tours.com.

    CIT also provides European Rail trips for independent travelers. 800-CIT-RAIL (248-7245). www.citrail.com.

Club Med offers all-inclusive resort vacations in the U.S. and around-the-world, such as Bora Bora, Egypt, and Costa del Sol. Price includes lodging, watersports and land activities (including instruction), all meals with beer or wine for lunch and dinner, night time entertainment. Specialty programs include singles, single parents, families, couples, adventure, faraway, and Forever Young (55 or older). Half the guests are 24–44 years old. Roommates are assigned or a 20–40 percent single supplement is assessed. Each Club Med resort specializes in a different program so be sure to ask about resorts that meet your needs. Rates are typically less than $1,000 per week. Ask about their annual low season "Wild Card Tropical Lottery." For less than $999, participants can enjoy a week-long all-inclusive vacation (all meals, entertainment, and air) to a Caribbean or Mexican beach. 800-CLUBMED or 888-932-2582. For groups: 800-453-2582. www.clubmed.com. e-mail: info@clubmed.com.

Discover Travel offers deep discount fly and drive packages to Mexico and the South Pacific (Australia, New Zealand, and Tahiti). Motorhomes with unlimited mileage are available, as well as airline tickets only or bus passes. 2192 Dupont Drive, Suite 116, Irvine, CA 92612-1322. 800-576-7770 or 888-TAHITI-1 or 949-833-1139. e-mail: info@discovertravel.net.

Eurovacations offers all types of economical ways to see Europe, such as cheap airfares or untours that include rail travel, hotels, sightseeing vouchers, and more. One of the best selections is their four night "combination deals." Choose two cities (London, Brussels, Amsterdam, or Paris) and stay two nights in each one. Round-trip airfare, transfers, hotels, sightseeing vouchers, train rides via Eurostar or Thalys trains, and some meals included. 1549 Glenlake Avenue, Itasca, IL 60143-1185. 888-281-EURO. www.eurovacations.com.

Footloose & Fancy Free is a Britain tour operator that offers participants a delightful walking tour, without a rigid tour itinerary. Travelers create their own itinerary from five possible locations in England, France, and Italy. Participants decide where to start and stop, as well as where to stay each night. Luggage is transported by Footloose & Fancy Free. Travelers are given a carefully marked map, a guidebook of recommended hotels and eating establishments, a list of background reading on the area, and suggestions on what to bring and wear for walking. 69-71 Banbury Road, Oxford OX2 6PE, United Kingdom. (44) 865-310355.

France Vacations has offered tours and untours throughout France and England for more than a decade. Their Web site reveals great deals in its Specials, Top Deals, and Featured Destinations sections. Their all-inclusive Getaway Specials include a week in Paris, the French Riviera, Painting in Provence, Waterways of France, and Discover Provencal Cooking. The company also offers Fly and Drive packages, as well as budget hotels in France, London, and Brussels for independent travelers. They even book Venice Orient Express rail trips. 800-332-5332. www.francevacations.net. e-mail: reservations@francevacations.net.

Transportation Tips...

Cable car rides in San Francisco are just a couple of bucks and tickets can be bought from an onboard conductor.

Stay away from the expensive gondolas in Venice and opt instead for water taxis. For less than $10, you get unrestricted travel all day versus about $50 for an hour-long gondola ride.

In Paris, buy a one-day pass that is good for the Metro subway and all buses, for just a few dollars.

For pocket change, passengers can ride Hong Kong's tram system.

A one-day unlimited travel pass on Amsterdam's trams is approximately $5—much cheaper than a taxi. The trams operate seven days a week and run every 10 minutes. Or, do what the locals do and peddle around this "bicycle-friendly" city. It is very safe for bicyclists here. There are bike lanes and traffic really does yield to bicyclists. There are bicycle parking garages everywhere and fairly level terrain.

Gate1 offers low-cost, cruises and all-inclusive worldwide tours, including photo tours and untours for independent travelers. Best deals are to Italy, China, and Spain. 101 Limekiln Pike, Glenside, PA 19038. 800-682-3333 or 888-88-Gate1 or 215-572-7676. www.gate1travelcom. e-mail: info@gate1travel.com.

General Tours/TBI Tours provides affordable tours, cruises, and independent travel packages to worldwide destinations. 53 Summer Street, Keene, New Hampshire 03431. 800-221-2216. www.generaltours.com. e-mail: info@generaltours.com.

Globus & Cosmos is a worldwide independent travel and escorted travel tour operator, offering both first class and budget travel. They offer approximately 110 budget tours to six continents. Discounts of 10 percent available for those 18 and under on land portion. Minimum age accepted is eight years old. 5301 S. Federal Circle, Littleton, CO 80123. 800-338-7092. www.globusandcosmos.com.

Go Ahead Vacations offers discounted tours, cruises, and independent travel packages, throughout Europe, as well as to Egypt, Israel, Kenya, Australia & New Zealand, China, Panama, and Costa Rica. If you have previously traveled on a Go Ahead vacation or bring five friends, you'll receive a substantial discount. Bring 10 people and travel free, plus earn a cash bonus. Apply to be a group leader and travel free(see Web site). Go Ahead offers several 7–10-day vacations, such as to Paris or London, for less than $1,000pp, including air from New York. One Education Street, Cambridge, MA 02141. 800-590-1170. www.goaheadvacations.com. e-mail: goahead@ef.com.

GoToday.com is an Internet reservations company that offers budget-priced land-only trips to South American and Europe. The company provides self-guided or escorted tours, European barge and worldwide cruises, walking and bicycling trips, and self-drive packages. Web site has Hot Deals section and e-mailers announcing specials and last-minute deals can be requested. Telephone reservations may be made for an additional fee of $10. 425-487-9632. www.GoToday.com

GPSC Charters Ltd. offers great deals on private yacht travel to the Greek Isles. Their Wake Up package includes round-trip air, hotel, and sailing through Greek Isles where participants have plenty of opportunity to explore historical and archaeological sites, visit quaint villages, and enjoy secluded beaches. 600 St. Andrew Road, Philadelphia, PA 19118. 800-732-6786 or 215-247-3903. www.gpsc.com. e-mail: com@gpsc.com.

New Frontiers offers bargain packages for independent travelers throughout Europe and a few other parts of the world, including the South Pacific. 12 East 33rd Street, New York, NY 10016. 800-366-6387 or 212-779-0600. West Coast Office: 5757 West Century Blvd., Suite 650, Los Angeles, CA 90045. 888-277-6058 or 800-677-0720 or 310-670-7318. e-mail: mailus@newfrontiers.com.

Pacific Bestour Inc., offers fantastic untours to Asia. 228 River Vale Road, River Vale, NJ 07675. 800-688-3288 or 201-664-8778. www.bestour.com. e-mail: webmaster@bestour.com.

Petrabax offers very good deals on escorted tours and untours to London and Spain, especially November through March. 800-634-1188. www.petrabax.com. e-mail: info@petrabax.com.

TIP: Mexico's version of the Grand Canyon is Copper Canyon, which has been dubbed the last outpost of civilization and renowned for its spectacular scenery. The Copper Canyon Lodge is a beautiful restored adobe hacienda that stretches the equivalent of a city block. There is so much to do and see within a three-hour radius of the lodge, such as cave exploration and remains of gothic mansions, you might have trouble deciding what to do first. This is perfect for independent travelers. The lodge will help arrange travel, transfers, land transportation and accommodations. Comfort is promised once travelers reach the canyon via the only road, a rugged terrain taking eight hours to travel. Many different packages available. Low single supplement. 800-776-3942 or 810-340-7230.

The Grand Canyon is an impressive 217 miles long, 18 miles at its widest point, and one mile deep. The deepest gorge is found in Hell's Canyon, Snake River, Idaho (7,900 feet). The Maswik Lodge and Yavapai Lodge, both located on the South Rim of the Grand Canyon, offer substantial price breaks for visitors during late fall and winter (November-March, excluding holidays). Children 16 and under stay free.

Some of the best deals on lodging for Yellowstone National Park are family-owned lodges, guest ranches, and dude ranches located at the park's eastern entrance. All these places offer activities ranging from white-water rafting to rodeos and horseback riding. Contact The Lodges of East Yellowstone for a free list of all member lodges and ranches. P.O. Box 21-RC, Wapiti, Wyoming 82450. 307-587-9595. www.yellowstone-lodging.com.

South Pacific Travel Shops offer independent travelers many wonderful ways to see Australia, New Zealand, Tahiti, and Fiji. For example, their 10 day Capital & Country Tour would be hard to beat. It includes air from Los Angeles and accommodations are guaranteed in Sydney and Melbourne. Vouchers are issued for the remaining nights for use on the journey between the cities, as well as a voucher for a car rental. A suggested itinerary is provided for the many sights en route to your destination city of Melbourne, but you are free to do whatever you choose. During the three day stay in Sydney, you will be issued passes on all public transport, including bus, train, and ferries. Some of the suggested sights include gold mining towns, wineries, animal park to see kangaroos and other native animals, camel farm, cave exploration, botanical gardens, wildlife and reptile park, battle re-enactment, the world's third largest castle, casino, and more! And, since your airline ticket allows up to a one-month stay, you may opt to spend time in New Zealand, Fiji, and/or Tahiti. 1720 Peachtree Street, NW, Atlanta, GA 30309. 800-894-7722 or 404-733-6202. www.inta-aussie.com.

♦ FYI: Australia was founded in 1812 as a British settlement where criminals were sent. Later, others moved there for its gold and rich farmland.

Travel In Style specialize in Mediterranean travel. Some untours are very affordable, despite the fact they include a first-class sleeping compartment on a train from Luxor to Cairo, luxury Nile cruise, and more. Spend free time roaming through the colorful bazaars or choose from options, such as a visit to The Egyptian Museum, the Pyramids, and the Sphinx. 1255 Post Street, Suite 506, San Francisco, CA 94109. 888-466-8242 or 415-440-1124. www.travelinstyle.com.

Travelnet's week-long self-drive Explore Costa Rica Vacation is the cheapest, and perhaps, most enjoyable way to independently experience northern Costa Rica. The packages includes rental of an air-conditioned 4 x 4 vehicle with unlimited mileage and insurance, stay in San Jose and at the base of the active Volcano Arenal, full day tour to Cano Negro Wildlife Refuge where you have a chance to spot exotic birds, iguanas, monkeys, and crocodiles, a couple days in Tamarindo on a white sandy beach, and all transfers. Other untours include photo safaris, and explore packages that offer different options, including golf, rafting, fishing, scuba diving, and casino gambling. 800-343-8300. www.centralamerica.com/travel. e-mail: travelnet@centralamerica.com

Untours offers independent travelers an exciting way to see European cities. For example, it offers a package to Venice that includes airfare from the states, apartment stay in Venice for 2–4 weeks, Italian Rail FlexiPass, and airport greeting and orientation. Some trips with no single supplements are offered each year. P.O. Box 405, Media, PA 19063. 888-UNTOUR1 (868-6871). www.untours.com.

◆　　◆　　◆

Ground Transport: Trains, Buses, And Cars

Trains
Have you ever thought about enjoying the scenic beauty of the Rockies by rail? How about a train adventure through Mexico's spectacular Copper Canyon? Or, how about hopping on Amtrak and discovering America? Trains are truly a hassle-free way to travel and there are a couple of ways to go about it. First, you may travel independently by purchasing a rail pass, or take a train tour. Train tours usually combine sightseeing and other activities with a rail trip, which varies in duration according to the type of tour. Some rail trips spend minimal time aboard, while others spend most of the time on the train. The best deals on train tours are usually through last minute specials and promotions revealed in electronic or printed newsletters, so be sure to get on the list.

Alaska Railroad--Scenic Rail Tours utilizes many trains, such as The Denali Star, The Coastal Classic and The Glacier Discovery. The Alaska Railroad, established 1914, has been designated a scenic railway by the Alaska Department of Transportation and Public Facilities. The scenic rail trips are offered in conjunction with a number of exciting options, including passage cruises, rafting, fly-fishing, wildlife tours, trolley and ferry tours and much more. P.O. Box 107500, Anchorage, AK 99510-7500. 800-544-0552. www.akrr.com. e-mail: reservations@akrr.com.

TIP: Alaska Heritage Tours specializes in independent travel to Denali National Park, Prince William Sound, and Kenai Fjords(877-258-6877, www.ahtours.com). NorthStar Trekking takes travelers on helicopter tours and glacier hikes (907-790-4530). For those looking for value-oriented places to stay, *How to Rent a Public Cabin in Southcentral Alaska* (Wilderness Press, 800-443-7227) is a handy guide. Or, contact the Department of Natural Resources at 907-269-8400, www.dnr.state.ak.us/pic /faq.htm. For more general information on Alaska, call 800-862-5275 or access www.travelalaska. com.

American Orient Express is far from cheap, but if you are a train enthusiast and really want to splurge, you may want to consider it. They promise "Deluxe Rail Journeys on North America's Only Private Luxury Train." Itineraries include National Parks of the West, Antebellum South, Pacific Coast Explorer, and Great Transcontinental Rail Journey. Early booking discounts are extended. 5100 Main Street, Suite 300, Downers Grove, IL 60515. 630-663-4550. www.AmericanOrientExpress.com.

Amtrak offers rail passengers many ways to save money, such as its Guest Rewards program. Participants accumulate points on all routes and the points can be redeemed for train tickets, airline frequent-flyer miles or other services/merchandise. Another option is Amtrak's North American Rail Pass, which is good for unlimited stops to 900+ destinations in U.S. and Canada, with the only restriction being travel must be during a consecutive 30-day period. Persons 62 or older receive a 15 percent discount and children (ages 2–15) accompanied by older adults receive 50 percent off the fare. Amtrak frequently runs specials, such as Explore America, which is good for discounted fares to one region, two adjacent regions, or any three or four regions.

Amtrak debuted Acela Express trains in late 2000, which will eventually replace all the Metroliners because they are sleeker and faster. For example, travel between Boston and Washington used to take over eight hours but Acela Express trains make it less than six hours.

Call to request a free copy of *Amtrak Travel Planner*, a 100-page brochure filled with specific adventures and travel tips. 800-USA-RAIL. The Web site shows specific train schedules and allows online booking. It also informs travelers of discounted fares--up to 90 percent off normal fares. www.amtrak.com.

Maupintour Rail Adventures offers numerous worldwide rail trips combined with other activities, such as trekking, rafting, and exploring. They also offer independent and escorted tours, as well as hotel barge trips on European waterways. 421 Research Park Drive, Suite 300, Lawrence, KS 66049-3858. 800-255-4266. www.maupintour.com.

Rocky Mountaineer Railtours provides travel on one of Canada's best trains. It has spacious, reclining seats, picture windows, air-conditioning, and a no smoking policy. They offer safe independent travel throughout Canada and the Rockies. 1150 Station Street, 1st floor, Vancouver, BC, Canada V6A 2X7. 800-665-7245 or 604-606-7245. www.rockymountaineer.com.

Trains Unlimited Tours has provided "spectacular rail adventures" since 1985. Trips take place in the U.S., Canada, Mexico, Russia, and Latin America. Best rates on Rio Grande, Fall Colors, and Copper Canyon trips. P.O. Box 1997, Portola, CA 96122. 800-359-4870 or 530-836-1745. www.trainweb.com/trainsunlimitedtours. e-mail: info@trainsunltdtours.com.

Uncommon Journeys/Train Holidays offers worldwide rail tour adventures, especially British Columbia and Canadian Rockies. Single occupancy and Suite accommodations are available on most trips. Very reasonable rates. Early booking bonus often includes free Amtrak travel to Seattle or low-cost airfare. 309 Lennon Lane, Suite 101, Walnut Creek, CA 94598. 800-543-2846, 800-323-5893, 925-938-0456, or 510-933-1072. http://trainholidays.com/th or www.uncommonjourneys.com.

Via Rail Canada has authentic 50s era cars and many amenities, such as observation dome, first-class lounge, and dining cars. Spectacular route through the Rockies, Vancouver to Toronto, including Churchill, Manitoba; Halifax, Nova Scotia; and Prince Rupert, B.C. Significant discounts for those over 60. 800-561-9181. www.viarail.ca.

◆ FYI: The world's longest railroad is the Trans-Siberian Railroad. It extends 5,770 miles, beginning in Moscow, stretching through the Ural Mountains and across all of Asia to Vladivostak, which is on the sea of Japan. You will cross seven time zones if you ride it the entire distance.

◆   ◆   ◆

One of the best travel experiences I've ever had was traveling around Europe using a Eurail pass, hopping on and off as desired. Rail passengers can comfortably spend the night on a train by getting a sleeping compartment, or may opt to stay in a hotel and catch a train another day. For more information on any of these rail systems, or to purchase train passes, contact your travel agent or one of these companies:

> **DER Travel Services**--800-782-2424. www.dertravel.com.
> **Europe Through the Back Door**--425-771-8303.   www.ricksteves.com.
> **Rail Europe**--800-438-7245. www.raileurope.com.
> **Rail Pass Express**--800-722-7151. www.railpass.com.

Eurailpass is the best deal if you are planning to visit three or more countries in Europe. A EurailPass is a discounted train pass available for unlimited first class travel for periods of 15, 21, 30, 60, or 90 days, good for 17 countries: Austria, Belgium, Denmark, Finland, France, Germany, Greece, Hungary, Italy, Ireland, Luxembourg, The Netherlands, Norway, Portugal, Spain, Sweden, and Switzerland. These passes are not valid for travel on private railroads. Passes for children ages 4–11 are half the cost of an adult EurailPass, and children under 4 travel free.

There are other types of Eurail Passes including **Eurail Flexipass**, Which Allows Only 15 Travel Days Within a two-month period but costs considerably less money. A Flexipass is a good deal if you plan to stay in France for a week and then travel to Switzerland and stay for a week before traveling on to Italy, etc.

Eurail Selectpass is the newest pass, introduced early 2001. It includes rail and ferry travel for three European countries, which must border each other. Passes are good for five to 10 days.

Eurail Supersaver Pass is a Eurail pass that is discounted because there are two or more persons traveling together. Travel is consecutive over 15 or 21 days, one month, two months, or three months.

Eurail/Drive Pass allows seven days of travel: four days of train travel with three days of car rental within a two-month period. Up to five additional days can be purchased.

A **Europass Drive** works the same way and pricing is very similar.

Eurail Youthpass is the same as the traditional EurailPass with these two exceptions: 1) The traveler must be under the age of 26, and 2) the traveler is confined to second class rather than first class.

TIP: Here are three ways to save money on rail passes. First, European rail pass prices usually increase after the first of the year, so buy your pass before December 31st to save money. The rail pass is still good for travel as long as it's used within six months of purchase. Secondly, several European Rail Passes are discounted for older travelers and youths. Be sure you pay the discounted price and/or obtain the right pass. And lastly, save money on lodging by traveling to your next destination on a night train. For a little more money, you can obtain a private compartment or a sleeping berth. Doing this just a few nights, rather than paying for a hotel, will add up to significant savings.

Protect your pass against theft or loss by enrolling in the pass protection program and paying the nominal fee. Ask your travel agent or whoever issues your rail pass for more information.

Europass lets you choose the number of days and countries you wish to travel to, with the one restriction being the countries must border each other. The main pass allows travel in the five most visited European countries: France, Germany, Italy, Spain, and Switzerland. The associated countries include Austria/Hungary (counts as one add-on), Benelux (Belgium, Netherlands, and Luxembourg), Greece, or Portugal. You have to know the associated countries you plan to visit when purchasing the pass. Due to these limitations, this pass is much cheaper than the traditional EurailPass. And, the second traveler receives 40 percent off his pass.

Alaskapass permits travel on the Alaska Marine ferry, Alaska Railroad, and several Alaskan bus lines. Travelers save more than 40 percent. This is the most affordable way to see Alaska's interior. 800-248-7598. www.alaskapass.com.

Train travel in Australia is not discounted for anyone, including children, youth, or seniors. The **Austrail Flexi-Pass** allows eight days train travel within a six month period. There are also some cheaper regional passes which are good for Victoria, Queensland, and Western Australia.

Austrian Railpass--Children under 7 free.

Benelux Tourail Pass--Belgium, Luxembourg, and the Netherlands. Children under 4 free. Reduced rate for two or more adults traveling together.

Britrail Pass And Britrail Flexipass--England, Scotland and Wales. Children under 5 free. Children 5–15 pay half fare. Discount for those 60 and older. Car rental discounts available for pass holders.

Britrail Southeast Pass--This is a flexipass good for travel to a large section of Southern England.

Britireland Pass--England, Scotland, Wales, Northern Ireland, and Republic of Ireland. Children under 5 free. Children 5–15 half fare.

Bulgaria--Children under 4 free. Children 4–11 half fare.

Czech Flexipass--Czech Republic only. Children under 4 free. Children 4-11 half fare.

European East Pass--Austria, Czech Republic, Slovakia, Hungary, and Poland. Children under 4 free. Children 4–11 half fare.

Finrail Pass--Children under 6 free. Children 6–16 half fare. Additional 20 percent discount for travel from October to April.

♦ FYI: The Eiffel Tower was completed in 1889 and stands 984 feet.

France Railpass--Discounts for two or more adults traveling together. France Youthrail available. Children under 4 free. Children 4–11 half fare. Combination passes, such as Rail/Drive or Rail/Fly available.

German Rail Passes--50 percent discount on second pass for two or more travelers. Children under 4 free. Children 4–11 half fare. Rail/Drive passes available.

Greek Railpass--Reduced rates for children 2–11. Children under 2 free. Rail/Fly passes available.

Holland Railpass--Children under 4 free. Discounts for seniors. Discounts for two adults traveling together.

Hungarian Flexipass--Children under 5 free. Children 5–14 half fare.

Indrail--good for travel within India.

◆ FYI: India's Taj Mahal was built as a tribute for Emperor ShahJahan's wife, MumtajMahal, in 1648. It took 20,000 men and 22 years to complete. When it was finished, it was valued at over $4 million. Today, the Taj Mahal is considered priceless.

Irish Emerald Card--Republic of Ireland & Northern Ireland rail and bus pass. Cards can be purchased through CIE Tours International, 201-292-3438. Discounted price for children under 12—if card purchased in Ireland.

Italian Railpass--Children under 4 free. Children 4-12 half fare.

Japan Rail Passes are rather expensive and the only discount available is children 6-11 pay 50 percent of adult fare.

Norway Railpass--Children under 4 free. Children 4–16 half fare.

Portuguese Railpass--Children under 4 free. Children 4–11 half fare.

Prague Excursion--Youth fare allows one round-trip from any Czech border to Prague within seven days. Children under 4 free. Reduced fare for children 4–11.

Romania--Children under 4 free. Children 4–11 half fare.

Scanrail Pass--Denmark, Sweden, Finland and Norway. Children under 4 free. Children 4–15 half fare. Offers youth passes and discounts for 55 and older. Rail/Drive passes also available.

Freedom Of Scotland--Allows transportation on most Caledonian MacBrayne ferries to the islands of Scotland. Discounts on several ferry operators, and on some bus companies in Scotland. 20 percent discount on Stena Sealink to Northern Ireland. No discounts for children.

Spain Flexipass--The pass is valid on most private railroads as well as public railroads. Children under 4 free. Children 4–11 half fare. Rail/Drive passes available.

Sweden Railpass--Two children, up to age 15, travel free with one accompanying adult. Additional children pay 30–40 percent less than adult fare.

Swiss Pass-- No additional discounts.

Companion Swiss Pass--This pass is valid on most private railroads as well as public railroads. Children under 16 free with parent. Rail/Drive passes also available.

New Zealand Travelpass--The Travelpass also entitles bearer to free unrestricted travel on all trains, buses, and ferries throughout New Zealand. Children pay 66 percent of adult fare.

◆ FYI: New York's Grand Central Station is the largest train station in the world. It covers 48 acres on two levels, with a total of 67 tracks. On average, around 550 trains pass through this station daily.

◆　◆　◆

<u>Buses</u>
Bus passes are available for just about any town or city in the world. Typically, these are the cheapest and most convenient way to utilize bus transport. When making travel arrangements, ask the tourist board or your travel agent for specific information.

Adventure Planet/Adventure Network (ANT) is a "hop-on, hop-off backpacker transportation adventure network that takes participants all over California and the southwestern United States. ANT pass holders are picked up at hotels or hostels. ANT offers many routes and participants also receive exclusive deals, such as discounts at certain independent hostels. Passes good for six months. 870 Market Street, Suite 416 San Francisco, CA 94102. 800-336-6049 for U.S. and Canada, or 415-399-0880. www.theant.com. e-mail: anttrip@theant.com.

Busabout is a "hop on, hop off" European bus company. It also has a membership club, which entitles participants to discounted hotel rooms and meals, free sightseeing admissions, baggage and mail holding, and more. 258 Vauxhall Bridge Road, London, England SW1 1BS. 44-(0)171-950-1661. www.busabout.com. e-mail: info@busabout.co.uk.

Eurolines is a "hop-on, hop-off" bus company that goes to 500 European cities in 25 countries, and offers many kinds of bus passes. Youth and senior passes available for less. Grosvenor Gardens, 52 Grosvenor Gardens, London SW1 W0AU. +44 (0) 1582404511. www.eurolines.com.

Green Tortoise Bus Tours have short and long U.S. and South of the Border adventures. The company was founded in 1974 for budget-minded travelers who appreciate the custom-converted sleeper coaches, which means you are horizontal and not propping your head on a window or seat back. By day, explore towns and countryside, and at night, soft music lulls you to sleep. Green Tortoise welcomes all ages, promises gourmet meals, and a unique opportunity to meet new people. I think it's most appreciated by young travelers. Points are accumulated on some trips and can add up to free trips. 494 Broadway, San Francisco, CA 94133. 800-TORTOISE or 415-956-7500. www.greentortoise.com. e-mail: tortoise@greentortoise.com.

◆ FYI: The top five tour bus destinations in America are Myrtle Beach (SC), Branson (MO), New Orleans (LA), Nashville (TN), and Washington, D.C.

If you want to see America by bus, **Greyhound** is the best option. The bus line offers 2,600 destinations in 48 states, and Canada and Mexico, with 18,000 daily departures. Greyhound also allows many discounts. Military personnel receive 10 percent off normal fares and are guaranteed a low rate. College students can choose from several options, such as a 15 percent discount or a special Spring Break fare. Those over 62 are entitled to a 10 percent discount off full fare tickets. Children under 2 travel free but only one free child per adult. Children 2-11 are half the adult fare with a limit of three children per adult. Companions accompanying and assisting disabled travelers are entitled to free travel. Always ask about special fares because Greyhound offers many different deals, depending on the time of year. P.O. Box 660689, Dallax, TX 75266. 800-229-9424 or 800-231-2222. www.greyhound.com. e-mail: ifsr@greyhound.com.

Greyhound Canada works the same way as Greyhound America. Some noteworthy deals are the Canada Travel Pass and Companion Fares Program, which is a buy one full fare ticket(one-way or return trip) and get the second ticket at 50 percent off. A 10 percent discount is given to those 60 or older on certain fares. 800-661-8747. In the U.S.: www.greyhound.com or in Canada: www.greyhound.ca.

♦ FYI: The five largest cities in the world, population wise, are :
Seoul, Korea (10,726,000); Sao Paulo, Brazil (10,063,110); Bombay, India (9,909,547); Moscow, Russia (8,801,500); and Mexico City, Mexico (8,236,960). New York is ninth on the list with a population of 7,322,564.

Some "hop-on hop-off" bus companies that go to unusual destinations include:

Australia--Oz Experience offers different routes and passes, such as a six-month pass with unlimited stops. 011-61-2/9368-1766. www.ozexperience.com.

Canada--CanaBus Tours pass. 877-226-2287. www.canabus.com.

South Africa--Baz Bus offers passes good for up to three years. 011-27-21/439-2323. www.bazbus.com.

Turkey--Fez Travel offers bus routes from Istanbul to Cappadocia. 011-90-212/516-9024.

New Zealand--Kiwi Experience allows travelers to do both North and South Islands for one low rate. 011-61-9/366-9830. www.kiwiexperience.com.

*Discounts vary so be sure to ask.

♦   ♦   ♦

Cars
There may be times during your travels that you need to rent a car. You might want to use a car broker agency as opposed to a car rental agency. These companies work similarly to traditional car rental agencies, except they offer three things those agencies cannot: lower prices and no tax, different types of vehicles, such as motorcycles and motorhomes; and services, such as driver, hotel, air, train, barge, and car packages.

When renting a car overseas, make all the arrangements from the U.S., if possible. It's often cheaper (up to 50 percent) and easier, due to language barriers and car shortages, to have advance reservations and confirmation. Because economy cars are the most requested, advance arrangements guarantee the best price.

There are other considerations. Manual transmissions are the most common vehicles in Europe and it may be difficult, as well as costly, to rent an automatic transmission. In Europe, rental cars are confirmed by category; i.e. economy, sports, and luxury—not make and model. Be sure you can take the car into all the countries you intend to visit. For example, travel into Eastern Europe is usually not allowed by car rental agencies.

Find out the difference in price if you are thinking about leaving the car at a different location than where you picked it up. Verify the drop-off time by checking the contract, as well as asking the representative. If the car is due at noon and you return it at 12:14 p.m., you may be charged for another full 24-hours, so be clear about the drop-off policy. If the car has a full tank of gas when you receive it, it is expected to be returned with a full tank of gas. Be sure to fill it yourself because it will cost less than what you will be charged if the company has to fill the gas tank.

As always, ask about discounts, such as getting a lower price if you use a certain credit card. Be careful of prices quoted on the Internet as they typically do not include surcharges, such as taxes, per day state surcharges, per day car licensing fees, airport access fees (try to avoid picking up a car at the airport because rentals are usually higher), and second driver or underage driver. You must be at least 21 to rent a car, except in New York where the age is 18, and those under 25 will pay a heavy surcharge. It's best to ask for a written price confirmation. Also, be forewarned that many European rental agencies won't rent to persons under 25 or over 70. These age restrictions also apply in other parts of the world, and vary according to location and company, so be sure to ask. Always check your bill before leaving the agency to make sure you receive any discounts you are entitled to and that you are not overcharged. Make sure you are not billed for gas fill-ups or optional insurance you didn't agree to purchase.

Car rental agencies and brokers push hard for insurance policies be taken out. This is a big moneymaker and you should only buy it if you are not covered by your own policy. Most policies do cover drivers of rental vehicles so be sure to find out from your insurance agent if your specific policy covers this before purchasing unnecessary insurance.

TIP: Most museums lower entrance fees after 3 p.m. because they close at 5 or 6 p.m. If two or three hours is all you need, this is a big money-saver. For example, the Louvre cuts its admission price in half for late afternoon patrons.

Additionally, buying tickets on the day of a performance usually entitles the recipient to 50 percent off the normal ticket price. For example, unsold tickets to shows can be purchased for London and New York Broadway shows at less than half the regular rate. The drawback is you will only have a few hours notice because unsold tickets are not offered until three or four hours before curtain time.

AutoEurope offers short-and long-term rentals and leases, air and hotel packages, chauffeured drives, motor homes, motorcycles, as well as escorted tours and safaris in Europe, Africa, and the Middle East. AutoEurope frequently runs specials, which include free airfare or hotel stay with every motorhome rental. 39 Commercial Street, P.O. Box 7006, Portland, ME 04112. 800-223-5555. www.autoeurope.com. e-mail:ae@autoeurope.com.

Europe By Car was established in 1954. Special low pricing for teachers/faculty or students. Discounts of at least 10 percent are available for clients at certain hotels/motels in Europe, or budget motels. Europe by Car offers big discounts for teachers and students. One Rockefeller Plaza, New York, NY 10020; 212-581-3040. 9000 Sunset Blvd., Los Angeles, CA 90069. 800-252-9401 or 213-272-0424. Nationwide: 800-223-1516. www.europebycar.com.

Kemwel Holiday Autos offer cars (rentals and short-term leases), campers and chauffeured drives, hotel and air packages, luxury hotel and barge trips, and luxury train tours in Europe, Middle East,

Africa, Canada, Caribbean, Central America, and more. The Kemwel Group, 106 Calvert Street, Harrison, NY 10528. 800-678-0678 or 914-835-5555. www.kemwel.com. e-mail: webmail@kemwel.com.

Renault Eurodrive leases cars, from compact to mini-vans, vans, and wheelchair access vehicles at low tax-free rates with full insurance and unlimited mileage for European travel. For a small surcharge, you can pick up the car in one city and drop it off in a different city. To lease, you must be at least 18 years old (no maximum age) and have a U.S. Driver's License, valid for at least one year. You will also be required to show your passport and Renault Eurodrive contract when you pick up the car or van. Minimum lease is 17 days, but there are no second-driver fees or drop-off charges. Rates include insurance. 650 First Avenue, New York, NY 10016. From Eastern states: 800-221-1052. From Western states: 800-477-7116. From Florida and Puerto Rico: 800-777-7131. In New York: 212-532-1221 www.eurodrive.net or www.renaultusa.com. e-mail: mail@eurodrive.com.

TIP: Attention Shoppers: Going to America's biggest shopping facility, the Mall of America, is a bargain in the winter. Many Minneapolis/St. Paul area hotels and motels offer weekend shopping packages November–March. Rates are drastically reduced at nearby hotels, including Baymont Inn, Days Inn, and the Hilton, *and* typically include free shuttles from the hotel to the mall and coupon books for mall discounts. And, no sales tax is charged on clothes!

If you're looking for somewhere to spend the savings, Mystic Lake Casino is less than 20 minutes from the mall. Northwest Airlines has a major hub in Minneapolis with incoming flights from dozens of cities(800-225-2525 or www.nwa.com).

Car rental agencies offer minimal discounts to travelers, only 5–10 percent. These price reductions are usually reserved for mature travelers. Always let the agency know if you are a member of AAA, Costco, Sam's Club, or AARP, because this usually entitles you to additional savings, although discounts vary according to city. People belonging to a travel club, or utilizing a credit card promotion, may be entitled to discounted rates. Periodically, both Visa® and Mastercard® insert discount offers, with monthly billing statements, good at leading car rental agencies. Avoid booking on Wednesdays because that is the highest demand day of the week. Always reserve a compact (economy) car because they have the lowest rental rates. Additionally, these cars sell out first, so you'll often be upgraded, free-of-charge.

Another possibility is to use a rewards program. For example, Hertz awards participants 10 points for every dollar spent in its Greenpoints Program. Points can be exchanged for free car rentals, airline tickets, or merchandise. Access a company's Web site or ask the customer service representative/sales agent to explain any discounts and rewards programs currently being offered.

Several agencies now have a car rental auction Web site area, such as Budget-Rent-a-Car's BidBudget (www.drivebudget.com). The program was initiated for "cost-conscious vacationers." Participants fill out an electronic form, which includes desired dates, car preference, major credit card, and bid amount. Budget notifies bid winners within 24-hours. A wonderful bonus is that Budget offers a money-back guarantee if you change your mind, as long as it's at least 48 hours prior to car pick-up.

Additionally, many car rental agencies, such as Budget, Hertz, and Avis, offer substantial discounts for those who rent cars online. My suggestion is to shop around before making a reservation to ensure you pay the lowest rate. Some of the bigger Internet travel sites may beat the prices offered by the car rental agency. These companies buy in volume, affording them a wholesale price that will often beat what the individual consumer is offered.

Alamo--800-327-9633. www.goalamo.com.

Avis--In the U.S.: 800 331-1212. Worldwide: 800-331-1084. www.avis.com.

Budget--800-527-0700. www.budget.com.

Dollar--800-800-4000. www.dollar.com.
Dollar is the first car rental agency to launch a first full service travel site, which features 500 airlines, 40,000 hotels, and 45 car rental companies.

Enterprise--800-325-8007. www.enterprise.com.

Hertz--In the U.S.: 800-654-3131. Worldwide: 800-654-3001. www.hertz.com

National--In the U.S.:800-227-7368. Worldwide: 800-227-3876. www.nationalcar.com.

Thrifty--800-367-2277. www.thrifty.com.

TIP: Want to rent a Harley Davidson and head out on the highway? Many Harley dealers actually rent the fancy motorcycles. The rental fee includes helmets, rain suits, short-term luggage storage, and 24-hour roadside assistance. Motorcycle license required. 888-HD-RENTALS. www.hdrentals.com.

A cheaper alternative (roughly 30 percent less) to using traditional car rental agencies, is 25-year old **Dial-A-Wreck** Most of the cars are only 2–3 years old and roadside assistance is promised is there is a problem. Another bonus: the company doesn't require a credit card, which all major car rental agencies do. Make sure you carry the mandatory (legally required) insurance only, and always read the fine print as each franchise is free to set its own rules. Dial-A-Wreck has over 500 locations in 48 states in the U.S. 800-535-1391. www.rent-a-wreck.com.

TIP: Some ways to save money on gas include driving 55 rather than 65 for a savings of 15 percent. Luggage tied onto the roof makes your car burn more gas because of wind resistance. Using the air conditioner is more fuel efficient than rolling down the windows, again, because of wind resistance.
For pit-stops over two minutes, turn off the engine to save almost a gallon an hour. Fast accelerations increase gas consumption, so slowly back out of a parking lot or resume speed when stopped at a redlight. For a list of cars that burn less fuel, access www.fueleconomy.gov. For the lowest gas prices, go to www.driveandsave.com and input the state, airport, or zip code.
The 10 most expensive places overseas to buy gasoline are Hong Kong, London, Amsterdam, Oslo, Finland, Tokyo, Copenhagen, Paris, Seoul, and Stockholm.

◆   ◆   ◆

Helpful Resources

<u>Trains</u>

Britain By Britrail by George and LaVerne Ferguson. Published by Globe Pequot.

Eurail And Train Travel Guide To The World is published by Houghton Mifflin.

Itinerary Planning With A Eurail Pass is a free booklet that can be obtained by contacting Rick Steve's Europe Through the Back Door, Edmonds, WA 98020. 425-771-8303.

Traveling Europe's Trains by Jay Brunhouse. Published by Pelican. This outlines rail trips throughout Europe including Europe's Lowest Train, the TGV, and other unique trains.

For information on specific trains and train travel in general, access Train Web's Web site, www.traintravel.com. **The Society of International Railway Travelers** is an excellent source for North America, Europe, and exotic rail destinations. 1810 Sils Avenue, No. 306B, Louisville, KY 40205. 800-IRT-4881 or 502-454-0277. www.irtsociety.com.

<u>Planning Guides</u>

America's Most Scenic Drives ($3.95+$2.95 postage) is a handy resource for anyone interested in exploring America and Canada by car. Each route, such as Shenandoah Valley, VA and Outer Banks, NC, includes highlights, distance, route and directions with sites of interest, accommodations, and contact information. The publication contains 45 interesting road-trips. Vacation Publications, 1502 Augusta Drive, Suite 415, Houston, TX 77057.

Chamber Of Commerce's national Web site provides information on all U.S. Chambers of Commerce, as well as Convention & Visitor's Bureaus and foreign tourism offices. www.chamberofcommerce.com.

Independent Travel Planner (G10, $5) is a very useful planner. Transitions Abroad, P.O. Box 1300, Amherst, MA 01004-1300. 800-293-0373. www.transitionsabroad.com.

International Association Of Convention & Visitor Bureaus lists 1,000 tourist bureaus in 30 countries. 202-296-7888. www.officialtravelinfo.com.

Map World has thousands of maps of any location in the world for sale, as well as globes. 123-DN E. Camino Real, Encinitas, CA 92024. 800-246-MAPS(6277) or 760-942-9642. www.mapworld.com.

Planning Your Trip To Europe is a free up-to-date guide to 28 European countries, including color photos, maps, and schedule of special events. 800-816-7532. www.visiteurope.com.

World Calendar's Web site includes over 40,000 events around-the-world and offers many useful links. www.worldcalendar.com.

TIP: *On the home front...*

Most hotels and cruise ships provide free postcards in the room, cabin, or lobby, but wait until you get home to mail them and you'll save all that overseas postage. Better still, use www.postcards.org to e-mail free ones! To save costly overseas or ship-to-shore calls home, use e-mail whenever possible. Hand-held computers, laptops, and organizers with e-mail capabilities, allow cheap and convenient home access. If you do much traveling, buying such a device would be a worthwhile investment. Some cruise lines have Internet cafes that passengers can use for fees that are less than those charged for making ship-to-shore phone calls. Never buy souvenirs at tourist shops because prices are inflated for tourists. Instead, buy goodies, such as coffee, tea, nuts, jams, candies, and cookies at local grocery stores, and arts and crafts at the open markets.

Safety

The Citizen's Emergency Center Of The Bureau Of Consular Affairs Hotline is for reporting emergencies, inquiring about travelers in emergency situations, or for obtaining current safety warnings, alerts, and conditions around-the-world. 202-647-5225

How To Protect Yourself From Becoming A Crime Victim And Avoid Problems While Traveling is a booklet filled with 100 ways travelers can protect themselves and includes Internet resources. Send $5 and SASE to Notebook Publications Inc., PMB 150, 2601 So. Lemay, Suite 7, Fort Collins, Colorado 80525. www.notebookpublications.com.

Travel Advisories (Official Warnings) and ***Background Notes*** (consular information sheets), as well as Visa and Passport information, can be obtained for any country or territory from the U.S. Department of State, 2201 C. Street NW, Washington, D.C. 20520. 202-647-4000. www.travel.state.gov/travel_warnings.html.

◆　　◆　　◆

Chapter Four--How To Get The Best Deals On Airline Tickets

Chapter Four--How To Get The Best Deals On Airline Tickets

Let observation wit extensive view
Survey mankind, from China to Peru.
Samuel Johnson, Vanity of Human Wishes (1749)

Ten Ways To Save Big Money

Most of us rely on heavily advertised "airfare price wars" or our travel agent to inform us about bargain fares, but there are several other methods to secure low prices. However, while travelers should not rely solely on airfare price wars, they shouldn't dismiss them either. During slow travel times, many airlines frequently slash their normal rates to entice travelers into buying tickets. The best deals go to the early birds, so regularly scan business and travel sections of the newspaper, watch Internet fares, and remind your travel agent to always let you know when special fares are offered.

1. Call the airlines between midnight and 1 a.m. (Monday–Friday) to get cheaper fares. At midnight, airline agents revise and load new fares into the computers. The best chance to obtain the handful of rock bottom fares offered is just after these fares have been updated.

2. Check into alternative airports. Many major cities, such as New York, Los Angeles, San Francisco, Dallas, Washington, and London, have two airports. Additionally, surrounding cities also have airports. Compare fares for carriers (including regional airlines) that fly into all these airports to find the lowest price.

3. Typically, the earlier you book, the better the savings. Most special fares have restrictions that include a minimum 7 to 30-day advance purchase. Special fares are usually nonrefundable so make sure you will be able to satisfy the advance purchase requirements. Conversely, there are last minute specials. Log onto www.smarterliving.com to sign up for e-mailers detailing last minute fares. For more on e-mailers, see Number 9 below.

4. Mid-week fares are usually cheaper. If you can fly out on Tuesday, Wednesday, or Thursday, and stay over a Saturday night, you can expect considerable savings over fares with departure dates on Friday, Saturday, Sunday, or Monday.

5. At times it is cheaper to purchase one-way or split tickets. For example, if flying from Raleigh to Boston, it may be cheaper to buy two separate tickets: one from Raleigh to Atlanta and one from Atlanta to Boston. This depends on the airline and where its connecting cities and hubs are located. For example, in the Southeast, major airline hubs are in Nashville, Atlanta, and Raleigh. It is often cheaper to drive or fly to these cities and depart from them. Regional airlines are an economical way to get you to a major city where fares are cheaper. If you book through a travel agent, a good agent will check all possibilities and find the best deal for your needs. Be sure to tell the agent if you are willing to fly out of other cities or airports to save money.

6. Another option is an "open-jaw" ticket. These are also used when a traveler is arriving and departing from different cities. The difference is that one ticket is purchased to cover both cities. Check the prices of each to determine whether (two) one-way tickets or (one) open-jaw ticket is the best deal.

7. Use an online service such as SideStep, FareChase, or Qixo. To utilize these types of services, simply download the program into Internet Explorer or Netscape (more options will soon be available). Enter destinations and dates and SideStep quickly searches more than two dozen affiliated regional and international airlines to come up with the absolutely lowest price. Sabre-powered services, which account for roughly 75 percent of all travel bookings worldwide, can be bypassed with

services such as SideStep. Since airlines and agencies don't have to pay for Sabre, they can offer cheaper fares. However, these fares are not always lower than other sources.

"Who has the best deal on airline tickets—Internet travel sites, airlines, or consolidators?" I could retire if I had a quarter for every time I've been asked that question. Unfortunately, there is no pat answer. Most of the time consolidators (Internet or otherwise) are hard to beat. However, there are times when add-on airfares offered by tours or cruise ships are the best deals. Sometimes, airlines provide unbeatable vacation packages during non-peak travel seasons or fares during price "wars." Always check all the possibilities before buying an airline ticket or booking any other type of travel.

8. When booking a flight, ask whether it's a "code share" flight, which means that the same flight is offered by two different airlines. If so, get the name of the other airline and contact it to find out the charge for the flight. Only one of the airlines is actually operating the flight, although both airlines are listing the flight as their own. The airline operating the flight will offer the cheaper fare so book with them. Code share flights are not unusual these days with all the airline alliances that currently exist.

9. Most of the major airlines offer supersaver deals they reveal in e- mailers. These are special deals and last-minute bargains on domestic and international fares and packages. Some of the offers expire at the end of the week, while others are good for months. The deals vary from air and hotel packages for independent travelers to fully guided vacation packages. For example, American Airlines once offered a week-long all- inclusive air and cruise package to the Galapagos Islands for less than half of what Galapagos trips typically cost. The only restriction was that travel had to occur within two months. American Airlines also offered a five day air and hotel package to Paris or London, including continental breakfast, transfers, and sightseeing vouchers, for less than $400pp. The specials vary from weekend getaways, with Friday or Saturday departures and Monday or Tuesday returns, to extended stays at international destinations.

The best part is that you don't have to go to each airline's Web site every week to see what they're offering. Most airlines provide a free weekly newsletter of their savings, which travelers can sign up for by going to an airline's Web site and clicking on "registration." The e-mailers are posted weekly and participants may unsubscribe at any time. Also, www.aol.com/directories/airlines.adp is a directory of all airlines and includes contact information. Free weekly e-mailers can be requested at this site. Additionally, airlines and contact information can be found later in this chapter.

Six airlines have joined up to form an online discount ticket company, www.hotwire.com. United, American, Northwest, Continental, America West, and US Airways sell unsold seats at deeply discounted prices. Roughly 3.5 million airline seats are left unfilled every week.

Also, pay attention to promotions advertised in travel publications. For example, South African Airways (800-2-SAFARI, www.saa-usa.com or www.flysaa.com) offers one of the best deals I've seen to South Africa. I have seen the bargain trip promoted in two or three travel magazines and yet I've seen nothing online, nor received any direct mail regarding it. The same holds true for America West Vacations (888-259- 9499, www.americawestvacations.com). Their air and hotel packages to Las Vegas are hard to beat.

10. Volunteer to be "bumped" and travel free. Getting bumped means that you are willing to give up your seat on the plane. Volunteers are asked to do this when the seats are overbooked, which is often these days. Airlines book more seats than are available because every passenger will not get on the plane, for various reasons, such as missing the flight, an emergency, or change of plans. For this reason, they oversell most flights; but every passenger does show up sometimes. The airline tries to solve this problem by asking for volunteers to be bumped to another flight.

Passengers willing to catch a later flight will be compensated with a voucher good for a free flight or discounted fare. If interested, you need to check in as early as possible and inform the gate attendant you are willing to be bumped. Make sure that before you give up your seat, the airline will guarantee you a seat on a later flight or with another airline. If you can't get a flight out until the next day, you will be responsible for any costs incurred. Furthermore, make sure you know an airline's voucher/ticket policy before agreeing to anything.

If the flight is overbooked, the agent will announce the names of passengers willing to give up their seats. The most likely day of the week for overbooking is Monday. The gate agent will issue a voucher worth a certain dollar amount that can be applied toward a future ticket. You should be given a seat on a later flight, as well as a voucher. If the airline is particularly desperate, you should be able to bargain for meal and hotel vouchers, as well. My advice to people looking to get bumped is to bring a good book and some snacks in case you have to wait a while for the next flight. Here's a list of some airline policies:

American--cash voucher good for one year.
Delta--cash voucher good for two years.
Northwest--cash voucher good for one year.
TWA--cash voucher good for one year.
US Airways--round-trip ticket good for one year.
Southwest--voucher worth a one-way ticket, plus $100.

If planning to use a voucher, certificate, frequent flyer miles, or a senior special, make sure that you will not be traveling during a blackout time. Blackouts are usually during peak travel season and major holidays. Vouchers or discounts are seldom honored at those times. Also, if your flight is canceled or arrives too late to make your connection, ask the clerk at the ticket counter to put you on another airline that will get you there in time to make the connection. Since many of the major airlines have reciprocal agreements, this can usually be accomplished. Remember, "be nice" because airlines are not required to compensate passengers for delayed or canceled flights. They are only required to compensate if they overbook a flight and you get bumped from that flight as a result. The earlier in the day you fly, the less likely you will experience delays.

One of the most common questions I am asked is "What happens if I buy my airline ticket and then shortly after that the airline offers a better fare than what I paid?" Most airlines will honor the better fare, if you qualify. In order to do so, you must satisfy the advance purchase requirement and there must be seats available on your travel dates. Assuming this, some airlines won't charge the $50–$100 ticket re-issue fee. Most airlines charge this fee any time a ticket has to be altered, regardless of the reason. United Airlines will waive the ticket re-issue fee if travelers opt for a voucher instead of a refund for the fare difference. Always ask.

♦ FYI: The five busiest airports in the United States are Chicago, Atlanta, Dallas/Ft. Worth, Los Angeles, and San Francisco. The good news is that some airlines are now putting in self-service stands at major airports. Air travelers may bypass long check-in lines and use the kiosks to obtain boarding passes, get seat assignments, answer security questions, and check luggage. Some airlines are even offering frequent flyer miles to passengers who use the kiosks.

♦   ♦   ♦

When And How To Use Consolidators

Another option for obtaining substantial savings is to use an airfare consolidator. A consolidator contracts with the airlines to get tickets at cheaper rates than what is offered to the public. The airlines do this because consolidators buy a large blocks of tickets. Regardless of whether the consolidator sells them or not, the airlines have sold many seats; he name of the game is quantity. These companies offer good deals, sometimes very good deals, but consolidators are not service-oriented.

Think of it as the difference between a stock broker and a discount brokerage company. A stock broker advises what stocks you should buy and acquires them for you, whereas you must tell a discount brokerage firm which stocks to buy. If you need personal attention and guidance, use a travel agent instead of a consolidator.

Shop around to verify the best rate. Typically, in the low and off seasons, consolidator fares are no better than the lowest advertised fares. However, during peak travel times, consolidators usually offer savings of around 20–30 percent. Another benefit of using a consolidator is that if you have to fly on short notice, tickets can be purchased for much less than airlines charge because they don't impose advance purchase penalties.

Be sure to choose a consolidator carefully and purchase tickets with a credit card. Some consolidators charge high fees for changing reservations or 2–5 percent for using a credit card. Make sure you are clear on the consolidator's cancellation and refund policies. Booking with a consolidator can be accomplished through most travel agencies for a small fee.

In addition to this list, check the phone book Yellow Pages under Airlines and review back issues of *Consumer Reports Travel Letter*, which can be found at most libraries or a subscription cost $39; it's a worthwhile investment. Consumer Reports does an annual in-depth review of consolidators, including the areas each company specializes in, such as Europe or Southeast Asia. Or, write and request this year's back issue that discusses airfare wholesalers and consolidators. Enclose $5 to cover costs. *Consumer Reports Travel Letter*, 101 Truman Avenue, Yonkers, NY 10703-1057. *An Advisory on Ticket Consolidators* can be obtained online at www.newyork.bbb.org. The United States Consolidators Association provides a free membership list, including contact information. Members of this monitoring organization can also be found on its Web site. 914-441-4166. www.usaca.com.

For only $5 an issue, *Jax Fax* (800-9-JAXFAX) details every charter flight taking place during the following six months. Seats are sold at substantially-discounted rates.

♦ FYI: The coldest place on earth is Vostok, Antarctica, with a chilling record temperature of -127°F (-88°C). The hottest place of record is Azizia, Libya, at 136°F (58°C).

Cheap Tickets sells more than 500,000 tickets each year for domestic and international flights. It has recently added discounted hotel rooms and cruises to its services. 800-AIR-PLUS or 800-247-7587 or 800-234-4522. www.cheaptickets.com. e-mail: cheapcruises@cheaptickets.com.

Council Travel Service offers great fares in the USA and worldwide(although mainly Europe) for budget travelers, especially to students and teachers. In addition to cheap airfares, Council provides independent vacations, car rentals, rail passes, paid internships, and work programs. 800-226-8624. www.counciltravel.com or www.ciee.org. e-mail: info@ciee.org.

Derair(affiliated with Der Travel Service)--International. 800-717-4247. www.dertravel.com.

Far Eastern Travel--China. 800-275-3384.

Fly Cheap--Domestic and international. 800-359-2432. www.flycleap.com.

Hari's World Travel--India. 888-889-2968 or 212-997-3300.

ITS Tours & Travel--International. 800-533-8688.

Kintetsu--Japan. 800-225-5543. www.kintetsu.com.

Lowairfare.com (merged with leading consolidator, Flyless)--Domestic and international. 800-359-4537.

Magical Holidays--Africa. 800-433-7773 or 800-228-2208.

Nova Travel--Eastern Europe. 818-222-8300.

Overseas Express--Europe and Africa, as well as part of Asia and the Middle East. 800-343-4873. www.ovex.com.

Picasso Travel-- Middle East, Africa, and Europe(mainly Turkey, Greece, and Italy). 800-462-8875 or 212-244-5454. www.picassotravel.com.

Pino Welcome Travel--Worldwide travel, but specializes in Italy, and Central, Latin, and South America. 800-247-6578 or 212-682-5400.

Solar Tours--Latin and South America. 800-388-7652.

Sophisticated Travelers--Eastern Europe. 800-801-1055.

STA--Specializes in student fares for domestic flights and flights to Europe. 800-777-0112. www.statravel.com.

Travac--Europe (scheduled and charter), Mexico, Africa, Middle East, Central and South America, Pacific and Orient. 800-TRAV-800 or 407-896-0014. www.travac.com.

Travel Bargains--Domestic. 800-AIRDEAL or 800-886-4988. www.airfare.com.

Travel Interlink--Asia. 800-477-7172.

Travel Network--U.S., South America, Central America, and Mexico. 800-933-5963.

Tzell Travel--Israel. 212-944-2121.

UK Consolidated--Ireland and United Kingdom. 800-577-2900.

Unitravel--Domestic and International. 800-325-2222. www.unitravel.com.

♦ FYI: The average fee airlines pay a film company for in-flight movies is $75 per showing.

Around-the-World Air Consolidators

Ever dreamed of circling the globe? Have you always wanted to but figured it would be cost prohibitive? Well, think again! The companies listed below offer an extremely economical way to see the world. The best part is that they offer so many routings, you are guaranteed to see the places you desire. Ground transportation, city tours, and lodging can be booked in advance or upon arrival. For increased savings, I recommend combining around-the-world airfares with train passes and hotel vouchers. If you are interested in a more unique experience than a hotel stay, see Chapter Six, which reveals villas and apartments that can be rented at a very reasonable rate. If you would like to rent a car and explore on your own, see "car brokers" in Chapter Three.

Around The World Travel (G7) is a planning publication for people interested in around-the-world travel. Transitions Abroad, P.O. Box 1300, Amherst, MA 01004-1300. 800-293-0373.

The best thing you can do for yourself is to eat a light meal and drink a sports drink at least 30 minutes before boarding a flight. Studies show that doing this enables the body to adapt better to low cabin pressure and dry air aboard the airplane. This means less likelihood of jet lag, dehydration, and air sickness because your body does not try so hard to adjust. The American Heart Association also supports this plan, stating that it may fend off in-flight fainting and heart attacks. Be sure to drink an eight-ounce glass of water for every hour onboard.

Air Brokers International, Inc. was established in 1987 and specializes in around-the-world travel with "Circle the Globe" and "Circle the Pacific" trips, starting at less than $999pp. Stay as long as you like in each location because travel is valid for up to one year. Sample world routings: Los Angeles, Hong Kong, Bangkok, Bali, Hawaii. Or, New York, Lima, Santiago de Chile, Buenos Aires, Europe, London, Iceland, New York. Or, Los Angeles, Auckland, Sydney or Brisbane or Melbourne, Tahiti, Easter Island, Santiago de Chile, Los Angeles.

Air Brokers also provides information concerning travel insurance, visas, and inoculations (recommended and required). Hotel accommodations and stopover packages are available upon request. 150 Post Street, Suite 620, San Francisco, CA 94108. 800-883-3273 or 415-397-1383. www.airbrokers.com. e-mail: sales@airbrokers.com.

Air Tickets Direct claims "lowest prices guaranteed on scheduled major airlines. No charters, no advance purchase on most fares, and no additional charge for credit cards." Worldwide flights starting at less than $200 one-way. 208 E. 43rd Street, 13th floor, New York, NY 10017. 888-888-TKTS. www.airticketsdirect.com.

Council Travel Service offers Around-the-World airfares, such as Los Angeles, Nadi, Auckland, Sydney, Bali, Singapore, Bangkok, Paris, Los Angeles. 205 East 42nd Street, New York, NY 10017. 800-226-8624. www.counciltravel.com or www.ciee.org.

High Adventure Travel has an Around-the-World Airfare Builder program. Prices start at around $1,000 and any place you want is probably included in one of their routings, such as: New York, Amsterdam, Prague, Moscow, Beijing, Los Angeles. Or, New York, Hong Kong, Bangkok, Delhi, Bombay, Frankfort, New York. 442 Post Street, Suite 400, San Francisco, CA 94102. 800-350-0612 or 415-912-5600. www.airtreks.com. e-mail: airtreks@highadv.com.

Ticket Planet offers Around-the-World, Circle-the-Pacific, and round-trip airfares to exotic destinations such as Bali, Nepal, Cambodia, Brazil, Egypt, Kenya, and the world. Fares start around $1,000pp. Sample route: San Francisco or L.A., Hong Kong, Bangkok, Kuala Lumpur, Bali, L.A. or San Francisco. 59 Grant Avenue, Level 3, San Francisco, CA 94108. 800-799-8888. www.ticketplanet.com. e-mail: trips@ticketplanet.com.

◆ FYI: The world's shortest flight is between Orkney Islands of Westray and Papa Westray, Great Britain. While check-in is required at least 20 minutes prior to departure, the flight itself is only two minutes in duration.

I am often asked, "What is the best way to upgrade to business or first class without paying more than you paid for your first car?" One way is to buy an economy ticket and then use frequent flier miles to upgrade. Another option is to use an airline coupon broker. These companies match up travelers who want to sell frequent flier certificates with buyers. The best airline coupon broker is First Class Traveler (800-558-0053). They guarantee all tickets. Brokering tickets is not illegal, but it is against airline regulations.

◆　　◆　　◆

Discount Programs, Coupon Books, Regional Airlines, and Air Passes

This chapter has discussed many techniques air travelers can employ to save money, but what about simple, year-round discounts? Child fares are typically free or reduced, depending on age. Students, teachers, and military are often entitled to lower rates. Unfortunately, the only adult segment of the population guaranteed discounts is seniors. For this group, most airlines offer at least 10 percent off normal fares.

For older travelers, airlines also offer "travel coupon books." These books come with 4–8 coupons and each coupon is good for (one) one-way flight anywhere within the continental U.S. The books generally cost between $600-700. Typically, travel must be used within one year of purchase and each airline may impose further restrictions.

I recommend asking an airline representative to tell you about all discounts and promotions they are currently offering, as well as any they are planning to offer in the near future. If a money-saving program will soon be implemented, you may want to put your travel plans on hold until then. Be sure to inquire before paying for a ticket because after a ticket has been issued, it's not likely you will get a refund. Also, beware that some airlines are initiating a fee for paper tickets. Internet vendors, such as Travelocity and Expedia, already charge an extra $10 to cover delivery. Some airlines, such as U.S. Airways and America West, allow grandchildren to fly free when accompanied by grandparents. be sure to inquire.

American Airlines, Aer Lingus, British Airways, Cathay Pacific, Finnair, Iberia, Lanchile, and Qantas formed an alliance recently that allows flyers to earn and exchange miles among the member airlines. www.oneworldalliance.com. Another alliance formed by five major airlines (American, Continental, Delta, Northwest, and United) is www.Orbitz.com. In addition to airline tickets, browsers will find hotel rooms, rental cars, and vacation packages. It promises travelers the cheapest tickets anywhere. Since $12 billion was spent on-line last year for airline tickets, look for more of these unions among airlines, agencies, and companies.

Alaska Airlines takes 10 percent off its published fares for those 62 and over to most markets, except Mexico. It also offers senior fares in some markets, which can be bought in advance or right up to boarding (if the flight is not sold out). 800-426-0333. www.alaska-air.com.

American Airlines offers those 62 and older 10 percent off all flights. Or, travelers over age 62 may opt to buy a coupon book which has four one-way coupons. Travelers have up to one year to use the coupon books and can travel anywhere in the continental U.S., Puerto Rico, and Virgin Islands. Two coupons needed for Hawaii. 800-433-7300 or 800-237-7981. www.aa.com.

America West offers 10 percent off the lowest fare available for 62 and older (published senior fare) for all cities served by airline. Or, you can purchase coupon books, which are good to all U.S. cities served by America West. 800-247-5692 or 800-235-9292. www.americawest.com.

Continental offers 10 percent discount to all U.S. cities for those age 62 and older. They also offer coupon books. One coupon required each way for Canada, Caribbean, Mexico. Two coupons each way for Alaska and Hawaii. Participants have one full year to use their coupons. Programs are always changing, so check with the airline to see what it is currently offering. For example, one option for those 62 and older used to be the Freedom Passport. This gave travelers the opportunity to do unlimited flying with these restrictions: 1) could not fly more than once a week, 2) had to include a Sunday stay over, and 3) could not fly more than three times to any one city. 800-248-8996. www.continental.com.

Delta gives travelers over the age of 62 a 10 percent discount on all their fares. The airline also offers a couple of programs including Senior Coupons, good for travel within Continental U.S., Virgin Islands, Puerto Rico, and Canada. Two coupons required for Hawaii and Alaska. Programs are always changing, so check with the airline to see what it is currently offering. For example, Delta used to offer a Senior Select Savings Program. For those 62 and older, membership in this program was something to consider. There are no Saturday stayovers required or limitations on number of times you can travel to a particular city. Currently, the only restriction is a 14-day advance notice must be given to receive these low fares. 800-221-1212. www.delta.com.

Delta also offers **Delta Express**, a shuttle that serves many cities. 800-325-5205.

Hawaiian flies from the U.S. to Hawaii, inter-island, and to the South Pacific. It has senior fares of 20 percent off on international fares for those over age 60, and its senior fares for domestic flights are not advertised because their lowest excursion fare is often lower than the senior fare. 800-367-5320. www.hawaiianair.com.

Midwest Express gives travelers 62 and older 10 percent off all fares. 800-452-2022. www.midwestexpress.com.

Northwest senior fares are discounted 10 percent or better. Price depends on departure and arrival cities. 14-day advance notice required when using coupon books. Canada and Puerto Rico require one coupon each way. Two coupons needed for Alaska and Hawaii. Sometimes only one coupon is required for Hawaii or Alaska, depending on departure city.
800-225-2525. www.nwa.com.

TIP: "Park 'N Fly" facilities are near most major airports and are cheaper than using an airport's long-term parking lot. A shuttle will pick you up on both ends of your trip. Look in the yellow pages for specific airport listings. Another trick is to use the farthest airport parking lots. I often fly out of Charlotte and when I do I use a satellite parking lot that charges $2.75 per day as opposed to the $7–12 per day charged for parking closer to the terminals. A free shuttle delivers passengers to any airline terminal.

Many hotels also offer good "park and stay" packages. Simply pay a daily rate if you need to leave your vehicle longer. Typically, your credit card is not billed (for parking) until you redeem your car. Ask when making hotel reservations.

There are also parking lots in most major cities that offer low daily rates for long-term parking, but they won't have a covered garage with 24-hour security like most hotels.

Check out www.AirportParkingLots.com for reservations and pricing of many airports nationwide.

United Airlines gives a 10 percent discount to anyone 62 and older. They also offer a coupon program that is good for travel in most U.S. cities, Canada, and Puerto Rico. Two coupons needed for Alaska and Hawaii. No minimum stay. Blackout period for Alaska and Hawaii is Christmas through New Years. If you are 55 or older, you can join United's Silver Wings Plus program (800-720-1765), which gives participants discounts on hotels, resorts, and cruises--up to 50 percent. 800-241-6522 or 800-633-6563. www.united.com.

US Airways offers a guaranteed 10 percent off all its flights to people 62 and older, and published senior fares, depending on cities. They also provide discounts for military personnel. And, they offer first class for the price of a full, unrestricted coach fare to 150 of its destinations. Or, mature travelers may take advantage of its Golden Opportunities Booklet, which is four one-way coupons good for the Continental U.S., Canada, Mexico, Virgin Islands, and Puerto Rico. US Airways also lets up to two children travel with you using the same book. For example, one adult and one child from New York to California is four coupons. 800-428-4322. www.usairways.com.

Note: Due to the recession of 2002, some of the airlines listed in this chapter may no longer be in business or may have revised their discount programs.

◆   ◆   ◆

Regional Airlines
Another option for getting cheaper fares is to use regional airlines. They are usually more affordable than major airlines, especially if you are unable to fulfill the requirements most airlines impose for cheaper fares, such as mandatory advance purchase and Saturday night stayover. However, these discount airlines are varied in their reputations and services.

Some regional airlines do not assign seats, so if a flight is crowded there can be a "cattle rush" for the best seats. However, many people prefer open seating to reserve seats. If you are assigned a seat next to a screaming baby or someone with a bad cold, you have no choice if the plane is full.

Some regional airlines are ticketless, which means you are not issued an actual ticket. Presenting a valid ID and the *credit card used to book the ticket* confirms your electronic ticket. Most travelers enjoy not having to keep up with tickets. However, if a flight is canceled or there is any other reason you have to use another airline, it is difficult to get an airline to honor your ticket without a written ticket to present.

Also, few regional airlines participate in frequent flyer programs or offer additional discounts for children or seniors because the fares are already deeply discounted. But, remember it never hurts to ask.

Increasingly, regional airlines are merging with each other or major airlines to stay competitive. New airlines start up every month and existing airlines go out of business just as quickly. Some of the bigger and more established airlines are listed below. To find discount airlines serving your market, look in the Yellow Pages under Airlines.

If an airline files for bankruptcy there's not much you can do to get a refund because once an airline files for protection, refunds on tickets purchased prior to that date won't get paid, most likely. According to *Consumer Reports Travel Newsletter*, the best thing to do is to get a "Proof of Claim" form at any U.S. courthouse or online at www.uscourts.gov. Send it to U.S. Bankruptcy Court, District of Delaware, Marine Midland Plaza, 6th floor, 824 Market Street, Wilmington, Delaware 19801. Be sure to send a photocopy of your airline ticket, including the cost of the ticket. You may get lucky and receive at least a partial refund.

Europe also boasts some good discount airlines, such as Ryanair (www.ryanair.com), Buzz (www.buzzaway.com), Virgin Express (www.virgin-express.com), Go (www.go-fly.com), and easyJet (www.easyJet.com). Check with your travel agent before booking any internal air travel in Europe because these airlines offer cheaper fares than major airlines—as much as 50 percent off regular fares.

♦ FYI: Roughly one million passengers fly on U.S. airlines every day.
Rule 240, created by the FAA, explains the only two events that make airlines accountable to consumers. The first thing is a Schedule Irregularity, which means overbooking, a mechanical problem, or mixed up reservation. The other is Force Majeure Event. This covers weather, civil unrest and war, labor disputes and strikes, and unforeseen occurrences. Obviously, the latter provides a big loophole for airlines. If you have a problem, the best advice is to be polite but persistent. Try to get another airline to honor the ticket, if all else fails.

Airtran Airways goes to many cities, but offers no discounts. It issues its own frequent flyer miles that are good for flight vouchers. For only $25, passengers can upgrade to business class. This can only be accomplished at the airport and is subject to availability. 800-AIRTRAN or 800-247-8726 or 800-825-8538 or 770-994-8258. www.airtran.com.

American Trans Air (ATA) goes to many cities. Ten percent discount to seniors and children 2-17. 800-435-9282 or 800-225-2995. www.ata.com.

Frontier Airlines (owned by Continental) offers many routes to major cities all over the country, such as Atlanta, New York, Portland, and Denver. Frontier provides Continental OnePass frequent flyer miles. Frontier has been awarded *Entrepreneur's* Business Travel Award "Best Domestic Low-Fare Air Carrier." 800-432-1359. www.frontierairlines.com.

Jetblue Airways 800-538-2583. www.jetblue.com.

National flies to several major U.S. cities, including New York, Philadelphia, Chicago, Dallas/Ft. Worth, Las Vegas, Los Angeles, and San Francisco. 888-757-5387. www.nationalairlines.com.

Southwest goes to many cities. Discounts for 65 and older, but the savings depend on destination. Seniors may receive discounts even when flying standby, and there is no minimum or maximum stay required. 800-I-FLY-SWA (435-9792). www.southwest.com.

Spirit Airlines goes to many cities, particularly resort or "favorite vacation destinations," such as Atlantic City, Myrtle Beach, New York, and Florida. 800-772-7117. www.spiritair.com.

Vanguard goes to most major cities. 800-826-4827. www.flyvanguard.com.

┌───┐
│ ◆ FYI: In 1976 the Concorde became the first passenger plane to fly faster than sound and began │
│ flights across the Atlantic. │
└───┘

◆　　◆　　◆

Air Passes

Most international airlines provide some kind of discount program for children and older travelers. Many of the major airlines also offer "air passes." For example, those interested in seeing Europe will delight in a program that was launched a few years ago. Most major European airlines participate in Europe by Air (formerly EurAir).

A Europe by Air Pass (also called a Flight Pass) allows flights to dozens of cities in 18 countries: England, Ireland, France, Germany, Netherlands, Belgium, Spain, Portugal, Italy, Greece, Finland, Denmark, Sweden, Poland, Estonia, Latvia, Lithuania, and Belgium. Each one-way flight costs $99. The coupons must be obtained from a travel agent or through Europe by Air (888-387-2479, www.europebyair.com) and are valid for up to 120 days. Minimum purchase is three coupons. There are no blackout dates or Saturday-night stay required.

British Airways has a Pass Program with low cost coupons. Fly from London to any European city serviced by British Airways (800-247- 9297, www.britishairways.com).

Aerolineas Argentinas Airlines (800-333-0276) offers a Visit Argentina Air Pass that allows four flights within the country. Additional flights can be purchased. The pass is valid for 30 days.

Austrian Airlines (800-843-0002, www.austrianair.com) recently began offering a Discover Europe Pass, which is for travel to more than 70 European cities. It must be purchased with a round-trip ticket from the U.S. or Canada to Vienna. The pass is good for 90 days.

Cathay Pacific's Asia Pass is one of the best airline passes ever offered. Reasonably priced at $999 for the last few years, it entitles participants to fly all over Asia for up to 30 days. For just a couple hundred dollars more, travel can be extended up to six months. Travelers receive unlimited air travel to most major Asian cities, such as Hong Kong, Bangkok, Singapore, Seoul, Bali, and Tokyo. This pass must be purchased through Cathay Pacific's Web site www.cathay-usa.com or a travel agent. Another option is Ticket Planet's Asia Pass. It cost about $100 more than Cathay Pacific's pass, but is good for six months (800-799-8888, www.ticketplanet.com). Malaysia Airlines offers the AccessAsia Pass, which entitles bearers to fly from Los Angeles to 24 Southeast Asia destinations within 30 days for less than $800 (800-552-9264, www.malaysiaairlines.com).

Aloha Airlines has a value Island Pass, which is a seven-day island- hopping pass, good for unlimited travel to Hawaii's 122 islands (800-367- 5250, www.alohaairlines.com).

Another consistently good deal is Thai Airways (800-426-5204) Discover Thailand Air Pass (approximately $200). It consists of four flight coupons, valid for two months.

Australia's Qantas Airlines (800-227-4500, www.qantas.com) offers a Boomerang Pass, but it has several restrictions, including it cannot be used for travel between Australia and New Zealand. The pass permits buying 2-10 discounted tickets that are good for as long as your international ticket is valid. The pass is fully refundable and/or changeable if not used. Ansett Australia Airlines(800-366-1300, www.qantas.com) offers a Visit Australia Air Pass that is very similar to the Boomerang Pass. To explore New Zealand, you might want to get the Air New Zealand Explorer Pass from Air New Zealand(800-262-1234, www.airnz.com). Or, purchase the Visit South Pacific Pass, available from Qantas Airlines(800-227-4500, www.qantas.com). It is good for travel between Australia, Fiji, and New Zealand.

A group of thirteen airlines joined together to form Star Alliance, which offers international air passes to 815 European cities. Passes are sold in books of 3-10. Destinations must be selected when buying passes, but travel dates can be determined later. Cost is dependent upon location and coupons are good for up to three months. Star Alliance also books hotels and rental cars. www.staralliance.com. 800-255-1555.

Most foreign airlines offer air passes. Always check with airlines to find out if they have started a new program or if they are running a promotional or off-season pass. Restrictions vary greatly so be sure to ask. Additionally, most airlines offer discounts for on-line booking. Also, don't forget some of the best deals are airline vacation packages.

Aer Lingus offers no discounted fares. 800-223-6537. www.aerlingus.com.

Aeromexico serves the U.S. to Europe, South America and Mexico, and offers a 10 percent discount for 62 and older. 800-AEROMEX (237-6639). www.aeromexico.com.

Air Canada offers restricted discounts for those 62 and older, and only for U.S. and Canada travel. www.aircanada.ca.

Air France allows a 10 percent discount for travelers 62 and older, with the restriction tickets must be purchased 21d in advance. No companion discounts. 800-237-2747. In Canada: 800-667-2747. www.airfrance.com.
Air India discounts vary. 800-223-7776. www.airindia.com.

Air Jamaica discounts vary. 800-523-5585. www.airjamaica.com.

Alitalia Airlines discounts vary. 800-223-5730. www.alitalia.com

British Airways flies from Great Britain to many worldwide destinations. Senior fares depend on destination cities. This airline is the first to offer a seat that converts into a flat six-foot bed, but is only available to those in business class. 800-247-9297. www.britishairways.com.

Canadian Airlines International gives 10 percent off its normal fares for those 60 and older. Ask about excursion fares from U.S. to Canada for additional savings. www.cdnair.com.

Cathay Pacific Airways offers no discounts for students or seniors, but they do accept American Airlines frequent flyer miles. 800-233-2742. www.cathay-usa.com.

China Airlines discounts vary. 800-227-5118. www.china-airlines.com.

Finnair offers 10 percent off normal fares for people 62 and older, if flying from New York to Helsinki. They do have youth fares for those under 25, but fares depend on destinations and time of year. 800-950-5000. www.finnair.fi.

Iberia gives people 62 and older 10 percent off normal fares. They sometimes have special youth fares. Iberia also has an America Express 2-for-1 deal. Buy one first class or business class seat and get the second ticket free. Ticket must be purchased using American Express credit card. 800-772-4642. www.iberia.com.

Icelandair offers no discounted fares. 800-223-5500 or 410-715-1600. www.icelandair.is.

Japan Air Lines offers no discounted fares. 800-JAL-FONE or 800-525-3663. www.jal.co.jp.

KLM Royal Dutch Airlines offers a 10 percent discount for those 62 and older from the U.S. to most markets, including Frankfort, Amsterdam, and Paris. 800-374-7747/225-2525. www.nwa.com.

Korean Air has a frequent flyer program, in conjunction with Delta's Sky Team program. 800-525-4480 or 800-438-5000. www.koreanair.com.

Lufthansa offers a 10 percent discount for those 65 and older. 800-399-LUFT or 800-645-3880. www.lufthansa-usa.com.

Mexicana gives 10 percent off most fares for those 62 and older. 800-531-7921. www.mexicana.com.

Qantas offers no discounted fares, but ask about their Boomerang Pass. 800-227-4500. www.qantas.com. Qantas also owns **Air Pacific**, which flies to many South Pacific destinations. 800-227-4446. http://airpacific.com.

Scandinavian Airlines gives 10 percent off for 62 and older from any U.S. cities through United Airlines gateway to Scandinavia. 800-221-2350. www.flysas.com.

Singapore Airlines discounts vary. 800-742-3333. www.singaporeair.com.

South African Airways discounts vary. 800-722-9675. www.flysaa.com.

Swissair discounts fares 10 percent for 62 and older. Companions, regardless of age, are also discounted if traveling with persons 62 and older. 800-221-4750. In Canada, 800-267-9477. www.swissair.com.

Virgin Atlantic Airways discounts its international fares by 10 percent for those 62 and older. A couple of years ago the airline began offering a program in conjunction with Continental Airlines for some domestic discounts. Recently, they began offering 12-25 percent off on fares to select cities for AARP members. 800-862-8621. www.virgin-atlantic.com.

♦ FYI: The longest scheduled flight currently is the 7,968 mile flight from New York to Johannesburg, South Africa on South African Airways. Time-wise, not distance, the longest flight is 15 hours and 10 minutes. The route is Osaka to Istanbul on Turkish Airlines.

♦   ♦   ♦

What You Don't Know About Courier Travel

Independent or adventurous travelers are best suited for courier travel since couriers make their own lodging, transportation, and sightseeing arrangements. This can be achieved either in advance or upon arrival. Couriers should also be flexible, spontaneous, and willing to:

  1. fly coach(economy) on scheduled U.S. and
     international airlines

2. give up your baggage space
3. transport time-sensitive business documents or
   packages for well-known air express companies
   to a waiting representative.

The **International Association of Air Couriers (IAA)** has around 1,400 round-trip flights each week to seventy-one cities worldwide. The best bargains are during the off-season to lesser-known or lesser-traveled destinations. Return tickets are typically good for one week, but sometimes longer. Most flights originate from major U.S. gateway cities, such as Miami, San Francisco, Los Angeles, New York, Atlanta, and Chicago. Participants are responsible for arranging transportation to the departure cities. Sample round-trip fares: Paris--$228. China--$395. Bangkok--$235. London--$199. Peru--$223. Australia--$650.

Some of the best deals are for those who can fly with 3–14 day advance notice. For example, the last time I checked, IAA was offering free courier flights to London and Bangkok. You can also participate as a non-courier because IAA has exclusive contracts with airlines to fill unsold seats to most major European cities, even during peak travel times.

In exchange for the annual membership fee, which has remained under $50 for many years, members receive 50 to 80 percent savings on airline tickets to exotic and remote destinations. Learn about them in the *Air Courier Bulletin* and *Shoestring Traveler* newsletters (alternate month publications), which are included as a part with membership. Members are also entitled to the ACA World Guidebook, MEDEX card, exclusive discounts, last minute specials, and all flight schedules. 8 South 'J' Street, P.O. Box 1349, Lake Worth, FL 33460. 407-582-8320. www.aircourier.org.

These are the two largest U.S. air courier booking companies. They serve as agents for many different courier companies. Contact them to learn specific prices and destinations:

Discount Travel International
169 West 81st Street, New York, NY 10024. 212-363-3636.

Now Voyager
74 Varick Street, Suite 307, New York, NY 10013. 212-431-1616.
www.nowvoyager.com

♦ FYI: The world's busiest airports are Heathrow (London); Tokyo International (Japan); Rhein/Main (Frankfurt, Germany); Kimpo International (Seoul, Korea); and Charles De Gaulle (Paris, France).

♦   ♦   ♦

Helpful Resources

Air Courier Bargains: How To Travel World-Wide For Next To Nothing. (Intrepid Traveler, $14.95).

The Airport Transit Guide details cheap public transport to and from nearly 450 airports worldwide. (Magellan, $9.95).

A Web site that searches most major Internet booking engines, including CheapTickets, TicketPlanet, Travelocity, and Expedia is **www.qixo.com.**

♦   ♦   ♦

Chapter Five--How To Get The Best Deals On Cruises

Chapter Five--How To Get The Best Deals On Cruises

As the Spanish Proverb says, "He, who would bring home the wealth of the Indies, must carry the wealth of the Indies with him so it is in traveling, a man must carry knowledge with him if he would bring home knowledge.
Samuel Johnson, April 17, 1778

What No One Tells You

The economic impact of the cruise industry on North America was $15.5 billion as of 1999. More than two million Americans took at least one three-to-five-day cruise last year, with an estimated 2.5 million Americans cruising this year. It's so popular now that companies are starting to market cruise-ship timeshares, ranging from $700–$20,000 a week.

Cruises appeal to many travelers because they go to the same places as most land tours and the participants are very much pampered. They can do as much or as little as they like while en route to the next destination. And, you don't have to jump on and off tour buses, struggling with luggage along the way. Cruising has also become a popular way to vacation because the vessels have so many amenities that they are considered floating resorts. Most cruise lines are building huge ships to accommodate more dining options, bars and lounges, activities, and larger staterooms.

Royal Caribbean's *Voyager of the Seas* is a $700 million ship that holds 3,115 passengers and another 1,220 crew. With that capacity and a weight of 142,000 tons, the vessel is almost equivalent to an aircraft carrier. And this is just the beginning. Royal Caribbean has already announced plans for an even bigger vessel, *Adventure of the Seas,* as well as three other mega-ships. Carnival is debuting the *Queen Mary 2* (not to be confused with the *QE2*) in 2003. Carnival claims that the ship will be the biggest oceanliner ever built. It will be 1,132 feet long (equivalent to four football fields) and have 17 decks that create a height equal to that of a 23-story building. Some of its features include five swimming pools, a three-deck-high restaurant, seven-classroom enrichment center and art gallery, planetarium, 90 suites (including six penthouses offering butler and concierge service), and five 1,650-square-foot apartments—all featuring private gyms. Even small ships have gone to tremendous lengths to improve service and amenities. Seabourn and Windstar have added marinas. Located off the ship's stern, marinas provide passengers with a shark-proof saltwater pool and place of origin for watersports. In a frantic effort to "one up" each other, 50 ships will be built by various cruise lines between 2001–2004.

Cruising used to be reserved for the wealthy, but bargains have become plentiful as cruise lines struggle to fill these whopper ships. Pricing is affected by several factors, such as whether it is peak season, off season, one-time sailing, or a "positioning" cruise. One-time sailings are when a ship is "killing time" until it repositions (positioning cruise) to a more profitable cruising destination. Passenger fares are generally bargain-priced so as to fill the ship and maximize revenue. The same holds true for repositioning cruises, which are when a ship leaves a region at the end of the season and makes it way to another region where the cruising season has just begun. For example, when the season ends for Alaska Inside Passage cruises, the ships relocate to the Caribbean and Panama Canal. Cruise season for Alaska runs mid-May to early September. Weather is cool in May, but dry. Peak season is late June to early August, but weather tends to be rainy mid-summer. When the ships leave the Caribbean for the summer, they cruise to northern Europe. Destinations, ship popularity (newer, larger ships are most sought after, which means the best fares are often on older ships), and types of cruise also determine the cost. Rates will always be lower to the Caribbean or Alaska as opposed to the Galapagos Islands or Antarctica. European cruises cost more than many destinations because they go to more ports so it cost the cruise lines more. Additionally, there is always a high demand and pricing is always determined by supply and demand. Prices are most reasonable for European cruises at the end of summer. Demand is highest in early summer, when the weather is most favorable. Cruises lasting ten days are more expensive than seven day cruises, but seven day cruises are often cheaper than two- to five-day cruises. Again, supply and demand. Currently, the biggest demand is for these short cruises. Better fares are practically guaranteed for people who use cruise consolidators or who wait for specially advertised offers. Cruises booked months in advance, or at the last minute, are greatly discounted.

Cruise lines are often charging extra for activities, such as miniature golf, in-line skating, and rock-climbing on these new, megaships,. Be sure to find out what activities are *not* included before making a commitment as these "fun fees" can really add up.

Typically, the cruise line or travel agent will advise you to purchase an air and sea package because it's easier and *often* cheaper than arranging your own transport to the ship embarkation. However, be aware that booking through the cruise line or travel agent does not make them accountable if you miss a flight connection. I suggest arriving early enough, preferably the day before, to ensure that if there are any problems, such as canceled flights, overbooked flights, or lost luggage, there is sufficient time to sort it out before the ship sets sail. Also, by arriving the day before, your body will have time to get adjusted and you will be recovered from the ordeal of airport/airplane traveling. Inquire if the cruise line offers a pre cruise stay.

Did you know that cruise lines may change itineraries after you have booked or even in the middle of a cruise? And, they do not owe passengers any compensation if they do so because of weather or political instability. The best thing you can do to protect yourself is to read the fine print before making a commitment. Pay using a credit card rather than check. Make sure you have all required inoculations and documents, including passports and visas. Don't rely on the cruise line or travel agent. Check yourself. For example, diphtheria immunization is highly recommended by the Centers for Disease Control(CDC) for people traveling to St. Petersburg, Russia (and has been since 1997). Yet, there was no mention of this anywhere in the literature sent to me by the cruise line when I booked a Scandinavia cruise that included two days in St. Petersburg. Furthermore, staff aboard the ship did not disclose this during the cruise. You may also wish to buy travel insurance from a reputable company, such as Travel Guard International, Access America, or Travel Insured. Make sure the policy covers you from *date of purchase* until you return home and all shore excursions and extensions.

For travelers who have never been on a cruise or maybe have only taken a two- or three-day cruise, here are some tips to ensure that you have a pleasurable experience.

√ Pick the right cruise line for your needs and budget. There are six categories of cruise lines:

1. budget
2. moderate
3. deluxe
4. ultra-deluxe
5. boutique cruise
   *between deluxe and ultra-deluxe but with smaller, all-suite ships
6. adventure or expedition

Most deluxe, ultra-deluxe, and boutique cruises require formal and semi-formal attire most nights in the main dining room. However, there are casual dress nights and cruisers have alternative dining options, ordering room service, or eating a late lunch and going to the midnight buffet. Furthermore, some cruise lines have introduced Freestyle Cruising, which means no dress codes for dinner, table assignments, or arranged seating times. Some experiments currently in the works include automatic tipping billed to your account and pay-as-you-go dining. Norweigan now automatically charges a *daily* tipping fee that covers cabin stewards, waiters, bus boys, and maitre'd. It is $10pp for ages 13 and older, $5pp, for ages 3-12, and no charge for children 2 and under. Be sure to inquire before booking.

Also, some cruises offer more port calls and pre- or post-cruise extensions. Is this important to you? Do you want a family-oriented cruise or a singles cruise? Some cruises are theme-oriented, such as investment strategies, big band music, or bridge (card game), which includes instructional seminars and a tournament. Do you want "sun and fun," sightseeing, educational/enrichment, or an expedition type cruise? Expedition cruises, such as those to Antarctica or the Galapagos Islands, offer less amenities. Instead, they focus on exploration and adventure. Caribbean cruises are "sun and fun" cruises, while sightseeing and educational/enrichment cruises combine the best of both.

Cruise lines have been slow to recognize and accommodate the physically challenged. The good news is that cruise lines are improving accessibility. Recently, Holland America became the first line to install inclined tracks on the gangways, thereby making it easier for travelers in wheelchairs to get ashore by tender. Furthermore, the tenders are being outfitted with hydraulic leveling systems that can be adjusted upon arrival at the port dock.

√ Choose the right duration for you. Cruises vary from two or three days to three weeks. Cruises lasting longer than three weeks are called "extended cruises." How long can you or do you want to travel? If you only have a week of vacation time, you can't take a cruise to Australia. Most cruises to the South Pacific take three weeks. However, a week is perfect for an Alaska Inside Passage cruise or Caribbean cruise. Most cruises to Central America, South America, the Mediterranean, Panama Canal, and Europe require 10 days to two weeks.

√ Select the right size ship for you. Ships come in five sizes:

1. intimate (up to 10,000 gross registered tonnage(grt)
2. small (between 10,000 and 20,000grt)
3. medium (between 20,000 and 30,000grt)
4. large (30,000grt to 90,000grt)
5. mega (over 90,000grt)

Typically, as ships increase in size, so do the number of passengers and amenities. If an intimate cruise (meaning one where you have the most opportunity to get to know other passengers and interact with them) is desired, a smaller ship may be best. You can get tired of "fighting" 3,000+ passengers for disembarking or pool chairs! However, costs are usually less on bigger ships because there are more fare-paying passengers. For travelers who prefer small ship cruising, www. smallshipcruises.com discusses ships that carry less than 500 passengers and provides links to small ship cruise lines, including barge trips, river cruises, theme cruises, and sailing vessels.

√ Decide how much are you willing to pay for a cabin. Outside cabins have portholes or big picture windows, which make outside cabins more expensive than inside cabins. If you're willing to forego the view, you save up to $1,000. There are some innovative ways around feeling claustrophobic or "cooped up". One way is to bring a night-lite and keep it plugged in during the day to brighten the room. Also, turn on the television and tune it to the channel that continuously shows the view from the ship's bridge. Some of the newer ships have windows in many inside rooms that "open" to the interior. For example, *Voyager of the Seas*, inside cabin windows reveal the bright, glitzy Bourbon Street shopping gallery.

Cabins on higher levels cost up to $3,000 more than cabins on lower levels. A suite or a cabin with a private veranda and balcony is the most expensive and it's very difficult to find bargains on these types of rooms.

The best rooms for avoiding seasickness are actually the lower levels and mid-ship for stability. Try to avoid rooms below the disco or gym; high traffic areas, such as stairs and elevators; near the engine room; or rooms with obstructed view. Diesel-powered ships may vibrate toward the stern (rear part of the ship). Passengers in cabins near the bow (front part of the ship) may be subjected to hearing the anchor raised and lowered every time the ship docks.

♦ FYI: Good news! Some cruise lines are now addressing environmental concerns by installing new sewer systems. The recycled water quality is so good that it is almost exceptable for drinking, except the salt content is rated too high.

♦   ♦   ♦

Ten Ways To Save Big Money

1. Senior citizen fares are available for travelers 55 and older on most cruise lines. Always ask when booking. Members of organizations, such as AARP or AAA, are entitled to reduced rates on certain cruises.

2. (2-for-1s). Most major cruise lines extend "buy one fare and the second passenger travels free" offers. These cheap fares are good on select cruises or are offered as last-minute deals to fill a cruise ship (see Chapter Eight: Last Minute Travel Clubs). A few cruise lines, such as Princess, often offer 2-for-1s, plus $500-$1,000 off the ticket price.

Some cruise lines, such as Holland America, frequently use the incentive "50–80 percent off the normal fare for the second passenger." Don't mistake this for the 2-for-1 deals. The second passenger in the cabin receives up to 80 percent off, but does not travel free. If both travelers split the total room cost, discounts equal 25–40 percent off per person.

3. Added Value or Free Days. *Book a seven day cruise and get three days free.* Or, travelers will receive free shore excursions or hotel rooms pre- or post-cruise. This is popular with Holland America, Royal Caribbean, Princess, and Norwegian Cruise Lines.

4. Flat-rate specials give one fixed price for the best available cabin at the time of booking. Norwegian, Crystal, and Princess frequently offer these deals.

5. Many cabins allow the possibility of four beds: two lower twin beds and two berths that pull down from the ceiling and make two upper twin beds. These upper level beds are as sturdy and comfortable as the bottom beds. If you're willing to share a cabin with others, the cost of the cabin is greatly reduced for the third and fourth passengers (sometimes free!). Share with two friends, another couple, or two family members, and divide the fare four ways. It may be close quarters, but if you don't plan to spend much time in the room (and who does with all the shipboard activities and amenities, not to mention port calls?) the additional savings make the trade-off very worthwhile.

I have done this on more than one occasion and my only advice is to make sure you are comfortable with your cabin mates because you will all be sharing a bathroom and sleeping in the same room for days or weeks, depending on the length of the cruise. All ships built after 1990 have fairly large staterooms. Ships built before then have many different sized cabins and often the cheapest ones are rather small and may not be suitable for four adults. Brochures also detail ship information, including date of entry into service.

6. Free or reduced airfare to the cruise embarkation point is another cost-saving method used by many cruise lines.

7. Free upgrades, such as better cabins, are offered by many cruise lines as a booking incentive. If you get on a mailing list or receive periodic e-mailers from cruise companies, you will receive information on upgrades. Popular incentives include discount certificates, 10–40 percent savings off advertised fares, and cabin upgrades.

8. Early Booking equals substantial discounts (10–40 percent) on some cruise lines. Princess, Carnival, and Holland America commonly offer them on their European and Alaskan cruises.

9. Group discounts are offered to associations, organizations, wedding parties, family reunions, churches, and corporate meetings. Round up 15 fare-paying passengers and you'll most likely cruise free. Even if you are only traveling with family or a few friends, ask if you qualify. The booking agent may knock 5–10 percent off your fare. Or, log on to www.vacation.com to choose from one of nearly 10,000 member travel agencies. Agencies belonging to a consortium can offer group rates to individuals because they buy in volume.

10. Stand-by rates. Participants are notified three weeks prior to departure if there is space. The fare is substantially discounted for the late notice.

Always ask about special deals and programs. For example, Carnival has a Fountain Fun card for travelers under 21. For less than $20, the bearer is entitled to seven days of unlimited soft drinks! One of the biggest expenses onboard is (you guessed it), alcoholic beverages. Buy liquor or wine on shore or in the ship's liquor store and have cocktails in your room or pool side. Your steward can bring ice and mixers. A glass of wine can easily cost $10. Multiply that by seven nights and two people and you will see how fast bar charges can add up.

Find out what beverages your ship charges for and which ones are included at meals. A few cruise lines provide complimentary soft drinks with dinner. If so, wait until then to get your daily caffeine and sugar jolt. Usually, juice drinks, tea, coffee, and lemonade are free onboard and readily available all day, so drink those instead.

If going on a shore excursion, bring a picnic or snacks from the ship rather than buy lunch or dinner somewhere. On most ships, the kitchen will put together a picnic if you request it in advance. Or, simply take some fresh fruit, yogurt, and croissants from the breakfast buffet and have a delicious snack. For dessert, be sure to save some cookies from yesterday's afternoon tea the day, or last night's midnight buffet!

If you opt to explore on your own rather than take a shore tour, share a bus or cab with some other passengers to reduce costs, or, set out on foot and walk off some of those cookies you've been enjoying daily at afternoon tea and midnight buffet. If you were born to shop, limit the amount of cash and credit cards you take on shore excursions. You can't spend more than you have in your wallet.

Cruise Line Addresses

Intimate - Small Ships

Alaska's Glacier Bay Tours & Cruises--226 Second Avenue West, Seattle, WA 98119. 800-451-5952 or 206-623-2417. www.glacierbaytours.com. Itineraries: Alaska.

American--One Marine Park, Haddam, CT 06438. 800-814-6880. www.americancruiselines.com. Itineraries: East Coast Intracoastal and inland waterways.

American Canadian Caribbean Line--461 Water Street, Warren, RI 02885. 800-556-7450. www.accl-smallships.com. Itineraries: Caribbean, Panama Canal, Central America, South America, Canada, Great Lakes, and U.S. inland waterways.

American West Steamboat Company--Two Union Square, 601 Union Street, Suite 4343, Seattle, WA 98101. 800-434-1232. www.columbiarivercruise.com. Itineraries: Columbia, Williamette, and Snake Rivers.

Clipper--7711 Bonhomme Avenue, St. Louis, MO 63105. 800-325-0010. www.clippercruise.com. Itineraries: Caribbean, Central America, South America, East Coast, Mexico, Alaska, Pacific Northwest, Panama Canal, Europe, Asia, South Pacific, Australia, Antarctic, and Arctic.

CruiseWest--2401 Fourth Avenue, Suite 700, Seattle, WA 98121. 800-888-9378. www.cruisewest.com. Itineraries: Alaska, Pacific Northwest, California/Baja, Russian Far East, Asia, and South Pacific.

Lindblad Expeditions--720 Fifth Avenue, New York, NY 10019. 800-Expedition (397-3348) or 212-765-7740. www.expeditions.com. Itineraries: Alaska, Pacific Northwest, California/Baja, Caribbean, Central America, South America, Panama Canal, Antarctica, Galapagos Islands, Trans-Atlantic, Europe, Africa, Middle East, and South Pacific.

Norwegian Coastal Voyages--405 Park Avenue, New York, NY 10022. 800-323-7436 or 212-319-1300. www.coastalvoyage.com. Itineraries: Norway.

Peter Deilmann Ocean Cruises--1800 Diagonal Road, Suite 170, Alexandria, VA 22314. 800-546-4777 or 866-263-0584. www.deilmann-cruises.com. Itineraries: Caribbean, Panama Canal, Europe, and Mediterranean.

Radisson Seven Seas--600 Corporate Drive, Suite 410, Ft. Lauderdale, FL 33334. 800-285-1835. www.rssc.om. Itineraries: Caribbean, Panama Canal, Alaska, Bermuda, Central America, South America, Trans-Atlantic, Europe, Middle East, Africa, Indian Ocean, Asia, South Pacific, Antarctica, and Worldwide.

RiverBarge Excursions--201 Opelousas Avenue, New Orleans, LA 70114. www.riverbarge.com. Itineraries: Gulf Coast and Mississippi River.

Royal Olympic--805 Third Avenue, New York, NY 10022. 800-221-2470. www.royalolympiccruises.com. Itineraries: Europe, Middle East, Caribbean, Central America, South America, and Panama Canal.

Seabourn--6100 Blue Lagoon Drive, Suite 400, Miami, FL 33126. 800-929-9595. http://seabourn.com. Itineraries: Caribbean, Bahamas, East Coast, Canada, Panama Canal, South America, Europe, Middle East, Africa, Far East, South Pacific, and Worldwide.

Silversea--110 E. Broward Blvd., Ft. Lauderdale, FL 33301. 800-722-9955. www.silversea.com. Itineraries: Caribbean, East Coast, Canada, Mexico, Panama Canal, South America/Amazon, Europe, Africa, Middle East, Indian Ocean, Far East, and South Pacific.

Star Clippers (sailing vessels)--4101 Salzedo Avenue, Coral Gables, FL 33146. 305-442-0550. www.starclippers.com. Itineraries: Caribbean, Trans-Atlantic, Mediterranean, Indian Ocean, and Far East.

Voyager--226 Second Avenue West, Seattle, WA 98119. 800-451-5952. www.voyagercruiseline.com. Itineraries: California/Baja.

Medium-size Ships

Crystal--2049 Century Park East, Suite 1400, Los Angeles, CA 90067. 800-446-6620. www.crystalcruises.com. Itineraries: Europe, Caribbean, Alaska, Mexico, Panama Canal, South America, South Pacific, Far East, and Worldwide.

Cunard--6100 Blue Lagoon Drive, Suite 400, Miami, FL 33126. 800-528-6273. www.cunardline.com. Itineraries: Caribbean, East Coast, Canada, Panama Canal, South Pacific, Far East, and Worldwide.

Mediterranean Shipping--420 Fifth Avenue, New York, NY 10018. www.mscruisesusa.com. Itineraries: Europe, Africa, Middle East, Caribbean, Panama Canal, and South America.

Orient--1510 Southeast 17th Street, Suite 300, Ft. Lauderdale, FL 33316. 800-333-7300. www.orientlines.com. Itineraries: Europe, Middle East, Africa, Indian Ocean, Asia, Antarctica, South Pacific, Central America, South America, Panama Canal, and Trans-Atlantic.

Regal--300 Regal Cruises Way, Palmetto, FL 34221. 800-270-7245. www.regalcruises.com. Itineraries: Caribbean, Bahamas, Mexico, Panama Canal, East Coast, and Canada.

United States--Robin Street Wharf, 1380 Port of New Orleans Place, New Orleans, LA 70130. 877-330-6600 or 504-586-0631. www.unitedstateslines.com. Itineraries: Hawaiian Islands.

Windjammer Barefoot Cruises (sailing vessels)--1759 Bay Road, Miami Beach, FL 33139. 800-327-2601. www.windjammer.com. Itineraries:Bahamas, Caribbean, and South America.

Windstar (sail-cruisers)--300 Elliott Avenue West, Seattle, WA 98119. 800-258-7245. www.windstarcruises.com. Itineraries: Caribbean, Central America, Panama Canal, Trans-Atlantic, and Mediterranean.

World Explorer Cruises--555 Montgomery Street, San Francisco, CA 94111. 800-854-3835. www.wecruise.com. Itineraries: Alaska, Central America, and Panama Canal.

♦ FYI: Here are just a few examples of what it takes to care for passengers aboard Princess line's *Grand Princess* for one week:

96,396 pieces of glassware	23,000 bed sheets
13,200 bath towels	18,000 rolls of toilet paper
910 pounds of ice cream	200 pounds of salt
551 pounds of butter/magarine	1,170 pounds of potatoes
1,600 pounds of beef	3,600 muffins

Large and Mega-size Ships

Carnival--3655 Northwest 87th Avenue, Miami, FL 33178. 800-327-9501. www.carnival.com. Itineraries: Bahamas, Caribbean, Bermuda, Canada/New England, Hawaii, Mexico, Panama Canal, and Alaska.

Celebrity--1050 Caribbean Way, Miami, FL 33132. 800-437-3111, www.celebrity-cruises.com. Itineraries: Bermuda, Caribbean, Mexico, Panama Canal, Hawaii, Alaska, Central America, South America, Trans-Atlantic, Europe, and Africa.

Costa--World Trade Center, 80 Southwest 8th St., Miami, FL 33130. 800-462-6782. www.costacruises.com. Itineraries: Caribbean, Trans-Atlantic, and Europe.

Disney--210 Celebration Place, Celebration, FL 34747. 800-951-3532. www.disneycruise.com. Itineraries: Bahamas and Caribbean.

First European--95 Madison Avenue, New York, NY 10016. 888-983-8767. www.first-european.com. Itineraries: Europe, Middle East, Africa, Trans-Atlantic, and Caribbean.

Holland America--300 Elliot Avenue West, Seattle, WA 98119. 800-426-0327. www.hollandamerica.com. Itineraries: Alaska, Caribbean, Mexico, Hawaii, Canada, New England, Europe, Panama Canal, South America, and Worldwide.

Norwegian Cruise Lines--7665 Corporate Center Drive, 800-327-7030. www.ncl.com. Itineraries: Alaska, Bahamas, Bermuda, Caribbean, Panama Canal, Mexico, Hawaii, South Pacific, Asia, Canada, New England, South America, Trans-Atlantic, and Europe.

Princess--10100 Santa Monica Blvd., Los Angeles, CA 90067. 800-421-0522. www.princess.com. Itineraries: Alaska, Caribbean, Bermuda, East Coast, Canada, Europe, Africa, Middle East, Indian Ocean, Far East, Asia, South Pacific, Mexico, South America, Panama Canal, and Worldwide.

Royal Caribbean--1050 Caribbean Way, Miami, FL 33132. 800-327-6700. www.royalcaribbean.com. Itineraries: Alaska, Bahamas, Bermuda, East Coast, Canada, Caribbean, Mexico, Panama Canal, Hawaii, Trans-Atlantic, Europe, Africa, Middle East, South Pacific, and Far East.

TIP: Houseboats are very affordable and can be especially appealing to vacationing families. For more information on houseboat rentals available in the United States, contact Houseboat Association of America, 4940 North Rhett Avenue, Charleston, SC 29405. www.houseboat.net/hbass2.html.

◆　　◆　　◆

Everything You *Must* Know About Consolidators

Cruise Consolidators, also known as brokers or discounters, operate the same way airline consolidators do. They can offer great deals (20–80 percent off normal fares) but you must know where you want to go before contacting them. Since most cruise consolidators provide discounts on all major cruise lines, it's advisable to go to a travel agency and pick up some cruise brochures or contact the cruise lines and request them. Many of the companies listed below have direct links on their Web sites to all cruise lines. Ship deck plans, maps and weather information, and much more, can also be accessed. After you have studied them and know where you want to go, when you want to go, and how much you want to spend, call the consolidators. Before booking, be sure to check with several others to make sure you get the best deal. Also, I recommend contacting some of the companies listed below and requesting free e-mailers and newsletters or direct mail brochures that detail "hot deals."

Cruise Brothers. 800-827-7779. www.cruisebrothers.com.

Cruise.com. 800-243-4103 or 800-217-1807. www.cruise.com.

The Cruise Marketplace. 800-826-4333 or 650-595-7750. www.thecruisemarketplace.com.

Cruisemasters. 800-242-9444 or 800-603-5755. www.cruisemasters.com.

Cruises Of Distinction. 800-434-6644.

Cruises Only (formerly The Cruise Line).800-545-7447 or 800-777-0707. www.cruiseworldwide.com.

Cruise Vacation Center. 800-803-7245. www.cruisevacationcenter.com.

Cruise Value Center. 800-231-7447. www.cruisevalue.com.

Discount Cruise Brokers. 800-682-5122.

eCruises.com. 800-223-6868. www.ecruises.com.

Galaxsea Cruises. 800-923-SHIP. www.funcruises.com.

Galaxy Cruise & Travel. 800-445-4177 or 407-321-4159. www.great-vacations.com.

Hartford Holidays. 11596. 800-828-4813 or 516-746-6670. www.hartfordholidays.com.

Mytravelco.com is the largest cruise wholesaler selling 10 percent of all cruises. 800-211-2936 or 888-CRUISES or 888-278-4737 or 516-266-0860. www.mytravelco.com, www.travelco.com, or www.cruiseoutlet.com.

National Discount Cruise Company is the American Express Cruise Discount Headquarters. 800-788-8108. www.cruiseonsale.com.

Ship 'N' Shore. 800-475-6226. www.ship-n-shore.com.

Spur Of The Moment Cruises also offers many very good prices. 800-343-1991.

Vacations To Go.Com. 800-338-4962. www.vacationstogo.com.

World Wide Cruises. 800-882-9000. www.wwcruises.com.

♦ FYI: On April 30, 2001, *The World of ResidenSea* made its maiden voyage around the globe. For between $800,000 to $6.6 million, you can own a 671 to 4,161 square foot condo or timeshare on this first-of-its-kind cruise liner. Choose from four floor plans, each including one to three bedrooms, a complete bath and kitchen, and walk-in closets. Many have a terrace with whirlpool and audio/visual equipment. *The World of ResidenSea* will have 40 resident suites, 183 guest suites, and 246 resident apartments. Extras will include seven restaurants, theater, library, and stock market room and business center. Christie's Great Estates in Santa Fe, New Mexico (800-799-9792) is overseeing sales of these sea apartments. More than $117 million worth of the ship's condos sold in the first 10 months.

♦   ♦   ♦

Barge Cruises

Most barge trips take place in Europe and offer an intriguing alternative to crowded tour buses and trains. Dress is casual and the average age of participants is 45. Theme cruises, such as "study French" or "learn to watercolor" are sometimes offered. Since barge trips usually occur on rivers, there is little possibility of seasickness. These canal cruises enable travelers to see sights up close, such as quaint towns, castles, gothic churches, medieval villages, blooming flowers, and beautiful countryside. Barges hold 6–30 persons and are very comfortable. Most have spacious cabins with private bathrooms, library, dining room, and sitting area, as well as panoramic windows. Adult and child-size bicycles are typically kept on board for use during stops. Most trips last a week. The downside is that barge trips average $1,500–$2,000pp for a one week cruise. However, rates are reduced for children and third and fourth passengers in a cabin. Additionally, if you charter a barge rather than take a cruise, the cost is considerably less. A family of four can rent a barge for less than $2,500 a week (which comes to $625pp) in the summer and the cost is further reduced in spring and fall. There are at least 3–4 cabins on most barges, so a couple may opt to share the boat with friends and split the cost.

Are you up to the task? According to Debbie Petermann, president of LeBoat, "If you have a driver's license, you are overqualified." Shirley Linde, editor of *SmallCruises.com* says "Since the

101

waterways are narrow and you are going in one direction, all you really have to remember is pointy end forward." Barges use a steering wheel and progress slowly (boats go a maximum of 5mph). However, I caution amateur captains to stay away from routes with locks or at least make sure locks are automatic. If you're still unsure, don't worry there is another option. For an additional $100 or so a week, you can hire a captain. He will leave you each evening, after safely docking the vessel, and return in the morning.

Avoid July and August; prices are highest during summer months and canal traffic is heavy. Shoulder and low season in Great Britain and northern France is May, June, and September. For south of France, it's April and October. Pack the same things you would if you were going to the beach; insect repellent, comfortable lightweight clothing, sunscreen, and sun hat or visor, etc. The difference between a charter and cruise is that a barge cruise has a set itinerary and fellow passengers. On a charter, the participants have the boat to themselves and decide when and where they want to stop, as well as how long they want to remain at each location. There are no stewards or chefs on chartered cruises so travelers are on their own to make meals or stop in a village and dine. Ask to be put on mailing lists and request free periodic e-mailers, which announce special deals and incentive offers. Many of these companies discount rates for online bookings. Additionally, some of these listings are consolidators (brokers), which often have the best prices on barge river cruises. As always, check with several companies to find out who has the best fare before making a monetary commitment.

♦ FYI: The Pacific Ocean is the largest body of water, consisting of 64 million square miles. The Atlantic Ocean is almost half that size at 31,830,000 square miles. The Indian Ocean is 28,350,000 square miles, while the Arctic Ocean is 5,440,000 square miles.

Abercrombie And Kent (A & K) provide several summer barge trips for families to Belgium, France, and England. A & K also offers chartered trips. Price is reduced in April and October. Single travelers may forego a supplement if they are willing to share a cabin with another single traveler of the same sex. 1520 Kensington Road, Oak Brook, IL 60523. 800-323-7308. www.abercrombiekent.com.

The Barge Broker offers self-drive barge trips in France. Prices start at $400pp per week. 800-275-9794. www.bargebroker.com.

The Barge Connection is a large broker providing many European barge trips. 888-550-8580. www.bargeconnection.com.

The Barge Lady is one of the leading brokers of European Canal and River Cruising. Trips start at less than $1,000pp. On several of their barge trips in England, France, and Ireland, single cabins are available with no single supplement. Barge Lady has been recommended by numerous publications, such as *Gourmet* Magazine, *Town and Country*, and *New York Times*. I'm told the chef doesn't make meals, he "creates incredible feasts." 101 W. Grand Avenue, Suite 200, Chicago, IL 60610. 800-880-0071 or 312-245-0952. www.bargelady.com.

Continental Waterways is a French company, established in 1966, which operates barge trips in Belgium, France, and Holland. Discounted rates, up to 30 percent, are usually extended mid-October to mid-November. For best rates, use Barge Broker, Barge Connection, or Barge Lady. 800-676-6613. www.continentalwaterways.com.

Crown Blue Line is the #1 barge-charter company. They rent barges in some of the U.S., as well as Ireland and Holland. 510 Sylvan Avenue, Suite 204, Englewood Cliffs, NJ 07632. 888-355-9491 or 201-569-9588. www.Crown-Holidays.co.uk.

European Waterways (affiliated with BV Associates), offer barge trips in France, Ireland, Holland, and England. Prices include all meals and wine, shore excursions by mini-van, and bicycle use. The company offers American Airlines Advantage miles for those who book barge trips. 140 East 56th Street, Suite 4C, New York, NY 10022. 800-755-8266 or 800-217-4447. www.ewaterways.com or www.europeanwaterways.com.

KD River Cruises Of Europe offer seven night cruises, including land tours, starting at $1,060pp. Kids under 14, accompanied by paying adult, usually travel free during the summer months. (Represented by J.F.O. CruiseService Corp., 2500 Westchester Avenue, Purchase, NY 10577. 800-346-6525). 800-346-6526. www.rivercruises.com.

LeBoat, Inc. provides hotel barges, gourmet meals and wine and guided excursion with bicycles and ballooning, and self-drive boats for exploring France, England, Scotland, Ireland, and Holland. The company also offers worldwide yacht trips. The self-drive boat trips start at less than $1,000 per week and include boat usage, license, VAT (value added tax), gas for cooking, and canal tolls. Price doesn't include fuel, insurance, or transfers. 10 South Franklin Tpk., Suite 204B, Ramsey, NJ 07446. 800-992-0291 or 201-236-2333. www.leboat.com.

River Barge Excursions offers "the only barging experience on America's rivers and inland waterways." All shore activities, port charges, tips and taxes, are included. Stay in spacious staterooms, all offering fantastic views. Open seating for meals and casual dress. Choose from 4-10 day trips. 888-GO-BARGE. www.riverbarge.com.

Uniworld offers dozens of cruise holidays on numerous cruise ships. The company claims..*only Uniworld offers cruises on all major European Rivers on privately chartered ships(the best in Europe)*...All shore excursions are included. These all-inclusive cruises start at around $2,000pp, including airfare. Note: These are not barge trips, but cruise ships that offer trips on European and Russian rivers. 16000 Ventura Blvd., Encino, CA 91436. 800-570-9630. www.uniworld.com.

Value World Tours offers river cruises in Australia, China, Russia, and Europe for well under $1,000pp (including all meals, entertainment, and shore excursions). Booking online entitles participants to additional savings.17220 Newhope Street, #203, Fountain Valley, CA 92708. 800-795-1633. www.RiverCruises.net.

Viking River Cruises provide five-star cruises on Europe and Russia's most scenic waterways, including the Danube, Volga, Rhine, and Moselle. Daily shore excursions, shipboard lectures, folklore entertainment, and cultural theme dinners are all included. These all-inclusive cruises start at less than $2,000pp, including airfare. 800-706-0938. www.vikingrivercruises.com.

◆ FYI: The five largest islands of the world are
1) Greenland (840,000 square miles, Atlantic Ocean)
2) New Guinea (312,000 square miles, Pacific Ocean)
3) Borneo (287,000 square miles, Pacific Ocean)
4) Madagascar (226,657 square miles, Indian Ocean)
5) Baffin (183,810 square miles, Arctic Ocean)

◆   ◆   ◆

Freighter Cruises

While this can be an exciting and unusual means of travel, there are some restrictions. Typically, there is not a doctor on board, so anyone age 60–78 must have a letter from a physician stating they are in good health. Travelers 79 and older are not usually eligible for freighter travel. Anyone requiring special attention cannot travel by freighter. Amenities vary according to the ship but are usually basic. Unlike cruises, there are no planned activities. The upside is that fares are lower. Also, there's a greater spirit of adventure because there are only a few passengers and you are on a real working ship. Some freighter trips last only a few days, but others make around-the-world voyages. For people interested in extended cruises, doing so by freighter may be the most affordable and interesting experience. I suggest taking a short freighter cruise before embarking on a lengthy one, just to make sure it's right for you. I would advise the same for any cruise or type of travel.

Freighter World Cruises is the largest provider of freighter cruises and has been in business for more than 25 years. 180 South Lake Avenue, Suite 335, Pasadena, CA 91101. 800-531-7774 or 626-449-3106. www.freighterworld.com. e-mail: freighters@freighterworld.com.

Maris Freighter Cruises provides short- and long-term voyages in North America and Europe. They produce a monthly, subscription publication detailing their trips. Standard cabins include port-side view with TV and VCR (extensive video library on board) and private bathroom. Ships carry 150–490 passengers, depending on ship. Each ship has elevator, pool, reading library, and dining room. No age limit. Maris USA Ltd., 215 Main Street, Westport, CT 06880. 800-99-MARIS(62747) or 203-222-9191. www.FreighterCruises.com.

> ♦ FYI: The world's busiest port is Rotterdam, Netherlands, and the largest is the port of New York and New Jersey.

♦   ♦   ♦

Helpful Resources

Ocean Cruises

AllCruiseNews.com. is a free weekly electronic newsletter full of Sizzling Hot Specials, tips, planning resources, and other valuable information, including a section written by kids for kids, "Cruisin' Kids Corner." It also permits airline miles redemption on some cruises *and* a miles awards program for booking cruises. 888-666-8120. www.cruise4miles.com.

Cruise Travel is a bimonthly publication that profiles cruise lines, ships, ports of call, agencies, and much more. World Publishing Company, 990 Grave Street, Evanston, IL 60201. www.cruisetravelmag.com.

The Cruise Vacation Planner is a free publication provided by the Cruise Lines International Association (CLIA). It's filled with facts, charts, and descriptions of cruises and ships, as well as frequently asked cruising questions. 888-Y-CRUISE. www.cruising.org.

If you're worried about seasickness, send for *Don't Miss the Boat!*, a free booklet on how to avoid it. 888-726-7724. www.transdermscop.com.

For information on Cruise jobs, cruise ship reviews, cruise line listings, links to many useful **Web sites**, and much more, log on to:

http://cruises.about.com.

www.cruise2.com.

www.cruisecritic.com.

www.theworkingvacation.com (dance host program).

www.cruisereviews.com.

Barge Cruises

About Travel is a barge travel specialist. 3548 S. Gateway Blvd., #302, Sioux Falls, SD 57106. 605-362-1741. www.AboutTravel.com/barge.html.

Contact the **American Society of Travel Agents** for a current list of agencies specializing in barge travel. See Chapter One for contact information.

The Barge Company books self-drive and barge cruises. 12 Orchard Close, Felton, Bristol, U.K. BS40 945. 800-688-0245. www.bargecompany.com.

The Barge Connection is a barge travel specialist. 888-550-8580. www.bargeconnection.com.

Freighter Cruises

If you can't find a book listed in this reference in your local bookstore, have the book seller special order it (no additional charge), or buy it online at www.Amazon.com, www.Barnesandnoble.com, or www.Borders.com.

A la Carte Freighter Travel books passenger freighters. www.freighter-travel.com.

Contact the **American Society of Travel Agents** for a current list of agencies specializing in freighter travel. See Chapter One.

Ford's Freighter Travel Guide & Waterways Of The World. Judith Howard. Published by Ford's Travel Guides.

Internet Guide to Freighter Travel books passenger freighters. http://people.we.mediaone.net/freighterman or www.geocities.com/freighterman.

Running Away To Sea: Round The World On A Tramp Freighter. Douglas Fetherling. Published by McClelland & Stewart.

Send Me A Postcard: Freighter Cruising With Frances Flynn. Published by North American Heritage Press.

Travltips Cruises And Freighter Travel Organization informs members about freighter trips and itineraries, answers FAQs, provides freighter directory, offers resources, and makes travel arrangements and reservations. 163-07 Depot Road, P.O. Box 580188, Flushing, NY 11358. 800-872-8584 or 718-939-2400. In Canada: 800-548-7823. www.travltips.com.

◆ FYI: The five longest rivers of the world are
1) Nile, Africa, 4,000 miles and the Amazon, South America, 4,000 miles
2) Yangtze, Asia, 3,430 miles
3) Yellow, Asia, 2,900 miles and the Congo, Africa, 2,900 miles
4) Missouri, USA, 2,710 miles
5) Amur, Asia, 2,700 miles.

◆　　◆　　◆

Chapter Six--How To Get The Best Deals On Accommodations

Chapter Six--How To Get The Best Deals On Accommodations

When a man is tired of London, he is tired of life;
for there is in London all that life can afford.
Samuel Johnson, September 20, 1777

There are nearly three-dozen different rates for hotel and motel rooms. The rate *you* get depends on many variables, including how much you know about the "art of negotiating" room rates.

For travelers looking for something different, you may be interested in http://boutiquelodging. com. This site lists moderate to deluxe, nonchain hotels and resorts. Look under "Irresistible Packages" for their best deals. For a booklet listing historic hotels throughout the United States, contact the National Trust for Historic Preservation. The listings include complete addresses, descriptions, amenities, and rates. 1785 Massachusetts Avenue, NW, Washington, DC 20036-6412. 800-944-6847. www.nthp.org.

Ten Ways To Save Big Money

1. Consider joining a travel club to obtain substantial savings on lodging. Many motels and hotels offer discounts, up to 70 percent off, to members of travel clubs. See Chapter Eight for specifics, including names and addresses of leading travel clubs.

2. Hotels and motels often provide rewards to frequent traveler program participants. Some, such as Hilton, Radisson, and Baymont Inns, offer airline miles and hotel points programs. Incentives and programs are listed below, along with contact information for all major hotel and motel chains.

3. Call and quiz the front desk staff or manager to find out when the property is most (and least) busy. Booking in advance and avoiding peak travel times increase savings because reduced rates are subject to availability. The highest demand for lodging is during holidays, summer, and annual events. For example, The Furniture Market is held twice a year in High Point, North Carolina. Every October and April, wholesalers and manufacturers come to High Point to conduct business. There are no rooms to be had anywhere within an hour's drive of the city. In fact, many people rent out their homes and make a great deal of money accommodating market participants. Lodging is usually booked at least a year or two in advance. If possible, travel during the low- or off-season and obtain accommodations at the cheapest rate. Consider staying on the outskirts of a city rather than downtown or the historic district. And remember, weekday rates are usually higher because of business travelers.

4. Check inserts that accompany monthly bills, especially credit card statements. As an incentive to stay at a certain hotel or motel, a discounted rate, free night stay, or special weekend getaway package, may be offered.

5. Make sure you really are quoted the lowest possible rate. I once called a hotel and told the desk clerk I would be there within the hour and needed one room at government rate. He quoted a price that seemed high to me. When I questioned it, I discovered it was $30 higher than the standard government rate "because I hadn't made advance reservations." I called another hotel that was a couple of miles from the property I had planned to go to and they charged me standard government rate. So, I stayed there instead.

6. Be sure to mention *anything* that might entitle you to a discount, such as being a government employee (including military), age, or membership in organizations such as AARP or AAA, *when*

making the reservation to ensure you are charged the best room rate. Discounts are often available for people 50 and older. If anyone in your group meets the criteria, be sure to book the room in their name to obtain the discounted rate. Child fares are typically free or reduced, depending on age.

Ask that a confirmation be faxed or mailed to you and be sure to take it with you. If a different rate is charged at check-in, show the written confirmation. The hotel or motel must honor the rate they promised, if you have written proof. I cannot emphasize enough how important that written confirmation will be if there is a bill dispute, which often occurs.

7. Never book through the toll-free number. Call the central reservation line only to obtain the local phone number. While you have them on the phone, go ahead and get their room rate, just to use for leverage when dealing with the hotel or motel directly. In rare cases, the rate quoted by central reservations may be less than the local rate. However, as a general rule, travelers save at least 10 percent off the rate by calling the property because the central reservation operators have no direct access to room availability and so they have no authority to negotiate or give a lower price than what is in their computer. Besides, the operator doesn't know where the hotel is in proximity to area attractions. The operator can only recite a street address or exit ramp number that's in the computer. After talking to a desk clerk, you may realize you would be better off staying closer somewhere more convenient.

Booking through a hotel's Web site often guarantees discounts of at least 10 percent. Be sure to check out a hotel's Web site before making a reservation. My advice is to compare the hotel's rate with central reservation rates and those found on the Web site to determine which one is the lowest.

Additionally, the best day to reserve a room is on Sunday. Typically, revenue management is not working, so better deals can be obtained. If possible, speak directly with someone in sales or the manager on duty. If you're willing to take chances, don't make a reservation. Walk into a hotel or motel after 8 p.m. As travel expert Wendy Perrin points out, "The hotel room is a perishable commodity. If there's room, the later you arrive, the more you can negotiate the rate down."

8. Another option is to use a coupon book. One of the best is the Entertainment Book series. There are Entertainment Books available for most major U.S. and Canadian cities. These coupon books offer 50 percent off hotels and motels, discounts on car rentals, cruises, and airlines, and 2-for-1's on dining, movies, and attractions. Entertainment Publications, 2125 Butterfield Road, Troy, MI 48084. 800-933-2605 or 877-688-8912. www.entertainment.com.

Some hotels, such as Holiday Inn and the Inter-Continental, are now offering prepaid gift cards, which are used like a debit card and money can be added to the account or it can be thrown away when used up. Increments are usually $25 or more. Talk about great Christmas and birthday gifts!

9. Use the Internet to help you find big savings. Additional listings can be found in Chapter Eight.

Budgethotels.Com reveals budget lodging and provides printable location maps. The company also has air and car discounts, as well as specials. P.O. Box 1129, Point Roberts, WA 98281. 877-779-7070 or in Canada: 250-868-1171. www.budgethotels.com. e-mail: info@bugethotels.com.

Worldhotel has more than 200,000 listings for U.S., Canada, Mexico, and other worldwide destinations. They even allow a hotel search within 5–25 miles of most U.S. towns. 4206 Enterprise Avenue, Naples, FL 34101. 941-403-7881. www.worldhotel.com.

10. Hotel Discounters. A hotel discounter is like a travel agent. They find the lowest price hotel that offers the amenities you desire. If you want a hotel in New York City for one week that's within walking distance of the theater district, it would be easier to use one of these companies than to call several hotels. Depending on the company, a hotel discounter will provide either a written confirmation or prepaid vouchers, which are presented at check-in.

Call the hotel and check its rate against a few brokers to verify the lowest rate. Hotel brokers aren't always lower. Also, do not use a broker that charges service fees, such as for booking or cancellation. Make sure to get a confirmation number. Use a charge card so that you may refuse payment if there's a problem.

Accommodations Express has listings for 1,300 properties in 190 U.S. cities, Bahamas, Turks and Caicos, Puerto Rico, Aruba, and Curacao Island. They promise up to 60 percent savings, but charge a small fee for booking or canceling. 801 Asbury Avenue, 6th floor, Ocean City, NJ 08226. 800-906-4685 or 800-444-7666 or 609-525-0800. www.accommodationsexpress.com.

Asia-Hotels.com has approximately 1,000 hotels and resorts in nearly 20 Asian countries, as well as Australia and New Zealand. The Web site contains photos of properties, descriptions, customer reviews, and more. www.asia-hotels.com.

Central Reservation Service has listings for 224 hotels in many major U.S. cities, promising savings of up to 40 percent. They also book other kinds of lodging, air, cruises, tours, theme parks, trains, RVs, and other types of transport. CRS does not charge a booking or cancellation fee. 800-686-6836 or 800-950-0232. www.reservation-services.com.

Euro-Hotels.com is operated by the same company that runs Asia-hotels.com. and has many properties all over Europe.

Hotelguide.com offers up to 70 percent off over 60,000 hotel listings in roughly 200 countries. The Web site includes time of day around the world, currency converter, and locator map. www.Hotelguide .com

Hotel Reservations Network is a free booking service that promises up to 70 percent off 1,500 hotel rooms in 29 U.S. and nine foreign cities, such as New York, Chicago, San Francisco, Boston, Orlando, Las Vegas, New Orleans, Los Angeles, San Diego, Miami, Washington D.C., Paris, and London. No booking fee, but $50 cancellation fee. They guarantee rooms available for sold out dates, although these rooms are not necessarily discounted. 8140 Walnut Hill Lane, Suite 203, Dallas, TX 75231. 800-964-6835. www.hoteldiscount.com or www.180096hotel.com.

Steigenberger Reservation Service offers hundreds of hotels throughout Europe, Middle East, Asia, Australia, and the United States, with discounts of up to 45 percent. Rates can be confirmed in U.S. dollars if the hotel is paid in cash or traveler's checks. There's a 48-hour cancellation policy. They will send you a free brochure of participating worldwide hotels, which are divided into three categories: deluxe, first class, and comfortable. The brochures provide photos, descriptions, prices, and amenities. 1155 South Semoran Blvd., Suite 1129, Winter Park, FL 32792. 800-223-5652. www.srs-worldhotels. com.

Quickbook does not charge a membership or service fee and claims to discount (up to 50 percent) 200 hotels in seven major U.S. cities. No booking or cancellation fee. Consumer Reports rated this the top hotel broker, citing their rate was lower 85 percent of the time. 800-789-9887. www.quikbook.com.

Travel Interlink has more than 3,000 hotels, from moderate to deluxe, in Asia, Australia, New Zealand, and South Pacific. The average discount is 40 percent and there is also a Consumer Discount Travel Program. Sherman Oaks, CA. 800-477-7172. www.travelinterlink.com.

1800USAHotels offers up to 65 percent off normal rates at 11,000 hotels in 1,500 cities worldwide, plus free frequent flyer miles program. They also have discounted rates for spas, cruises, bed and breakfasts, and tours. No booking or cancellation fees. 860 Wyckoff Avenue, Mahwah, NJ 07430. 800-USA-HOTELS (800-872-4683) or 201-847-9000. Outside U.S.: 800-252-331-1555. www.1800usahotels.com. e-mail: info@1800usahotels.com

---

TIP: If traveling with your pet, you might want to check out www.Dogfriendly.com and www.Petswelcome.com for listings of pet-friendly hotels, B & Bs, and campgrounds.

◆   ◆   ◆

Discount Programs For Hotels And Motels

Remember that special deals and promotions are advertised on hotel Web sites and that some chains provide additional discounts for online bookings. Some properties listed below have been grouped together because they are all owned by the same corporation, which means programs are usually reciprocated.

Adam's Mark--Discounts vary according to city and are available only to AARP members. 800-444-2326. www.adamsmark.com.

Amerisuites-- Children under 18 free and 10 percent off for members of AARP, AAA, and Sam's Club. They also have an AmeriClub program, which is a frequent stay program. Receive a free night's stay for every 12 paid stays. 800-833-1516. www.amerisuites.com.

Baymont Inn and Suites--Their Frequent Traveler Program, Ovation, provides a free night stay for every 12 nights paid. Additionally, frequent flyer miles, American Express rewards, and free merchandise can be acquired. Senior discounts vary according to location. 800-428-3438. www.baymontinns.com.

Best Inns offers 10 percent off the normal rate for people 50 or older, as well as lower rates for government employees, AAA and AARP members. In 2000, they began offering "Evergreen" rooms for allergy sufferers and health-conscious travelers that are allergen-free, chlorine-free shower, and pure, filtered, drinking water. 800-237-8466. www.bestinn.com.

Best Western--Children under 12 free and 10 percent off for 55 or older. 800-528-1234 or 800-937-8367. www.bestwestern.com.

Country Hearth Inns--10 percent discount to travelers 50 and older. Their frequent travelers program is called Country Club. 888-HEARTH or 800-848-5767. www.countryhearth.com.

Days Inn--Children under 12 free (staying in room with adult), 10–50 percent off for those 60 or older, and 10 percent discount for AARP, AAA, and CAA members. Their September Days Club gives 15–50 percent off for 50 and older, as well as additional discounts for rental cars, tours, on-site restaurants, free stay for spouses, free six month subscription to *Budget Travel*, and three $5 coupons.

Small annual membership fee ($15). Also, be sure to ask about their Super Saver rate (available to travelers who make reservations at least 29 days in advance). 800-544-8313 or 800-241-5050 or 800-329-7466. www.daysinn.com.

Doubletree Hotels--Discounts vary according to location. Usually, children under 18 free and 10 percent senior rate. They offer 40 percent off for AARP members who book 21 days in advance. 800-528-0444 or 800-222-TREE (8733). www.doubletree.com. **Embassy Suites**--Children under 18 free and 65 and older receive 10 percent off room rates. Free cooked to order or continental breakfast. 800-EMBASSY (362-2779). www.embassysuites.com. **Hilton Hotels**--Children under 18 free and 10 percent discount for seniors. The Senior Honors Plan gives 50 percent off rooms for retirees 55 or older or for those 60 or older (retired or not). And, 20 percent discount at their restaurants, as well as cash certificates, according to how much you spend at Hilton Hotels annually. Hilton offers a HHonors program, which rewards guest with both air miles and hotel stay points. Annual membership fee. 800-HILTONS (445-8667), 842-4242, 800-492-3232 or 800-HHonors. www.hilton.com. **Hampton Inns**--The LifeStyle 50 program allows four persons over the age of 50 to stay in a room, with two double beds, and pay a single rate. Children 18 and younger stay free in room with adult. 800-HAMPTON (426-7866). www.hamptoninn.com.

Drury Inns--10 percent off for people 55 or older. They also offer Drury Member Rewards Program, whereby participants can earn points good for rooms, airlines, and cruises. Drury Gold Key Club is their frequent traveler club. 800-DRURYINN or 800-378-7946. www.druryinn.com.

Econo Lodges--55 or older receive 10 percent off room rates. Econo Traveler's Club gives travelers one free night for every six nights they stay at participating motels. Participants do not have to stay six consecutive nights to receive free night. 800-55-ECONO (553-2666). www.choicehotels.com.

Extended Stay America--No discounts available. Everyone gets one flat rate, which starts at $209 for a week stay. Each room has a kitchenette. 800-398-7829. www.extstay.com.

Holiday Inn/Holiday Inn Express/ Holiday Inn Resorts/ Holiday Inn Crowne Plaza Hotels/ And Staybridge Suites--50 or older get 20 percent off room rates and 10 percent off at their restaurants. Holiday Inn has a frequent traveler program. Children 12 and younger eat free in dining room if they order from Kids Eat Free Program Menu. 800-HOLIDAY (465-4329) or 800-343-1122. www.holiday-inn.com. **Inter-Continental Hotels**--Discounts are offered by individual properties, and vary accordingly. Reduced rates cannot be obtained through central reservations. They offer many programs, such as Points Program, Six Continents, and Priority Club. 888-567-8725. www.interconti.com.

Howard Johnsons--59 or older receive 50 percent off rooms. For those who belong to Mature Outlook or AARP, the requirement is 50 and older to receive 50 percent discount. Participants in their free SuperMiles Program are awarded one point for every $1 spent and that includes phone calls, restaurant, and taxes. Points are good for rooms, airline tickets, car rentals, and gift certificates. Children 18 and younger stay free in room with adult. 800-406-1411 or 800-634-3464 or 800-446-4656. www.hojo.com.

Hyatt Hotels & Resorts--Discounts for AAA members and up to 50 percent off for those 62 or older in most cities, depending on time of year. Gold Passport Program awards certificates to participants. 888-591-1234 or 800-228-9000 or 800-233-1234. www.hyatt.com.

Inn Suites--The Silver Passport Program awards 10 percent off room rates and free quarterly magazine to people 55 or older that details promotions. 888-INNSUITES or 800-842-4242. www.innsuites.com.

Knights Inns/Arborgate Inns--AAA and AARP members, and travelers 55 or older, are entitled to 10 percent off room rates. Sam's Club members receive 15 percent. Discounted rates for those staying seven nights or longer. 800-682-1071 or 800-418-8977. www.knightsinn.com.

La Quinta Inns--55 or older receive 15 percent discount. Returns Club is their frequent traveler program. Members receive free check cashing, no additional charge for spouses or children 18 or younger, and more. Join online and receive bonus reward points. 800-531-5900. www.laquinta.com.

Marriott--Discounts vary according to location (10–50 percent). AARP members are entitled to 50 percent off rooms. Two rooms can be reserved at the discount rate, depending on time of year. If you're not a member of AARP, you must be 62 or older to qualify for 50 percent discount. Additional discounts include 25 percent on restaurant meals for up to eight people. And, 10 percent off at gift shop. There's no membership fee. Participation in the Marriott Rewards program can earn members a free vacation and earn points and frequent flyer miles. 800-249-0800 or 800-236-2427. www.marriott.com. **Courtyard Inns By Marriott**-- Discounts vary according to location and availability. 800-321-2211. www.courtyard.com. **Residence Inn By Marriott**--Discounts vary according to location and availability. 800-331-3131 or 800-228-9290. www.residenceinn.com. **Fairfield Inn**--Discounts and availability vary according to dates and cities. Typically, discounts are 15 percent for travelers age 65 or members of AARP. Marriott Rewards Program members earns points toward a free vacation. 800-228-2800. www.fairfieldinn.com.

Microtel Inn & Suites--Discounts vary according to location. 800-771-7171. www.microtelinn.com.

Motel 6--Discounts vary according to location, but usually there's a 10 percent discount for AARP members. Children 17 and younger stay free in room with adult. Small pets allowed, free of charge. 800-4-MOTEL-6 or 800-466-8356. www.motel6.com.

Omni Hotels--AARP members receive 50 percent off rooms and 15 percent off meals in on-site restaurants. They also offer an Omni Select Guest Program. 800-THE-OMNI (843-6664). www.omnihotels.com.

Quality Inns/ Comfort Inns/ Clarion/ Choice Hotels--Children 18 and under are free(in same rooms as adults) and 60 and older receive 10-30 percent off rooms depending on location. Ask about this senior saver rate and its restrictions. 800-221-2222 or 800-424-6423. www.comfortinns.com, www.qualityinns.com, www.clarioninns.com or www.hotelchoice.com. **MainStay Suites** (extended stays) are the best deals for families because rates usually run $199-299 per week. 800-660-MAIN (6246). **Rodeway Inns** (U.S., Canada, Mexico)--Anyone 50 or older who is a member of a senior organization gets 10–25 percent off rooms. If you don't belong to a senior organization, you must be at least 55 to be eligible for the discount. Rodeway Choice is a free program that offers extends mature travelers rooms with special amenities. 800-424-6423 or 800-228-2000. www.rodeway.com. **Sleep Inns**--This chain provides a Prime Time rate, which is 30 percent off as long as someone staying in the room is at least 50 (subject to availability) or a guaranteed discount of 10 percent for those age 50. There is a frequent traveler program and coupons and additional discounts are offered on-line. 800-SLEEP-INN(753-3745). www.sleepinns.com.

In an interesting experiment, MainStay Suites (extended stays) and Sleep Inn, both part of Choice Hotels International, were built as *one* 148-room hotel in a Philadelphia suburb. The idea is to utilize the staff and amenities to provide better service to all guests. For example, guests of both hotels will check in at the same front desk, as well as enjoy the same continental breakfast, patio and grill area, indoor swimming pool, meeting rooms, coin-operated washer and dryers, and high-speed Internet access. If the experiment goes well, other chains are sure to follow.

Radisson Hotels--Children under 19 free and 65 and older are entitled to 25–40 percent off rooms. Radisson Partner Miles program gives participants up to 500 miles/points through 20 different travel programs, including airlines, car rental agencies, etc. Radisson also offers family discounts and Bed & Breakfast Breakaway Rates program. Radisson's rewards program awards points for the room, room service, phone calls made from your room, restaurant and gift shop purchases, and taxes. No blackout dates. In addition to free stays, points can also be redeemed for gift certificates at top retailers, such as Barnes and Noble and Eddie Bauer. Free sign-up points available. Members are also entitled to 10–20 percent off room rates. 800-333-3333. www.radisson.com.

Ramada/ Plaza Hotels--Children under 18 free and 10-30 percent discount for seniors. Many programs available, including frequent traveler, Club Ramada. 888-298-2054. www.ramada.com.

Red Carpet Inns/ Master Hosts Inns/ Scottish Inns--55 or older get 10 percent off rooms except for some blackout times. 10 percent off for Allstate, Quest, or AAA members. 800-251-1962. www.reservahost.com.

♦ FYI: The Top Ten Famous Haunted Hotels in the United States

1. Chateau Marmont--Hollywood, California
2. Chelsea Hotel--New York, NY
3. The Equinox--Manchester Village, Vermont
4. Hotel Monte Vista--Flagstaff, Arizona
5. Hotel de la Poste--New Orleans, Louisiana
6. Rosario--Orcas Island, Washington
7. Don CeDar Beach Resort & Spa--St. Pete Beach, Florida
8. The Logan--New Hope, Pennsylvania
9. St. James Hotel--Cimarron, New Mexico
10. The Pfister--Milwaukee, Wisconsin

Red Roof Inns--60 or older receive 10 percent off rooms. Redi Card Rewards Program rewards travelers 60 or older with free road maps, additional discounts on car rentals, and future stays at participating Red Roof Inns. 800-RED-ROOF or 800-843-7663. www.redroof.com.

Ritz Carlton--Discounts vary according to location. 800-241-3333. www.ritzcarlton.com.

Sheraton Hotels--Children under 18 free and 15–20 percent for seniors. AARP members receive 50 percent off the published fare. Non-members of AARP must be 60 or older to receive the 50 percent discount. There's also 25 percent off room rates on most international Sheraton properties. 800-325-3535. www.sheraton.com.

Shoney's Inns--10 percent off rooms for those 55 or older and 15 percent off for AARP members. Frequent travelers program is ShoBusiness.800-552-INNS(4667). www.shoneysinn.com.

Sonesta International Hotels And Resorts--10–15 percent at most of their hotels for AARP members. 800-766-3782. www.sonesta.com.

Super8--No discounts available, but they do offer 10 percent off room rates to members of their VIP program. Participants must pay and join Traveler's Advantage to receive this perk. Children 12 and younger stay free in room with adult. Some properties allow older children to stay at no additional charge. 800-800-8000. www.super8.com.

Travelodge/ Travelodge Hotels/ Thriftlodge Inns/ Viscount Suite Hotels (all two room suites)-- Members of any senior organization receive 15 percent off room rates or 10 percent off for people 50 or older. There is also a Travelodge Miles Guest Rewards Program. Discounts and coupons available online. 800-255-3050 or 800 578-7878 or 800-527-9666. www.travelodge.com. Viscount: 520-745-6500. www.viscountsuite.com.

Vagabond Inns--Club 55 gives participants 10–30 percent off rooms and other benefits, such as a quarterly newsletter and tour packages. AA discounts and frequent traveler program also available. Coupons and discounts can be obtained online. 800-522-1555. www.vagabondinns.com.

Westin Hotels And Resorts--Restrictions, ranging from age to location, result in discounts that vary from 10–50 percent off room rates. 888-625-5144. www.westin.com.

Westmark Hotels (Alaska)--65 and older are entitled to cheap room rates, which vary according to location and time of year. There is also a frequent traveler program. 800-544-0970. www.westmarkhotels.com.

Wyndham Hotels & Resorts--Wyndham awards discounts on U.S. and Caribbean hotels and resorts to members of AARP. Discounts vary according to location. 877-999-3223. www.wyndham.com.

◆   ◆   ◆

Home Swapping

Home swapping allows travelers to go anywhere in the world and stay, briefly or for an extended period of time, without paying for accommodations. This may be right for you if you're interested in trading the use of your home for the chance to vacation elsewhere. Participants can experience a vacation with all the comforts of home, including full kitchens and total privacy, and no rigid check-in or check-out times. Additionally, travelers are afforded the chance to stay at places and for periods of time that might otherwise not be financially feasible. For example, participants can spend the summer in the south of France or January in Aspen, Colorado.

If you are considering moving or retiring to an unfamiliar area, home swapping allows ample time and leisurely exploration to determine if the potential location is desirable. Participants can swap as many times a year as they like, assuming suitable property is found and that the owners are interested in reciprocating. Success in this program is paramount on having a desirable location and property. If seriously interested, you may want to get a copy of *Home Exchange Vacationing* by Bill and Mary Barbour, published by Rutledge Hill Press.

All home-swapping organizations charge listing fees.

Homelink U.S.A. (formerly Vacation Exchange Club) members receive five directories a year. Listings are in America and range from apartments to mansions. P.O. Box 650, Key West, FL 33041. 800-638-3841 or 305-294-1448. www.homelink.org.

International Home Exchange Network is an Internet-based company with over 1,000 members. No charge for searching lists. P.O. Box 30085, Santa Barbara, CA 93130. 866-898-9660 or 805-878-9600. www.homeexchange. com.

Intervac U.S. members receive five catalogs a year that contain more than 10,000 homes in over 30 countries, including Iceland. Senior rates are cheaper. P.O. Box 590504, San Francisco, CA 94159. 800-756-HOME(4663) or 415-435-3497. www.intervacus.com.

Senior Vacation And Home Exchange is an Internet resource for those over 50 who are interested in exchanging houses, motor homes, caravans and/or nonexchange commercial travel accommodations including B & B's, hotels, inns, and resorts (such as the 7 Gables Inn in Fairbanks, Alaska, and the Black Duck Inn on Corea Harbor, Maine). There are more than 600 listings in 20 countries, including Ireland, Australia, Brazil, and Belgium. Seniors OnLine. 2107 Danforth Avenue, Suite 133, Toronto, ONT M4C 1K1. www.seniorshomeexchange.com.

TIP: Ever heard of Margarita Island? This Caribbean hideaway has white, sandy beaches, golf, incredible eateries and night-life, as well as spas and first-class shopping. Eight-day packages start at a few hundred dollars, including airfare, unlimited drinks, meals, and more. For more information, contact Moment's Notice. Membership in this discount travel club entitles participants to savings on vacation packages, cruises, and more. Their Web site reveals Hot Deals. 7301 New Utrecht Avenue, Brooklyn, NY 11204. 888-241-3366 or 718-234-6295. www.moments-notice.com.

◆   ◆   ◆

Camping and RVing

More and more travelers are realizing the advantages of camping and RVing—more than 9 million recreation vehicles are currently on the road in America. Interestingly enough, more vehicles are owned by families than by retirees. Besides having the advantage of being a "portable home" and an affordable alternative to hotels, this type of travel is a good way to meet people, exchange information, and even make new friends. As with most travel, campground and RV park rates will be further reduced for travelers willing to go at nonpeak times.

The Recreation Vehicle Industry Association (RVIA) states flexibility as the number one reason motor coaches have become so popular. A survey RVIA conducted last year showed that 87 percent of owners plan three impromptu trips yearly and 8 in 10 keep their vehicles packed and ready to go. Survey participants said they planned to log more than 1,800 miles and spend 25 days on the road.

The most affordable is the folding camping trailer (pop-up). Other types include the truck camper, travel trailer, fifth wheeler, and motor home. These range from $3,500 (pop-up) to $35,000 (small motor home). Prices are even less for those willing to buy used models. Top-of-the-line motor homes are now equipped with lap-top computer stations, walk-in closets, DSS satellite systems, king-size beds, heated tile floors, automatic awnings, slide-out patios, retractable sunroofs, spiral staircases leading to a rooftop deck, and much more. For more information:

Coleman--800-532-2318, www.colemantrailers.com.
Jayco--219-825-5861, www.jayco.com.
Starcraft RV--800-945-4787, www.starcraftrv.com.
Viking--616-467-6321, www.vikingrv.com.
Thor/Aero Coach--219-457-8787, www.aerocoach.com.
Aliner--724-423-7440, www.aliner.com.
Chalet--541-791-4610, www.chaletrv.com.
Palomino--616-432-3271, www.palominorv.com.

A must for campers and RVers who are 62 or older and planning to visit America's park system is the "Golden Age Passport." It's available for a one-time cost of just $10 and sometimes it's offered on site at no charge. The Passport entitles the holder to free admission to all national parks, monuments, forest and recreational areas *and* anyone traveling in the same vehicle also gets in free! Plus, the passport is good for 50 percent off federal user fees for camping, swimming, parking, cave admissions, and boat launches.

These passports can be obtained at any national park, or you can request one through the National Park Service(NPS), P.O. Box 37127, Washington, DC 20013. www.nps.gov. Do not confuse these with a new product, Passports, sold at many NPS outlets. These booklets resemble passports but do not offer discounts. They are merely a way travelers can record where they have been in America's national park system. NPS recently introduced the National Park Pass ($50 annually), which allows entrance into all 379 American parks, including Grand Tetons, Yellowstone, Grand Canyon, and Mt. Rushmore. It comes with a pop-out map of the parks and a free newsletter. Most of the revenue goes to wildlife protection and trail maintenance. In case you're wondering what normal park entrance fees are, Yosemite ($20), Olympic Park ($10), and Yellowstone ($20). For more information or to obtain a pass, contact the National Park Service, P.O. Box 37127, Washington, DC 20013. 888-467-2757. The Web site also has links to other useful sites. www.nps.gov.

If you enjoy RVing and have an interest in seeing Europe, Motorhomes International may be of interest. The company provides travelers the opportunity to tour Europe by motorhome. 4906 Turtle Creek Trail, Oldsmar, FL 34667. 813-771-1027. For cruising around North America, you might want to rent an RV. This is a good idea for people who are considering buying a recreational vehicle. Cruise America Rental & Sales has 25 locations. 800-327-7799. www.cruiseamerica.com.

If you would like to consult a travel agent who specializes in camping vacations, First Discount Travel is a member of ASTA. 3000 American Way, Missoula, MT 59802. 406-549-9991.

Many campgrounds will exchange labor for free camping. Jobs include cleaning, security, check-ins, activity directors, tour guides, entertainment, and maintenance. *Workamper News* lists hundreds of job openings across the country. 501-362-2637. www.workamper.com. Additionally, Camper Clubs of America (800-369-2267, www.camperclubsofamerica.com) and Escapees RV Club (888-757-2582) are useful resources. Members of Camper Clubs receive RV camping for $10 a night. Another interesting option is to utilize family summer camps. Camp Mather in Groveland, California, is only one mile from Yosemite National Park. Twenty tent sites and 100 rustic cabins are available. There's a cafeteria on site, as well as a lake, swimming pool, tennis courts, and supervised kids' activities ranging from horseback riding to an arts and crafts program. Cost start at $850 for a family of four. For more information on these facilities, contact the American Camping Association. They have information on more than 2,000 accredited camps. www.ACAcamps.org.

♦ FYI: According to Guiness Book of World Records, the largest camper was built in 1990 by Sheik Hamad Bin Hamdan Al Nahyan of Abu Dhabi, United Arab Emirates. It is a five-story vehicle, measuring 66 feet in length, 39 feet wide, and 39 feet tall. Weighing 120 tons, it has eight bedrooms and eight bathrooms, as well as four garages and water storage for up to 6,340 gallons.

♦   ♦   ♦

What You Don't Know About Hostels

Hostels are one of the cheapest ways for people of all ages to see the world. If you haven't considered this kind of lodging before, you really should. They're not just for college kids or backpackers—at least not anymore. In fact, Elderhostel has appreciated their value and used them for years in many of their programs.

Hostels began in Europe around 100 years ago, as a cheap lodging alternative for students. So, they were very basic and similar to dorm rooms. But, hostels have become more sophisticated. Some are converted jail-houses and log cabins, so they offer more ambiance than motels. Some have large rooms with many beds, while others have private rooms with two beds in each room.

The main appeal is still its low cost. Lodging in big cities can be outrageous. For example, hotel rooms in Manhattan, New York, average $200pp, per night. However, Big Apple Hostel charges travelers a fraction of that rate, and not only is it in the heart of Manhattan, it's just a block from Times Square.

Stays at ski resort areas are usually quite expensive, averaging $150pp, per night. Again, hostels provide a reasonable alternative. Most of the facilities charge less than $50pp, per night. For example, Castle Mountain Hostel in Alberta, Canada. has 36 beds, is less than 30 minutes from Lake Louise, Sunshine Village, and Mt. Norquay Ski Resorts, and costs $20pp, per night. Lake Tahoe Mellow Mountain Hostel in Lake Tahoe, California, also charges $20pp, per night, and provides free coffee and tea to lodgers. Even travelers who don't ski can find plenty of other wonderful things to do in these places, such as hiking, snowboarding, sledding, shopping, and dining.

You don't have to belong to a hostelling organization to stay at one, but nonmembers will pay more than members. Members also receive directories that list hostels, rates, and amenities/facilities. I strongly recommend making reservations. The Internet is a good place to start for additional information on hostelling. www.hostels.com.. Or, write to Trojan Horse Hostel for the latest edition of *The Hostel Handbook for the U.S. and Canada: 500 North American Hostels,* Trojan Horse HG, 44 Andorer Street, Ludlow, VT 05149. Another good publication that's available at most bookstores is *Hostels U.S.A.* (Globe Pequot Press).

Note: In Europe, many hostels offer private "family rooms."

Hostelling International–American Youth Hostels (HI-AYH) allows its members extremely low-cost lodging at any of its many hostels, such as New York City, Florida, Sydney, Australia, and Paris, France. Most hostels also offer special discounts on everything from museums to ski lifts. All ages welcome.

Membership includes a directory of hostels, plus discounts on rail passes and more. AYH also offers several trips catering to the over 50 crowd through their "50+ Young At Heart Travel" Program. Dues have remained less than $20 a year for many years. 733 15th Street, Washington, DC 20005. 202-783-6161. www.hiayh.org. e-mail: hostels@hiayh.org.

Hostelling International–Canada (HI-C) is Canada's largest budget travel organization with more than 40,000 members and 80 hostels. Hostels are located across Canada from Prince Edward Island to the Yukon. Accommodations range from cabin-style to quaint cottages, such as the Kamloop's Old Courthouse hostel, log cabin hostel in Val David, or the old Carlton County Jailhouse hostel in Ottawa. HI-C offers international booking so you have a confirmed reservation upon arrival. When you arrive in Canada, you will be given a complimentary copy of the Hostelling North America, an official guide to hostels in Canada and the United States. HI-C also offers a GO Canada Budget Travel Pass. Hostellers can choose from either a 15- or 30-day package, which includes either 15 or 30 overnight vouchers good for stay at any HI-C hostels, and either a 15- or 30-day unlimited Greyhound Canada coach pass. Participants also receive a prepaid long distance phone card, a souvenir T-shirt, and a welcome package of extensive travel information with additional discounts available on tours. The hostels have 24-hour access, activity programs, private rooms, self-service kitchens, and laundry facilities. HI-C offers more than lodging. HI-C takes a more interactive role, allowing travelers safety and comfort to see folk festivals, explore local marketplaces, visit museums and galleries, take a guided nature hike to see bears, take a deep-sea fishing excursion, or go whale watching, etc. They have numerous brochures at each site listing companies that offer these kinds of activities. The Web site also has links to international hostels, including Japan, New Zealand, Switzerland, and the Netherlands. 400-205 Catherine Street, Ottawa, Ontario, Canada K2P 1C3; 613-237-7884. www.hostellingIntl.ca. e-mail: info@hostelling.intl.ca.

♦ FYI: The Top U.S. States visited by overseas travelers are Florida, California, New York, Hawaii, and Nevada.

Some independent operators offer private hostels. Since they are independently operated, some are more desirable than others. Generally, the rates are slightly lower than other hostels. Most charge less than $25pp. For budget B & Bs in Australia, log onto www.homehostel.com. Low single, family, and weekly rates are available. For information on hostels throughout Europe, check out www.eurotrip.com/hostels. Additionally, here are a few noteworthy places:

Hawaii--Arnott's Lodge on the Big Island has dorms and private rooms. 98 Apapane Road, Hilo, Hawaii; 808-969-7097. Or, try Banana Bungalow Maui, 310 North Market Street, Wailuku, Maui. 800-846-7835 or 808-242-8999.

L.A.--Venice Beach Cotel. It has a dozen or so dorm rooms and 16 private rooms. Basic, but clean. 25 Windward Avenue, Venice Beach, CA. 310-399-7649. www.hostels.com/cotel.

New York City--Banana Bungalow. Conveniently located on the Upper West Side, this hostel even has a rooftop deck. No private rooms. The Web site has information on hostels in Santa Barbara, Miami Beach, Hollywood, San Diego, and Waikiki, Hawaii. Some of these facilities offer private rooms. 250 West 77th Street, New York City, NY. 800-3-HOSTEL. www.bananabungalow.com.

Pescadero, CA--Pigeon Lighthouse. Located 25 miles north of Santa Cruz and 50 miles south of San Francisco, the Pigeon Lighthouse, est. 1872, stands 115-ft. and has 144 steps to the top. The keeper's house has been restored and is now a hostel with dorms and a handful of private rooms. Self-service kitchen, hot tub, and parking. Reservations required January-September and weekends year-round. Whale-watching January–April. The Web site includes information on northern California hostels. 210 Pigeon Point Road, Hwy. 1, Pescadero, CA. 650-879-0633 or 800-909-4776 (for reservations only). www.norcalhostels.org.

San Francisco--Pacific Tradewinds Guest House. This hostel is near Chinatown. No private rooms. Travelers can earn free stays by doing a few hours of cleaning. 680 Sacramento Street, San Francisco, CA. 800-486-7975 or 415-433-7970. www.hostels.com/pt.

◆ FYI: The four smallest countries in the world are:
1. Monaco (French Riviera on the Mediterranean) is four square miles.
2. Nauru (Western Pacific Ocean) is eight square miles.
3. Tuvalu (South Pacific) is nine square miles.
4. Vatican City, (Rome, Italy) is 16 square miles.

Seattle--Green Tortoise Backpackers Guesthouse. This downtown hostel has 24 dorm rooms, with discounts for those with a student ID), and a dozen private rooms. They also operate a hostel in San Francisco. Free breakfast, backpacker dinner, movie night, and city tours available. 1525 Second Avenue, Seattle, Washington. 888-4-HOSTEL or 888-424-6783 or 206-340-1222. www.greentortoise.com.

Washington, D.C.--Columbia Guest House. This is actually a mansion that has been converted to a hostel. It has seven private rooms with rates less for those who show a student ID, and three dorm rooms. Quiet and clean. 2005 Columbia Road, N.W. 202-265-4006.

◆   ◆   ◆

Renting Affordable Villas, Castles, Inns, Houses, Condos, And Apartments

There are apartments, country houses, farmhouses, villas, inn, condos, and chateaux that vacationers can rent for short or long-term use. While not all are bargains, there are some incredible deals to be had. Rent-a-Home International offers has many listings for less than $900 a week. The rate remains the same no matter how many people stay. For example, a luxury apartment in Innsbruck, Austria, with a private garden patio, hardwood floors, and oriental rugs, was recently offered for that rate. So was a two-bedroom condo, within walking distance to Sun Valley, Idaho's River Run Ski Resort. Furthermore, the condo has a view of Mt. Baldy and a fireplace. How about a luxury one-bedroom condo at the base of the mountain at Whistler, British Columbia, which has a sofa that coverts to a bed, hot tub, gas fireplace, private patio, and is across the street from a big shopping center?

Below is a list of companies, including their areas of expertise and the type of accommodations they lease. The agent's job is to assess your needs and handle all arrangements. However, these agents vary as much as the lodging they offer. Some will handle everything once you tell them where you would like to go and your price range. Others do nothing more than let you know what is available. Be sure to choose an agent that will guarantee the accommodations. Remember, lodging will cost less if you avoid peak times, such as holidays and late summer (July and August).

For more information on these kinds of accommodations, see Travel Clubs and Resources in Chapter Eight or access www.travelguides.com. Also, try different search engines using keywords, such as "inns," "villas," "vacations and rentals," or "lodging." Check with tourist boards in the countries you plan to visit for a list of rentals available. For example, the French Ministry of Tourism provides interested persons with fully equipped apartment listings in Paris that cost less than $100 per night (or even less for rentals of a week or more).

At Home Abroad offers villas and apartments in England, France, Ireland, Italy, Spain, Portugal, the Caribbean, and Mexico. 405 E. 56th Street, 6-H, New York, NY 10022-2466. 212-421-9165.

Barclay International Group provides short-term rentals for 2,500+ apartments in London and eight buildings in Paris, more than 50 deluxe British country cottages and a few apartments, villas, and cottages in Europe, North America, Southeast Asia, and Australia. They will also arrange rail passes and theater tickets. 150 East 52nd Street, New York, NY 10022. 800-845-6636 or 212-832-3777. www.barclayweb.com.

Bridgestreet Accommodations give travelers the option of staying in a luxury apartment or condominium rather than a hotel room. BridgeStreet leases apartments or condos and then sub-leases them to travelers for a one week or less. This often makes lodging cheaper than hotels, especially with their double occupancy policies. All accommodations are fully equipped and furnished. The company currently has approximately 400 listings in 35 U.S. cities, as well as Canada and England. Rates vary from $43 per night for a one-bedroom apartment in Toronto to $2,682 for a week stay in a two-bedroom flat in London. In the United States and Canada: 866-405-3153 or in United Kingdom and Europe: 800-278-7331. www.bridgest.com.

Cyberrentals has chalets, condos, and houses in the U.S. and Canada, Caribbean, Mexico, South America, Europe, and Asia. 802-228-7158. www.cyberrentals.com.

Global Home Network has small hotels, villas, condos, and apartment rentals in Asia, Europe and South America. 800-528-3549 or 703-318-7081. www.globalhomenetwork.com.

Home Abroad offers villas and apartments in Italy for less than $999 a week. I am told the owner inspects each listing before accepting it and that many of the rentals are much less in the low and off-seasons. 413-528-6610. www.homeabroad.com. e-mail: info@homeabroad.com.

Hometours International Inc., offers short and long-term villa and apartment rentals in Portugal, Spain, Israel, Britain, France, and Switzerland. 800-367-4668 or 423-690-8484.

Interhome has nearly 20,000 villas and apartments available in most European cities and claims to be the International leader in Vacation Rentals. 305-940-2299. www.interhome.com.

Lacure has villas and yachts in Jamaica and Barbados available for short-term rental. 275 Spadina Road, Toronto, Ontario, Canada M5R 2V3. 888-4LACURE (452-2873) or 416-968-1095. www.lacure.com. e-mail: info@lacure.com.

Laterooms.com offers discounted rooms at more than 3,500 worldwide hotels and motels, especially Australia, New Zealand, France, Italy, Britain, Spain, India, and the U.S. They also rent villas, inns, chalets, guesthouses, apartments, condos, and resorts. Reservations can be made less than two weeks before arrival. 44 (0) 161 819800. www.Lateroom.com. e-mail: sales@laterooms.com.

Paris Apartments has apartment rentals for Paris and surrounding area. 63 Avenue de La Motle Picquet, Paris, France 75015. 33 1 43 06 78 79. www.locaflat.com.

Parker Company has many weekly rentals on homes in Italy: Tuscany, Umbria, Veneto, Lake Como, the Italian Riveria, Campania, and Sicily. 800-280-2811. www.zparkercompany.com.

Rentvillas.com offers some exceptional deals houses, apartments, and villas in Europe(mainly Italy, France, Spain, Greece, Portugal, and Great Britain. 800-726-6702. www.rentvillas.com.

Vacation Home Rentals Worldwide provides listings for estates, villas, apartments, chateaux, condominiums, private islands, and gourmet barge rentals in the Bahamas, Caribbean, Europe, Mexico, Central and Latin America, and the U.S. 235 Kensington Avenue, Norwood, NJ 07648. 800-633-3284 or 201-767-9393.

Vacation Spot offers rental houses, villas, cabins, condos, B & Bs, and chateaux. See the Bargain section of its Web site for special deals. Best of all, Vacation Spot has photos for almost all of its listings so you can preview the lodging. 877-EXPEDIA or 425-564-7235 (outside U.S.). www.vacationspot.com.

VillaNet (formerly Rent-A-Home International Inc.) offers rentals in the U.S., including Hawaii, as well as Europe (especially Italy), Australia, Canada, Caribbean, and Mexico. 7200 34th Avenue, Seattle, WA 98117. 800-964-1891 or 206-417-1832. www.rentavilla.com.

Villas and Apartments Abroad Ltd. provides villas, chateaux, apartments, and farmhouses in Morocco, Portugal, Spain, France, and Italy. 800-433-3020 or 212-759-1025.

Villas International Ltd. has villas, cottages, chateaux, apartments, and castles for rent in western Europe, Turkey, Mexico, and the Caribbean. 605 Market Street, San Francisco, CA 94105. 800-221-2260 or 415-281-0910.

Virtualcities.Com offers many properties in U.S., Canada, Mexico, Australia, and Europe, including houses, B & Bs, inns, and small hotels. Short and long-term rentals available. 800-809-7111 or 972-720-8779. www.virtualcities.com

Unusual Villas And Island Rentals offers Caribbean listings. 101 Tempsford Lane Penta, Richmond, VA 23226. 804-288-2823. www.unusualvillarentals.com.

West Indies Management Company has 1-2 week villa rentals in the Caribbean and south of France. P.O. Box 1461, Newport, RI 02840. 401-849-8012. www.well.com/~~wimco.

TIP: Want to stay on a private island? Garden Cay is a seven-mile island in the Bahamas. The vacation fee includes a secluded beach house, two guest cottages, wraparound decks, and a rooftop Jacuzzi. 812-386-6155. www.gardencay.com.

Or, stay in a lovely English cottage and pay significantly less than you would for a hotel room by utilizing self-catering accommodations in Great Britain. All are inspected and rated by the English Tourist Board so you are assured that lodging will be want you expect. Prices range from $250-$1,000, with most available for less than $500. To get a comprehensive listing of these cottages, read *Self Catering Holiday Homes*, available from Elstead Maps, P.O. Box 52, Elstead, Godalming, Surrey GU8 6JJ, England. www.elstead.co.uk.

Also, consider using Britain's Landmark Trust to rent very affordable historic cottages, farmhouses, and apartments in castles. 802-254-6868. www.landmarktrust.co.uk

◆   ◆   ◆

Homestays

This is a type of travel for people seeking something different. Participants are hosted by someone who takes the "traveler(s) under his or her wings." Exactly what the host provides varies significantly according to the particular program and what the host(s) and participant(s) arrange among themselves. This is a loose arrangement; the host and traveler have great flexibility to make up an itinerary that suits them.

American-International Homestays (AIH) offers the opportunity to stay in the home or apartment of a host. This is a chance for a more interactive experience than a general sightseeing tour provides. Participants are met upon arrival (and escorted to their departure airport or train station). Itinerary is set by participant and host. Typically, the host provides breakfast and dinner, plays tour guide for roughly four hours a day, interprets local language and culture, and provides a private bedroom in a single-family apartment or house. A local AIH representative will also be available in each city for assistance.
Single accommodations can be arranged, as well as smoking or non-smoking preferences. Local transportation, restaurant meals, and entrance fees are not included. Special programs include Customized Group Trip, Customized Individual Trip, Bed & Breakfast Accommodations, Long-Term Trip/Apartment Rental, Extra Weeks Beyond Scheduled Trip, Single Accommodations, Single Hotel Accommodations, and Special Language Programs. The organization has an extensive list of references, including the Columbia Business School, Better Business Bureau, and former travelers. The paperwork AIH sends to you fully explains procedure and policy. P.O. Box 1754, Nederland, CO 80466. 800-876-2048 or 303-258-3234. e-mail: ash@igc.apc.org. www.2ihttravel.com.

Cultural Homestay International (CHI), established 1980, is a nonprofit organization for exchange students. CHI also offers Outbound Programs that are for travelers "looking for a more profound and intimate experience of another country than you receive from the window of a tour bus, there is no better way..." 104 Butterfield Road, San Anselmo, CA 94960. 800-395-2776 or 415-459-5397. www.chinet.org. In Canada: 546 E. St. James, North Vancouver BC V7N 1L5 Canada. 800-463-1061 or 604-983-0950.

Servas offers short-term homestays (2-3 nights) in 80 countries. 11 John Street, Room 505, New York, NY 10038. 212-267-0252. www.usservas.org.

World Homestay Network Center is a membership organization that was founded in 1997 to introduce guests to qualified hosts. It offers worldwide placements and membership benefits include optional home swapping, directory with photos of all listings of host homes, and no annual placement fees or dues. www.whnc.org. e-mail: homestay@whnc.org.

◆　　　◆　　　◆

Helpful Resources

Camping and RVing

AAA Campbooks are available for members of AAA.

Beyond the National Parks (Smithsonian Institution Press), a 400-page guide describes lodging and food around America's parks. 800-782-4612.

Go Camping America--800-47-SUNNY or 888-RVING to request free camping and RV vacation planners.

Guide to Free Campgrounds by Don Wright and published by Cottage Publications, is a comprehensive directory of 6,300 free U.S. campgrounds.

Living Aboard Your RV, Great Eastern RV Trips, Cooking Aboard Your RV, and other RV-related titles, are written and self-published by Gordon and Janet Groene. The couple lived full-time in an RV for a decade. www.gordonandjanetgroene.com.

The National Park's Camping Guide (Publication #024-005-01028-9) is a very useful resource. Government Printing Office, Washington, DC 20402.

Official Guide to Christian Camps and Conference Centers is published by Christian Camping International.

Official National Park Service Map & Guide covers 365 park sites and monuments and is provided by the National Park Society. 888-GO-PARKS. www.nationalparks.org.

Rand McNally's Campground and Trailer Park Guide is published by Rand McNally & Company.

For a **free video and list of RV dealers and campgrounds**, call 888-Go-RVing or log onto www.GoRVing.com

Renting Affordable Villas, Castles, Inns, Houses, Condos, and Apartments

America's Favorite Inns, B & Bs, & Small Hotels, Sandra W. Soule. Published by St. Martin's Press.

Campus Lodgings Guide lists 597 colleges and universities (including 94 available year-round) that often charge less than $20 to rent dorm rooms in Europe and the United States. The guide also lists home-exchange programs, hostels, B & Bs, budget motels, and more. Published by B & J Publications. 714-525-6683. www.amazon.com.

Educators' Value Travel is an organization that arranges cheap lodging worldwide for teachers by utilizing other teachers' homes. Typical cost is $32 for two people. Membership fee and small one-time joining fee. 800-956-4822. www.educatorstravel.com.

Europe's Wonderful Little Hotels And Inns by Hilary Rubenstein and Carolina Raphel. Published by St. Martin's Press. This guide includes 1,000+ places to stay in 17 European countries.

Guide To Vacation Rentals In Europe includes listings and rental agencies. Published by Globe Pequot Press.

Hideaways International offers home rentals, discounts on car rentals, resorts, boutique hotels, condos, yacht-like cruises, and low airfares. Membership includes a semi-annual guide and quarterly newsletters that include worldwide listings with accompanying photos and detailed descriptions. Money-back guarantee if requested within 60 days, if not satisfied. 767 Islington Street, Portsmouth,

NH 03801. 800-843-4433. Within NH or outside U.S. and Canada: 603-430-4433. www.hideaways.com. e-mail: info@hideaways.com.

◆　　◆　　◆

Chapter Seven--50 Ways To Travel Free Or Get Paid To Travel

Chapter Seven--50 Ways To Travel Free Or Get Paid To Travel

*In God's wildness lies the hope of the world--
the great fresh unblighted, undeemed wilderness.*
John Muir, 1890, Alaska Fragment

How Almost Anyone Can Write Off A Vacation As A Tax Deduction

In addition to tax write-offs, there are ways to earn money from your travels to further reduce expenses—even make a substantial profit. Talk to an accountant to learn which expenses are tax deductible. Read Internal Revenue Service Publications #535 and #463. These free booklets are available at your local IRS office or may be requested online or over the telephone. 703-321-8020. www.irs.ustreas.gov or www.irs.gov. How much business is conducted and whether it's in the States or overseas, are the primary factors concerning how much of a trip can be deducted.

For example, some costs may be subtracted for attending conventions, seminars, or similar meetings held on cruise ships. However, you must establish that the meeting is directly related to your trade or business. All ships that sail are considered cruise ships. If you use your own vehicle or lease a car when traveling on business, the IRS allows a mileage deduction. Additionally, a significant amount of business-related entertainment and meal expenses (including taxes and tips) are deductible. As a general rule, accommodations and transportation may be completely written off by business travelers. A trip that's categorized as "primarily vacation" cannot be written off, but if it's "primarily business," all of your trip *may* be tax deductible.

If the trip was mostly business but there was some personal time or vacation involved, the trip is only partially tax deductible. However, there are loopholes. If you arrive on Saturday for business Monday because a Saturday night stayover made the flight cheaper, then the IRS considers Saturday and Sunday as part of your business trip. Therefore, costs incurred on those days are fully deductible. If attending a meeting on a Friday and again on the following Monday, the IRS allows the entire weekend to be considered business-related, making it a 100 percent tax write-off. Expenses incurred by a spouse and children are never deductible, except cabs, rental cars, and accommodations that you would use whether they were with you or not. If in doubt, check with an IRS agent or an accountant. What is paid to an accountant is a business expense and can be a tax write-off. Expenses cannot be deducted if you use a 1040EZ form.

1. Do anything business-related. Set up a meeting with a prospective client. Look at land for potential business expansion. Make sales leads by stopping in at a business and introducing yourself. I know a Web site designer who made some business contacts while on a vacation in England. Not only was he able to write off part of his travel expenses, he landed an account that requires quarterly business trips to London. If you own a restaurant, take the manager of a successful restaurant where you are visiting out for dinner and see if you can get ideas on how to make your restaurant more successful. Discuss the feasibility of opening another restaurant, adding a patio and music platform to your establishment, or talk about diversifying your menu by adding ethnic items to it. You get the idea. While you won't be able to write off all of the trip under current tax laws, you can get credit for a significant portion.

2. Attend a trade show, workshop, seminar, or conference. Many trade associations offer conventions, usually at resort areas, where members can network at cocktail parties or banquets and attend as many seminars as they like. Everyone, from tire manufacturer sale reps to dental hygienists,

can find trade shows, workshops, seminars, or conferences. Since these are business trips, expenses are considered business-related.

Typically, you don't even have to belong to the trade association to attend, just so long as you are affiliated with the industry. However, nonmembers will pay a higher fare than members.

3. Put together a business trip. I know a gentleman who owns a printing company and every year he takes his employees on a cruise. Not only is this great for morale, but he gets to travel free by bringing a group *and* he gets to write-off most of the trip as a business expense. A friend told me about a sales rep who really wanted to go to North Carolina's exclusive Bald Head Island but didn't want to pay the steep prices. He shrewdly arranged a sales meeting there so that he could deduct many of the expenses from his taxes.

4. A trip is business-related if you are collecting images for your stock photography portfolio. Photographic images are bought by stock photography agencies, which sell them to magazines, advertising agencies, etc., either for one-time use or serial usage. The biggest sales of stock photography are travel-related images. Most of the pictures you see in travel brochures and magazines came from stock photography files. *Writer's Market* and *Photographer's Market* are good references for finding publications and agencies looking for images. They are available at most major bookstores and libraries.

5. Write off a trip as a charitable deduction by volunteering. Participants get to make a difference, see and learn about a new place and culture, *and* get tax credit for it. Although the experiences may cost about the same as general sightseeing or adventure trips, these opportunities are often partially tax deductible, which make them less expensive than a normal vacation. Plus, these types of vacations permit participants a chance to play a more interactive role and have experiences the average tourist will never know, as well as knowing that they did something during their vacation that made a difference. Contact nonprofit organization, **Service Civil International** (est. 1920), for a free directory filled with volunteer projects available in more than 50 countries. Projects last two or four weeks. Ask for the *International Workcamp Directory*. 206-545-6585. www.sci-ivs.org. *Volunteer Vacations* is another good resource. Bill McMillon (Chicago Review Press). The Web site www. idealist.org has links to many worldwide agencies and reports from former volunteers. Here is a list of some excellent charitable organizations:

American Hiking Society is a nonprofit organization that was established to preserve our country's hiking trails. One and two-week volunteer vacations are extended for approximately $60pp–$75pp. Jobs all take place in national parks and are usually outdoors so participants can enjoy the scenery. 301-565-6704. www.americanhiking.org.

Participate in **Archaeological Digs** throughout Israel and receive either free room and board or small daily wages. A complete annual listing of Israeli digs is released in the Jan./Feb. issue of Biblical Archaeology Review (BAR), which can be purchased. 800-221-4644. www.mfa.gov.il/mfa/go.asp?mfah00wk0.

Archaeological Institute Of America is "dedicated to the support of archaeological research and publication and to the protection of the world's cultural heritage for more than a century." A nonprofit and educational organization chartered by the U.S. Congress, it is the oldest (est. 1879) and largest archaeological organization in North America, with more than 11,000 members around the world. It has many ongoing projects seeking volunteers. Boston University, 656 Beacon Street, Fourth Floor, Boston, MA 02215. 617-353-9361. www.archaeological.org. e-mail: aia@bu.edu.

Crow Canyon Archaeological Center is "dedicated to long-term archaeological research on the ancestral Pueblo Indian occupation of the Mesa Verde region." But, their programs vary and extend to many worldwide locations, such as their Family Excavation Program, Human Origins in East Africa: A Unique Experience with the Leakeys, and Mountain Biking to Ancient Ruins. Early bird discounts and annual service programs offered. Registration Manager, Crow Canyon Archaeological Center, 23390 Road K, Cortez, CO 81321. 800-422-8975 or 970-565-8975. www.crowcanyon.org.

Earthwatch is a terrific nonprofit organization that offers numerous U.S. and worldwide projects in which volunteers can make a difference tracking black rhinos, preserving Russian folklore, etc. Accommodations range from camping, hotels, field stations, hostels, boats, houses, lodges, bed and breakfast inns, ranch houses, cottages, apartments, and mansions, depending on the project. P.O. Box 9104, Watertown, MA 02471-9104. 800-776-0188 or 617-926-8200. www.earthwatch.org. e-mail: info@earthwatch.org

Explorations In Travel offers adventure tours and volunteering opportunities around the world. See Chapter Two for more information regarding volunteer vacations. 1922 River Road, Guilford, VT 05301. 802-257-0152. www.exploretravel.com. e-mail: women@exploretravel.com.

Folkways Institute is a "nonprofit school without walls for lifelong learning." It offers Global Study Projects, Overseas Volunteer Service Projects, as well as various Senior Studies Programs of cultural exploration, natural history, wildlife, performing arts, art, architecture, folk arts, and history. There are two types of programs, ranging from 7–28 days. One is called Open Projects and is for anyone aged 21 or over. The other program, ElderFolk, requires participants to be at least 55 and active. Both programs vary in length and seasons, geographic location, and activity focus. 14600 SE Aldridge Road, Portland, OR 97236. 800-225-4666 or 503-658-6600. www.folkwaysinstitute.org. e-mail: folkwaysdc@aol.com.

Global Volunteers was founded in 1984 as a private, nonprofit U.S. corporation with the "goal of helping to establish a foundation for peace through mutual international understanding." It has teaching, agricultural, and construction programs in the U.S. and around the world, lasting one to three weeks in duration. Airfare and program are tax-deductible for U.S. taxpayers. 375 E. Little Canada Road, St. Paul, MN 55117-1628. 800-487-1074 or 651-407-6100. www.globalvolunteers.org. e-mail: email@globalvlntrs.org.

Habitat For Humanity can provide volunteers with working vacations. You'll be sent to the project of your choice in the U.S. or other parts of the world. Volunteers build homes for needy families, in return they receive free room and board. 121 Habitat Street, Americus, Georgia 31709. 229-924-6935. www.habitat.org.

Health Volunteers Overseas is for health-care providers who wish to teach other health-care providers in third world countries. The duration is typically one month and volunteers pay their own airfare and lodging. P.O. Box 65157, Washington, DC 20035-5157. 202-296-0928. e-mail: hvo@aol.com.

International Workcamps brings 10-20 volunteers, from different countries, together for 2–4 weeks. During that time you work on environmental or community service projects in many countries such as Morocco, the Netherlands, Tunisia, Turkey, and the Czech Republic. Anyone over the age of 18 who is "open-minded, flexible, and self-motivated" is invited to participate. Volunteers pay their own travel expenses and a placement fee per project, but room and board is provided. CIEE, 205 E. 42nd Street, New York, NY 10017. 212-661-6464. www.ciee.org or www.counciltravel.org.

Experience life on an **Israeli Kibbutz,** which is a collective farm. This adventure involves a mix of work and play. Work is six days a week from 6 a.m. to 2 p.m., and ranges from waiting tables in a kibbutz guesthouse on the shores of the Sea of Galilee to working in a citrus orchard at Sde Nehemia. Participants pay their own airfare and a registration fee, but receive free room and board, as well as a small stipend. All ages over 18 are welcome. Kibbutz Program Center, U.S.. 800-247-7852. e-mail: kibbutzdsk@aol.com.

National Trust Working Holidays offers 400+ working holidays throughout Britain. Sample projects, which typically last one week, include wildlife surveys and conservation work. Six month projects available. Meals and dorm-style accommodations are provided. Send five International Reply Coupons (ask any postal clerk) to National Trust Volunteers Office, 33 Sheep Street, Cirencester, Glos. FL7 1RQ, Scotland. (44-1285) 644-727 or (44-20) 8315 1111 or 020 7222 9251 or 0870 458 4000. www.nationaltrust.org.uk.

The **Oceanic Society** offers travelers the chance to become a part of a legitimate scientific research team by observing and recording data. The society has several different expeditions, including Antarctica. No research experience is necessary. Trip fees go toward the cost of the field work. Participants will receive a pre trip research plan and on-site training. Oceanic Society Expeditions, Fort Mason Center, Building E, San Francisco, CA 94123-1394. 800-326-7491. www.oceanic-society.org.

The **Peace Corps** currently has many different programs in 91 countries with 6,419 volunteers (the oldest participant is 76). Married couples are placed together. Room and board, as well as a small salary is provided in return for your 27-month commitment. Room P-301, Washington, DC 20526. 800-424-8580. www.peacecorps.gov.

Sierra Club has many worthwhile service trips. 85 Second Street, Second floor, San Francisco, CA 94105. 415-977-5522. www.sierraclub.org/outings.

United Children's Fund needs teachers and teaching assistants (no experience required), clinic workers, builders, administrative aid, and many, many other positions. The cost is $820 (tax deductible) for one week and this includes all expenses except airfare. The work day ends at 4 p.m. and you are off on weekends. P.O. Box 20341, Boulder, Colorado 80308-3341. 303-674-2176. www.unchildren.org.

University Research Expeditions Program (UREP) offers projects through the University of California by partnering interested persons with school scientists on tax-deductible research expeditions. University of California, One Shields Avenue, Davis, CA 95616. 530-757-3529. www.urep.ucdavis.edu.

Visions In Action, established in 1989, is a grassroots organization that places participants in Africa and Mexico for six-month to one-year assignments, including one month orientation and language immersion program. Placements include human rights, youth, education, health, refugee relief, environment, community development, housing, and more.

In addition to volunteering opportunities, 15 to 40-hour week internships are available in public relations, newsletter writing, fundraising, special projects, and more. 2710 Ontario Road, Washington, DC 20009. 202-625-7402. www.igc.org/visions. e-mail: visions@igc.org.

Volunteers For Peace create and repair homes in the U.S. and abroad. Projects last 2–3 weeks with food and lodging included. Cost is $175. 43 Tiffany Road, Belmont, VT 05730. 802-259-2759. e-mail: vfp@vfp.org.

6. Check out travel sections of newspapers and the classified ads in travel publications for volunteering opportunities and other special travel arrangements. *Alternative Travel Directory* is a compilation of alternative travel resources and programs. The publication has more than 2,000 listings of specialty travel adventures, vacation language study programs, volunteer opportunities, and much more. It discusses travel for seniors, families, independent travelers, and students. Transitions Publishing. 800-293-0373. www.transabroad.com.

Transitions also produces an electronic travel newsletter, *TA News*, which discusses overseas educational programs and opportunities. To subscribe, e-mail request to: Listserv@Peach.Ease.Lsoft .Com, Transitions also publishes a magazine, *Transitions Abroad*, that Transitions describes as "The Guide to Learning, Living, and Working Abroad" and is for "travelers who want practical information on affordable alternatives to mass tourism...readers are experienced travelers who are looking for economical ways to work, study, or travel independently abroad. It offers information ranging from teaching English in Asia to consulting in Africa. The publication is for "the kind of people who have always dreamed of traveling by buffalo to study the remote hill tribes in Vietnam, preserving the environment in Antarctica, or for those who might want to take a beginner course in hat-making in England." Transitions Abroad, P.O. Box 1300, Amherst, MA 01004-1300. 800-293-0373 or 413-256-3414. www.transabroad.com.

7. There are alternatives to traditional charitable programs. Your place of work may be involved with or sponsor worthwhile volunteering opportunities. Ask your boss or contact company headquarters to find out if there's a way for you to "volunteer and vacation." Even if you don't work for a big corporation, your company may have discretionary income and be willing to contribute a few hundred dollars toward a philanthropic vacation. Or, you may be able to get co-workers, family, and friends to contribute.

You cannot write off a trip that others funded. You can deduct some expenses that you paid out-of-pocket. Be sure to ask an accountant or read the IRS's exemption policies.

◆　　◆　　◆

How Your Vacation Can Earn You $$$

8. Write an article or present a photo essay about your trip for a newspaper or magazine. Depending on the publication, you can earn up to several thousand dollars. Subsequently, you can write-off part of the expense of the trip. Your images don't have to look as good as *National Geographic's*. They need to be sharp (meaning in focus), and should tell a story, such as what it's like to live along the Amazon River or your interpretation of the London Underground. You are most likely to sell your work if you present a different perspective, rather than a general travel piece. "On Tuesday, we took our first walk into the rain forest and found it to be very interesting experience...."

Instead, give the reader (and editor) something unexpected and something compelling, such as, "I thought I was going to die when we took our first trek into the Brazilian rain forest. Dozens of unidentifiable insects collected on tree leaves and swarmed about in the air. It seemed like everywhere we tried to step, something was scurrying across our path. As I was trying to take it all in, our guide shouted 'Run! Fire ants!' Our small group half-jogged, half-ran until...." You get the idea. *Writer's*

Market and *Photographer's Market* are good references that list publications, including contact information and submission guidelines. Both books, which are updated annually, are available at most major bookstores and libraries. The Web sites, www.travelwriters.com and www.itravelsyndicate.com provide useful information and valuable links.

I advise novices to start with local newspapers and regional magazines. Get some credits to your name before tackling more circulated publications. You may submit the same article or photos to other regional newspapers or magazines to make more money. Just check with the editor at the publication where you sold it initially about their policies. Typically, if it's not in the same readership area, the publication will have no problem with you're-selling it. Also, foreign publications tend to be better resources for new freelancers than American publications. British magazine *Adventure Travel* (P.O. Box 6254, Alcester Warles, B49 6PF UK), and Canadian magazine *Explore* (54 St. Patrick Street, Toronto, ON M5T 1V1 Canada) are a couple of good publications that pay fairly well.

9. Enter your best travel photos in contests and win great prizes or cold, hard cash. www.travelphotocontests.com, onlinephotocontest.com, or www.phototrust.com. These Web sites all have links to other contests and useful resources.

10. Put together an armchair traveler presentation and show it to schools or civic organizations. Most schools, civic groups, and nursing homes have funds to pay speakers and entertainers. Sometimes the group can only pay a small sum to cover expenses, but many have discretionary funds that pay a few hundred dollars. Two or three speaking engagements can add up to several hundred dollars. Cultural centers, community theaters or centers, and specialty stores such as luggage vendors, outdoor provisions stores, and clothing gear outlets often present travelogues and will pay for a good presentation. An informative discussion and slide show or video will suffice.

11. Local and regional writers groups have "speakers on call." These are individuals who are interested in speaking to area organizations. Check the Community Organizations Directory at the local library to obtain the names and addresses of these groups and then call and have your name added to their speaker roster. Again, fees paid range from expenses only to a few hundred dollars.

12. Teach a travel class at the community college, such as Everything You Must Know Before Going to Italy, or How to Pack for any Trip Using One Small Suitcase and a tiny Carry-on Bag, or Twenty-five Fun Family Adventures. Most community colleges offer travel classes as part of their continuing education special interest program. While you don't have to have an advanced degree to teach continuing education courses, you should be an authority on the subject or have some credentials to support why you are qualified.

13. If you are an artist or photographer, get the local artist co-op to display your work. There's no fee for your work to be exhibited, but the co-op receives a commission on every item that is sold. The same holds true for galleries, museums, and cultural centers. Also, most communities have local restaurants or merchants that are willing and eager to showcase local talent. For example, the restaurant behind my house has decorated its entire interior by displaying paintings created by local artists. The amount the artist would like to receive for the piece (this is almost always negotiable), as well as contact information, is put on a card that is hung beside each painting. Libraries often have space they donate to local artists. Additionally, most places have some sort of annual crafts fair or arts festival, which is a great way to sell your work. A booth has to be rented, but the cost is usually nominal. You can even opt to split the cost of the booth by sharing it with another artist.

14. Make money by turning your artwork or photos into postcards, posters, notecards, tee-shirts, etc. Several years ago I started a stationery company by having a dozen of my most marketable images printed onto folded notecards. My first client was a local copy shop that had a small stationery section. I worked out a deal with the owner; he got a commission for each card sold. Every month I restocked the cards and collected my part of the money. The extra income I made from this arrangement gave me the incentive and confidence to wholesale the cards to other shops, museum

stores, and stationery vendors. Travel to obtain images, attend sales meetings ar
business expenses that I deducted on my taxes.

◆   ◆   ◆

How To Travel Free

15. Stay in religious institutions for free (well, almost). Convents and churches on
safe, no-frills rooms in many cities worldwide for as little as $5 a night. Check with tourist boards
churches. For example, Seventh Day Adventists allow visitors to stay in their school dorms for $10 a
night, on average. This depends on availability and preference is usually given to those of the same
denomination. In Spain, there are over 70 monasteries and convents that take in travelers. For a free
list, contact the office of tourism where you'll be traveling. See Chapter Three--Helpful Resources for
additional tourism information.

16. Attend a timeshare meeting and you may receive a free vacation. This is a common tactic of
timeshare companies. "Come to a meeting or visit our resort and stay free for a weekend if you agree
to attend a timeshare meeting." Usually, additional incentives are offered, such as restaurant gift
certificates, sightseeing tours, one free spa service, or day of golf including green fees. There are a few
qualifying restrictions, such as you must be married and earn a certain income. That information
should be disclosed in the advertisement or when you call to RSVP. If you're the type that succumbs
easily to sales reps, don't go!

17. Another option is to buy a timeshare and trade it for other vacation options. While it's not
free initially and there are some annual administrative/maintenance fees, it's very cheap in the long
run. The key to timeshare is to have a desirable location so as to get the best trade-offs. For more
information, check out *TimeSharing Today*, an independent magazine that reviews resorts in its
investigative reports and articles, and has hundreds of classified ads. 26A Franklin, Tenafly, NJ 07670.
888-463-7427. www.tstoday.com.

Timeshare originated in Europe during the latter part of the 1960s and hit the U.S. in the early
1970s. Since participants become fractional owners, the concept is especially appreciated by people
who cannot afford a second home. It's now the "hottest segment of the resort industry," according to
Gregory Cory, senior vice president of Economics Research Associates. With total worldwide
timeshare sales exceeding $6 billion, it would be hard to argue this statement. Many upscale resorts,
such as Four Seasons, Hyatt, and Ritz-Carlton, now operate timeshare resorts. Some of the biggest
names include Disney Vacation Club (800-500-3990, www.disneyvacationclub.com), Marriott
Vacation Club International (800-845-5279, www.vacationclub.com), and Trendwest Resorts (800-
722-3487, www.trendwestresorts.com). These are all members of the American Resort Development
Association(ARDA), which monitors the industry. The concept is simple: use your time at the resort in
which you are a partial owner, or, swap your time and vacation at another resort. The world's largest
re-seller of timeshares is Era Stroman (800-745-4410, www.stroman.com).

18. Rent a timeshare for next to nothing. Sometimes timeshare owners are unable to use their
time and rent them out dirt cheap to recoup some money. Some companies that buy, sell, and rent
timeshares include Holiday Group.com (800-704-0307), Century 21 (800-515-4441), and Timeshares
By Owner (800-246-7653, www.timesharesbyowner.com). For more information on renting
timeshares, log on to www.tug2.net or www.timesharing.com

A twist on the timeshare concept is "shared ownership." Individuals who could not otherwise
afford to own an expensive vacation home, may buy shares in one. Developers sell a home to 8–13
owners who share the vacation home. Club Corp. has sold over 1,000 memberships in its Owners Club,
which has luxurious homes in resorts areas, such as Telluride, CO, Hilton Head Island, SC, and Puerto

Mexico. Another perk is that upkeep is taken care of by the management company. The
~ is that majority rules when it comes to making decisions.

I: Two million Americans own time shares at 1,600 U.S. resorts. On average, a one-week, two-
room package costs about $10,000. The timeshare is deeded, so there is no restriction on the
~mber of years the package can be used. The leading U.S. timeshare states are Florida, North
Carolina, South Carolina, California, Colorado, and Hawaii.

19. Barter your services. You'll be amazed at the results. I have a friend who is a videographer.
He found a Web site for a rustic resort in the Tennessee mountains and contacted them to see if they
might be interested in doing a commercial. The owners said they weren't ready to do that, but they did
need some video clips for their Web site. They offered him free room and board in exchange for some
video footage. The owners asked him to come back and shoot in the fall to show how pretty it is in the
mountains when the leaves change colors, so he received another free vacation.

20. Play tour guide, lecturer, or guest speaker, and travel free. I know a wildlife photographer
who got a free trip to Antarctica just for escorting a tour group from the airport to the cruise ship,
giving one talk on wildlife photography, and helping passengers in and out of the inflatable boats that
were used for daily exploration. While this photographer is not "world renown," he has been published
in several magazines. The point being that you need to have some credentials to present to a company
or cruise line to verify why they should choose you.

To obtain credentials, start small. Write or photograph for local newspapers and magazines (for
free in the beginning, if necessary) and present the clippings to companies. Escort a small group
through a local company that offers day excursions or weekend trips (again, for free in the beginning,
if necessary). Give talks to local groups, such as the Rotary Club, Jaycees, and Chamber of Commerce,
and then ask for written references from them.

21. Offer to make a speech at a trade show or conference and your expenses may be paid for
you. No matter what you do for a living, there is at least one annual trade show or conference and you
might be able to receive monetary compensation for making a speech or leading a discussion. Even if
there's not enough money in the budget to pay you, your expenses will be almost always be
reimbursed. Read trade publications and junk-mail, ask co-workers if they know of opportunities, and
get your name added to mailing lists.

22. If you are self-employed, join a couple of pertinent organizations and sign up to be a
speaker or get a scholarship to a conference. Members receive information on workshops, retreats,
conferences, and symposiums. Most organizations have a form that can be submitted by anyone
willing to be a speaker. If you don't see it in the initial paperwork, ask for it. Sometimes, there's
enough budget to pay you, as well as your expenses.

Usually, organizations offer a few scholarships for conference participants. Again, if you don't
see anything about it, be sure to ask. Most Chambers of Commerce have a directory detailing all
community organizations and nonprofit groups, as well as area businesses. They also provide Business
Expos and Networking After Hours programs where members meet other self-employed people and
discover many resources and opportunities available. Additionally, the local library should have a
community organizations directory, which is often accessible online.

23. If you are asked to travel somewhere, ask for money to cover travel expenses. The first time
I was asked to make a speech, I was so flattered that anyone wanted me that it never occurred to me to
ask for compensation. But, I finally wised-up after I gave a few more free speeches and interviews. A
television producer asked me to travel six hours to be interviewed for a special that was going to air
nationally. Although it was good exposure, I declined because he didn't offer me any compensation.
He called me back and offered to pay all my expenses (including two nights at a beautiful inn where

I'd always wanted to stay), plus an interview fee. I use this as an example, but you don't have to be an author or celebrity, just remember it should be worth your while. It's not unreasonable to expect your expenses be paid.

24. Get together family, co-workers, friends, acquaintances (even strangers), and travel free. Tour companies and cruise lines typically offer free or substantial discounts to travelers who bring in groups. Some companies offer discounts if you sign up two or three adults. Most companies require 10 people before they grant free travel. Rounding up groups of 5–9 usually gets a 50 percent discount. Don't be shy about bargaining. For example, explain that you only have five people going on this trip, but you plan to take another trip next year (assuming you do plan to or are at least seriously considering it) and would like it to be with the same company. This should get you a bigger discount or free travel on the next trip.

25. Enter as many contests as possible. Earlier in this section I advised you to enter photography contests, but I am now suggesting you enter other kinds of contests, as well. In fact, you should enter every contest you come across! The more you enter, the better your chances of winning. Somebody has to win and it could very well be you, especially if you are a lucky person. The odds of winning are greater the more effort that is required because fewer people will bother to do what is necessary to enter.

Where do you find good contests? Watch the travel channel. They are always sponsoring some kind of travel-related contest. Scan the newspaper. Read magazines. Look at publications you don't subscribe to the next time you're at the library or sitting in a waiting room. Be on the lookout. Have you heard about the "pudding guy?" When Healthy Choice ran a promotion a couple of years ago exchanging barcodes off their products for free flyer miles, the promotion was well-received, especially by one man who bought $3,140 worth of pudding in order to obtain 1,250,000 flyer miles. HealthyChoice has offered other contests for free flyer miles, including instant-win game pieces off HealthyChoice products. The company has given away more than 65 million miles. www.healthychoice.com.

The *Contest News-Letter* says it is "one of America's most widely read sweepstakes and contest publications...showing people how to win big prizes for over 20 years." They promise no less than 30 sweepstakes and contests per issue, and they have offer a complimentary copy. A recent issue listed sweepstakes that awarded prizes, such as a trip for two to the Hawaiian islands, trip for four to the Grand Canyon, 17-foot runabout boat, two Amtrak North America Rail Passes, vacation for four to Orlando or L.A., and a trip for four to Australia. Contest News-Letter Reader Service, P.O. Box 9234, Dept. P300-PA, Islandia, NY 11722-9234. Another good, low-cost publication is *Sweepstakes Advisor*. It reveals the same kinds of prizes. P.O. Box 561528, Dallas, TX 75356-1528.

Contests can also be found on the Internet: www.totallyfreestuff.com, www.iwon.com (currently one of the Internet's busiest sites), www.Treeloot.com (hides $25,000 daily in a virtual money tree and participants must find it), or http://FreeLotto.com. Each Web site has links to other online contest giveaways. If you don't want to enter all these contests, enroll in www.ezsweep.com and you'll automatically be entered in multiple contests. They offer a free trial membership. It doesn't get any easier! Use the Web sites given in Chapter Eight to find additional sweepstakes and contests possibilities.

Tour operators have random drawing contests for people who take the time to answer the postage-paid questionnaires inserted in catalogs. One of my former students won a 10-day trip to Turkey because she took the time to answer nine questions.

26. Airline frequent flyer and hotel points programs are another way to travel free. If you do much flying, you are probably already enrolled in at least one frequent flyer program. If not, shame on you! Members receive great perks, such as discounted hotel rooms and car rentals, free seat upgrades, priority seating, and unadvertised airfare deals. It used to be that passengers had to fly with the same

airline and the miles expired at the end of the year. Nowadays, airline "marriages" allow mileage points to be credited to one account, despite flying with other airlines. Many major U.S. airlines have become partners with major international carriers, which means miles can be earned and exchanged between airlines. Additionally, most airlines have gotten more generous in their rollover policies for mileage points, which means they don't expire at the end of the year. Some carriers, such as United and America, have recently announced that their frequent flyer miles will never expire, providing a purchase is made once every three years, using their credit card. US Airways and Delta are emphatic that you must fly *their* airline, not a partner airline, to keep your miles from expiring. Be sure you understand the rules of a program before signing up.

These airlines offer free miles to people who use their credit cards to make purchases. At time of publication, it was one mile for every dollar spent.

Alaska Airlines
(800-552-7302)

American Airlines
(800-950-5114)

British Airways
(800-859-3758)

Continental Airlines
(800-377-0601)

Delta Airlines
(800-SKYMILE/323-2323)

Northwest Airlines
(800-360-2900)

Southwest Airlines
(800-792-8472)

United Airlines
(800-537-7783)

US Airways
(800-341-7568)

Beware of programs that offer enrollment bonuses but do not dispense them until a credit card purchase is made or a card is renewed. Some programs cut off heavy spenders with annual caps of 50,000 or a monthly limit of 10,000 miles. Northwest claims it does not restrict mileage, but participants earn only a half mile for every dollar spent after reaching 50,000 miles.

Capital One Platinum Visa allows points/miles to be used on *any* airline. Capital One offers one point/mile per dollar spent and a very reasonable mileage redemption total—18,000 points/miles. (most programs require 40,000). The miles must be used within five years. 800-553-2194. www.milesone.com. American Express Membership Rewards program is unique because accumulated miles never expire and can be transferred to many airlines, several hotel programs, or redeemed for gift certificates at top retailers. Balances must be paid in full every month. 800-942-2639. Diners Club also offers a rewards program. The miles can be cashed in with any airline and are good on most major hotel chains and car rental agencies. However, Diners Club is not accepted everywhere. Participants in the WebMiles Program receive free miles upon joining, plus opportunities to earn more miles through referrals. One mile is earned for every dollar spent on the WebMiles MasterCard. No blackout dates or Saturday stay required. Redemption may occur with just 8,000 miles, which entitles the traveler to $100 off the airline ticket or get a free ticket with 25,000 miles. www.webmiles.com. Several cruise lines and credit card companies, such as Carnival Cruise Lines and iCruise.com Visa, now offer points (usually $1 = one point) that are good toward cruise category upgrades, shipboard credits, and free cruises.

An important thing to remember, whether you use an airline credit card or a bank-issued credit card, is that you don't want to make charges you can't pay off in an attempt to obtain points/miles. It's

138

not free travel if you are paying high interest rates every month to obtain it! If possible, pay off the charges at the end of the month. Also, weigh the pros and cons. Will you get enough points/miles to justify the annual cardholder fee?

How do you know if you're getting a good deal? When should you cash in your miles? For most of us, this shouldn't be too hard to figure out, but for those using multiple credit cards and frequent flyer programs, it can be hard to know when it is best to cash in miles. One option is to pay a small fee and use a bookkeeper/tracking service, such as MaxMiles (www.maxmiles.com). This site will track your frequent flyer miles and related programs once account numbers are entered. You'll receive e-mailers as often as requested and notification of bonus miles opportunities. You still need to double-check that miles are getting properly credited by checking your statement after each flight.

Or, do the math yourself. A good rule of thumb is to get at least a penny a mile—unless your miles are about to expire. For example, to cash in 25,000 miles, the ticket value should be at least $250. *Money* magazine once provided a good rate chart:

<u>Example</u>

1. Estimate the dollar value of the reward.	$400
2. Multiply line 1. by 100	40,000
3. Enter miles needed to earn reward.	25,000
4. Divide line 2 by line 3 to see how many cents you're getting per mile.	1.6

Milesandpoints.com is another way members can easily keep track of points and miles and earn miles through promotions offered by airlines, hotels, credit cards, car rental agencies, and retail merchants (shopping). *Consumer Reports Travel Newsletter* annually evaluates the country's most popular travel cards. To obtain it, send $5 and a request for this year's review issue of travel cards. CRTL, 101 Truman Avenue, Yonkers, New York 10703-1057. 800-234-1970.

Participation in some programs such as American Express Membership Rewards and Marriott rewards can result in free cruises because they have partnered with many cruise lines. For 100,000 points, participants can sail free to many destinations, such as the Caribbean, Greek Isles, Alaska, and Europe. Hilton HHonors program awards both hotel points and airline miles from the same visit. Hampton Inn and Doubletree Resort also participate. For more information, see hotels in Chapter Six.

For people looking to cash in miles for greenbacks, Milepoint.com is the only program that permits frequent flyer miles to be redeemed for online currency at places like SkyMall and Amazon.com. Most major airlines, such as Delta, US Airways, and Northwest, are part of this program. Travelers looking to *buy* miles will also find Miles4Sale.com a useful resource. The miles are good on several airlines, including America West, Continental, and Delta. They are sold as "gift baskets" but can be used by the purchaser by naming yourself as beneficiary. Minimum purchase is 500 miles and you, or the lucky recipient, have one year to redeem miles. Some airlines, such as Continental and Delta, also sell miles so be sure to check around to find the best deal. Webflyer offers a free electronic newsletter that reveals unusual ways to obtain miles/points and latest promotions. www.webflyer.com. e-mail: Mileslink@webflyer.com

◆ FYI: In 1998, 2.5 trillion frequent flyer miles were disbursed and 15 million free tickets were issued. Sadly, 75 billion miles (enough for 1.9 million trips to Europe) expired last year, according to *InsideFlyer.*

27. Telephone companies, mortgage companies, and realty agencies now offer points programs. MCI awards free points/miles on all long distance phone calls. MCI is one of the best ways to earn free miles/points because they don't require a fee-based credit card, minimum balance, or other such stipulations. MCI gives customers five miles for every dollar spent. They issue free miles just for enrolling. Sprint (800-308-2011) has a similar deal with another airline. MCI recently added MCI WorldCom Internet service (800-359-3733), which means they now offer Internet access for a monthly service, and 100 free miles every month, plus bonus enrollment miles. So does Sprint. Both Sprint and MCI offer five miles for every dollar spent on their calling cards *and* miles for choosing their wireless phone service. With these kinds of deals, it doesn't take long to get a free ticket. The best way to find out about these things is by carefully reviewing your billing statements and enclosures. If you don't see information on mileage programs, be sure to inquire.

Some airlines offer miles for buying a car from a participating dealer, such as United (800-733-2062). The carrier offers 10,000 miles for doing this and American Airlines has a Buy to Fly Program (800-882-8880).

Many mortgage companies and realty agencies offer frequent-flyer miles when you buy a house, sell a house, or refinance a mortgage. A couple of big companies that offer free miles are Countrywide Home Loans (800-837-3080, www.countrywide.com) and North American Mortgage Company (800-500-6262).

28. Shop on the Internet and receive free travel. Many companies offer miles just for buying products over the Internet. The home page will inform consumers if the company participates in a mileage program. One on-line service, Clickrewards (www.clickrewards.com) awards one mile (good for travel on eight airlines) for every dollar spent. Participants include Gap Online, Barnesandnoble.com, and the Disney Store. Consumers can earn free tickets or miles by booking travel online. Many airlines award free miles to those who buy a ticket online. Again, the home page of the Web site will let you know what the company offers.

29. Find out what your employer offers. Faculty and staff at most universities are often entitled to discounted tickets to area events and attractions, such as theme parks. Many big companies arrange discounted entertainment and travel packages for their employees. Government employees are often privy to discounted rates and special deals. If your company uses a travel agency to book corporate travel, ask the agent to put together a couple different budget-oriented vacation packages and cruises for employees. If your employer doesn't offer anything, initiate something. Work out an employee discount to a popular regional attraction, resort, or spa.

If you become a referral or outside travel agent (see No. 35), be sure to put up a notice at work to let everyone know that you can help them with their travel needs. Make everyone aware of especially good deals you learn about. Don't be overly aggressive, just let people know that if they're interested, you will be glad to help them with travel arrangements.

30. Find out about resident discounts. Most states offer reduced rates to state attractions for residents. For example, Florida residents receive low rates to DisneyWorld, California residents receive substantial savings to Disney's California Adventure in Anaheim, and Universal Studios Hollywood gives discounts to residents of Southern California. State-run attractions such as zoos, science centers, and history museums often extend free admission to residents at certain times, such as the first Wednesday of the month. Most times, you will be asked to show a valid driver's license.

Many historic sites, museums, sporting events, shows, and attractions are free to the public year-round or through promotional programs, such as free admission on a certain day for "first timers" or to a particular game for fan appreciation night. Free tickets can be found in the newspaper or at area fast-food restaurants and other merchants.

Value-added promotions are becoming increasingly popular: visitors pay admission to one attraction and receive a "bonus" of free admission the next day to that same attraction or to another area attraction.

31. Numerous online travel packages are auctioned off every week. Although it is not free, it's a way to travel cheap. The bids start as low as $9 for cruises, hotel packages, tours, and airfares. The bids are made in $10 increments and the packages are fully explained, including bid cut-off times and dates.

SkyAuction (www.skyauction.com) is an online auction company that offers airline tickets, hotels, car rentals, and vacation packages. The bids start at $1 and increase in $5 increments. Bid1travel.com is also an online auction company and bids also start at $1. Egghead.com and Gavel.com are a couple more online auction companies that offer various vacation packages. Sometimes the final bids turn out to be as much as special fares, or even normally published fares. Make sure you think it is a good deal, don't just get caught up in a bidding "war." Chapter Eight lists more Internet sites that offer special deals.

Note: Nearly 50 percent of all online frauds occur through online auctions, according to the Federal Trade Commission(FTC). Check out their Web site at www.ftc.gov/bcp/conline/pubs /online/auctions.htm and www.scambusters.org for tips on how to avoid becoming one of these statistics.

32. If you're willing to be a caretaker, you can stay free at lodges, resorts, estates, and farms around the world. For a free report on how to accomplish this, send a self-addressed stamped envelope to *The Caretaker Gazette*, P.O. Box 5887, Carefree, AZ 85377.

33. Give a lecture aboard ship and cruise free. For travelersinterested in being speakers for cruise lines, the most popular areas are motivational/inspirational, special interest, ship's destination/port of calls, historians (maritime or cultural), naturalist/wildlife experts, art, and how-to, such as "how to play bridge better." Taboo topics include health, culinary demonstrations, cosmetics, entertainment, or anything that will detract from a passenger's enjoyment or the ship's own services or features.

When applying, send a typed resume outlining your credentials to the Entertainment Director. Do not call or e-mail. Also, submit a current photograph, three professional references, and a proposal or sample video. You will not be notified unless selected and your materials will not be returned. Typically, you are required to give one 45–55 minute lecture per day. In return, you will receive a free cruise and some cruise lines even pay speakers a small daily stipend. The key is to be perky or outgoing, and to be an expert on the subject matter you are presenting, whether it's wildlife of Costa Rica, Renaissance art, maritime history, or stress management.

Compass Speakers is a lecture booking agency for many cruise lines. 757 SE 17th Street, PMB 308; Ft. Lauderdale, FL 33316. Other useful Web sites include www.CruiseshipJob.com, www.ShipJobs.com, www.CruiseJobLink.com, or www.Cruisecareer.com.

34. Participate in The Gentleman Host Program and cruise free if you're interested in being a dance partner or instructor. Contact the cruise lines or see www.workingvacation.com for more information on the dance host program and which ships use them.

TIP: If you're interested in cruising *and* earning academic credit, contact the Continuing Education Inc./University at Sea (800-926-3775), Institute for Shipboard Education, 811 William Pitt Union, University of Pittsburgh, Pittsburgh, PA 15260. Or, contact Lifelong Learning, Inc. for information on "worldwide journeys for the inquisitive traveler" to exciting places, such as Antarctica, Africa, and the Pacific Rim. 101 Columbia, Suite 150, Aliso, Viejo, CA 92656. Holland America Cruise Line offers University at Sea programs. 800-926-3775. www.universityatsea.com.

◆   ◆   ◆

How To Get Paid To Travel

35. Become a referral agent and receive commissions for everyone you refer to the company that books travel. Agents make hundreds of dollars every year by referring friends, co-workers, family, and acquaintances to a travel agency. The best part is that you don't have to go to travel agent school or pay for expensive software programs. The travel agency does everything. All you do is hand out business cards (usually printed by the agency and sent to referral agents, free of charge). If the company doesn't supply them, have some printed at a local copy shop or Kinko's for less than $20 for 1,000 cards. If someone books a trip, you receive 5–10 percent (depending on what your arrangement is with the company) on airfare, cruises, and tour packages. Most travel agencies will accept referral agents because they don't risk anything. Cruise.com and sailandsave.com are a couple of Internet companies that utilize referral agents. Look in the yellow pages of a local phone book for "travel agents" or contact one of the agencies included in this publication.

36. Another option is to be an outside agent for a travel agency. This involves signing a simple contract or agreement with the company, authorizing you to use the agency's IATA or CLIA number to book travel. There are no quotas or fees, or special equipment or software necessary. Booking forms, provided by the agency, are processed through the agency. Your responsibility is to make reservations, give a credit card number to the vendor or send in the client's check to the agency, and dispense the tickets forwarded to you by the agency. The agency sends your cut of the commission after it receives payment from the vendor, which is usually 30–60 days after travel is completed. You can earn money just for booking airline tickets, hotel rooms, tours, cruises, resort stays, car rentals, and vacation packages for yourself, family, friends, and co-workers. Commissions issued are reported to the IRS by the travel agency. I recommend purchasing liability insurance through the agency. It is less than $100 a year and a prudent investment. Additionally, *you* can also take advantage of being a travel agent to obtain reduced rates on land tours, cruises, airfares, and hotel rooms. You won't get commissions on anything you were granted a travel agent rate on.

One company that utilizes outside agents is Global Travel International (GTI), a multi-national travel agency. Commissions received from airlines, cruise lines, hotels, car rental agencies, and tour operators are split 50/50 with GTI. Another perk is toll-free reservations, 24-hour a day/seven days a week, plus worldwide electronic ticketing. The drawback is that GTI charges for their program, which includes the start-up kit, official travel agent photo ID, and a GTI agency identification number needed to receive commissions. There's a money back guarantee. 888-699-0882. www.GTIWeb.com.

Agencies are more reluctant to use outside agents than referral agents because they have to give out confidential information, including IATA and CLIA numbers, as well as private booking phone numbers and passwords to travel agents-only areas on Web sites. However, agencies are increasingly relying on outside agents. Cruises Only, one of the world's largest cruise agencies (877-714-4072 or 800-211-2936), welcomes outside agents. Keep an eye out for opportunities and information on Web sites, look in the Yellow Pages under "Travel Agencies," or contact a company listed in this reference. I've found that it never hurts to ask and often it *pays* to inquire.

If you're interested in becoming a full-time travel agent, American Express Travel Services hires trainees and leisure travel counselors. www.staffing.americanexpress.com/travelcareers.

37. Anyone 18–80 willing to work four hours a day can stay free on St. John's Island in the U.S. Virgin Islands at the Maho Bay Camp. Stay in lovely, tented bungalows and receive 40 percent off meals. For more information or to obtain an application, write Attention: Four-Hour Worker Program, Box 310, Cruz Bay, Virgin Islands 00831. No telephone queries.

38. For those interested in teaching, opportunities are tremendous. Spend a summer anywhere in the world teaching English. There are numerous programs that pay anyone who has a Bachelor of Arts (B.A.) degree in any subject, from any college or university, to teach English a few hours a day. Popular places include China, Italy, Argentina, Thailand, and Spain. New World Teachers. 888-GO-TEACH. www.goteach.com.

Council on International Educational Exchange (CIEE) offers numerous teaching opportunities. 800-2COUNCIL. www.counciltravel.com or www.ciee.org. e-mail: info@ciee.org. In addition to teaching jobs, CIEE also has information on paid internships and work programs in France, Ireland, Germany, Canada, China, Australia, New Zealand, and Costa Rica. For about $20, teachers or students can purchase cards that provide insurance (including emergency evacuations), a 24-hour toll-free help number, and discounts on museums, airfare, and more.

39. Go on sabbatical and let someone else pick up the tab for your much-needed vacation. Teachers aren't the only ones eligible for sabbaticals. They are provided by many companies and foundations. In fact, one of every three Fortune 500 companies offers them. Additionally, many companies now offer sabbaticals for employees who have worked for them for at least five years. Grants are now being awarded for sabbaticals. I recently read in the local newspaper that Z. Smith Reynolds Foundation gave a $15,000 grant to a public benefits specialist with Central Carolina Legal Services for a three month sabbatical. The article cited other examples, including a couple of local law firms that award partners, who have worked there 10 years, three month sabbaticals. Participants are free to use the money and time however they see fit. Employees at nonprofit agencies are sometimes entitled to sabbaticals, but they must commit to remain with the organization for one year after the sabbatical. Because jobs in the public sector usually cannot pay as well as those in private sector, sabbaticals are used as employment perks.

Check to see if area foundations offer sabbatical grants. If not, check with your boss to see if your company has a program or might be interested in starting one. Present a carefully detailed plan of how your responsibilities would be handled during your absence and that you would be willing to help cover another employee's duties when she's on sabbatical. Volunteers, interns, and other employees are typically used to handle duties of people on sabbatical. Point out to your employer that it would help prevent job burn-out, thereby increasing employee retention, morale, and productivity. Circulate a petition to show your boss how many employees support such a program.

40. Make the government "employ" you. The National Park Service takes applications for paid part-time and full-time employees, as well as volunteer positions, in national parks such as Yosemite, Badlands, and Grand Canyon. Park staffs range from 7–630 (peak season in Yellowstone). These are seasonal and permanent positions that range from administrative to park rangers. Volunteer lighthouse "keepers" and tour guides are needed at many locations. Duties include greeting visitors, leading tours, picking up beach debris, and keeping an eye on the property. In exchange, volunteers live free in a former lighthouse keeper's dwelling, receive a food stipend, and mileage reimbursement (when appropriate).

Volunteer positions are hard to get, particularly in the Southwest and Alaska due to the large number of applicants. These well-sought after jobs include historians, concessions, visitor assistants, campground rangers, lifeguards, and naturalists. Seasonal Employment Program, Human Resources, National Park Service, P.O. Box 37127, Mail Stop 2225, Washington, DC 20013. 202-208-5074. http://nps.org or www.nps.gov/pub_aff/jobs.htm.

41. For those who are good with children, au pair programs are a great way to see the world. Au pairs(nannies) are given a round-trip airline ticket, small salary, and room and board. Often, they receive other perks, such as extra paid time-off, use of a family vehicle, and travel expenses when traveling with the family. Interviewing and placing qualified applicants into au pair positions, can earn participants free travel. I know an elementary school teacher who does this part-time at night and on

weekends and has earned a free Caribbean cruise and trip to Sweden. EF Au Pair (International Live-in Child Care. 800-333-6056. www.efaupair.com.

The American Institute for Foreign Study is another way to work and study, abroad. Live with a European family and take care of their kids for up to 30 hours per week, and study a foreign language or culture in Paris, London, or Madrid. 800-727-AIFS. www.aifs.com.

42. Take part in a work program. Antarctic Support Associates, a Colorado-based company, hires approximately 1,000 men and women every year to go to Antarctica. The company receives about 10,000 applications every year because the pay is so good. The well-paid employees spend four months maintaining and readying three of the American research stations for scientists who will return in the summer. Each station has a gym, bar, church, bowling alley, and even a museum. All kinds of workers are needed, such as cooks, plumbers, administrators, dentists, electricians, and pilots.

Alaska has some work programs where lodges and hotels pay employees a small wage, as well as room and board, during their tourist season. Additionally, there are better paying employment opportunities, ranging from banking to seafood industries. Alaska Tourist Board, P.O. Box 11801, Juneau, AK 99811. 907-465-2010. www.jobs.state.ak.us. e-mail: GoNorth@ commerce.state.ak.us. Alaska Jobs Center's Web site has hundreds of listings, including teaching positions and government employment, as well as links to other job opportunities and information regarding living in Alaska. www.ilovealaska.com/alaskajobs. A good place to look for planning Alaskan travel is www. myalaskavacation.com.

The British Universities North America Club (BUNAC) is a nonprofit organization that has helped U.S. and U.K. students and recent graduates (must be at least 18 years old) participate in work and travel programs in North America, England, Scotland, Wales, Northern Ireland, and Australia for up to one year. BUNAC participants receive work permits, which can otherwise be difficult to obtain. I participated in the BUNAC program when I was in college and highly recommend it. They provide a great support system and help find employment and a place to live. BUNAC USA, P.O. Box 430, Southbury, CT 06488. 800-GO-BUNAC or 203-264-0901. www.bunac.org. Or, BUNAC UK, Incoming Programs, 16 Bowling Green Lane, London, ECIR 0QH England. (0171) 251-3472. e-mail: wib@bunac.org.uk.

43. Get a temporary or permanent job that takes you overseas. A good source for temporary overseas employment is British organization, PayAway. www.payaway.co.uk. e-mail: jobs@payaway .co.uk. Underground Travel helps travelers find work and volunteer opportunities around the world. 8330 Rayford Drive, L.A., CA 90045. 310-670-5968. www.undergroundtravel.com. e-mail: info@underground.com.

Another source for U.S. and worldwide employment, as well as useful links, is www.dbm.com/jobguide/atoz.html. For numerous work/study/travel programs worldwide, check out www.istc.org or www.gotajob.com. A good book on the subject is *Work Abroad: The Complete Guide to Finding a Job Overseas* (Transitions Abroad Publishing, 800-293-0373). It provides names, addresses, good Web sites, and much more.

44. Many of the companies listed in this reference are often looking for seasonal employees. U.S. dude ranches need extra help in the summertime. Vista Verde Ranch (20 minutes north of Steamboat Springs, Colorado) offers white-water rafting, hot-air ballooning, horseback riding, fly fishing, rock climbing, and more. The dude ranch always needs winter and summer help, such as housekeepers, waitstaff, kid's wranglers, and fishing guides. P. O. Box 465, Steamboat Springs, CO 80477. 800-526-7433 or 970-879-3858. e-mail: jobs@vistaverde.com.

Club Med has resorts all over the world and they are always in need of employees, from "gentle organizers" to tennis instructors. 800-CLUBMED or call 561-337-6660 to hear a pre-recorded message instructing how to apply for employment. www.clubmed.com.Green Tortoise Adventures was recently seeking trip leaders and bus drivers. Backroads was looking to hire leaders for their biking adventures.

Log on to www.seasonalemployment.com or www.jobsinparadise for 200,000+ summer job listings in U.S., Canada, Caribbean, and South Pacific. If you're interested and feel qualified, submit your resume to any of the companies listed in this book.

45. Contact the International Tour Management Institute), which offers classes in several U.S. cities on how to become a tour escort. 800-442-4864 or 415-957-9489. www.itmitourtraining.com.

46. Global Ship Services hires maintenance personnel, hosts, youth counselors, deck hands, and cleaning personnel for most major cruise lines. To apply, send a resume and recent photograph, along with a cover letter outlining your qualifications to Personnel-Shipboard Operations of each cruise line that interests you. Or, contact Global Ship Services at 305-374-8649. Cruise lines offer many skilled and unskilled positions and hire all ages and nationalities. It's hard work, but employees are paid to travel and typically receive free room and board.

47. Apply directly to the cruise lines. Cruise lines that accept unsolicited resumes are:

Cunard/Seabourn Cruise Lines, 6100 Blue Lagoon
Drive, Suite 400, Miami, Florida 33126.
Holland America Cruise Line, 300 Elliot Avenue,
West Seattle, WA 98129.
Royal Caribbean International Cruise Line,
1050 Caribbean Way, Miami, Florida 33132.

48. Another possibility is serving as crew on a charter or private yacht. There are thousands of yachts worldwide, each employing between four and 25 crew members. Positions vary from deck hands, which make about $26,000 annually, to stewards/stewardesses who make between $24,000–$40,000 per year. On chartered yachts, the crew also splits a tip, which is 15 percent of the price of the charter. This equals additional earnings of $1,000–$2,000 per charter, and the average charter boat does 20–30 charter jobs annually. Room and board is free on charters or private yachts. Yacht Crew, Inc. places applicants (with charter or private yachts), for a one-time/lifetime fee of $40. Yacht Crew Inc., 1323 SE 17th Street, Suite 110, Ft. Lauderdale, Florida 33316. www.yacht-crew.com. e-mail: info@yacht-crew.com.

49. Get paid to ski. Ski resorts are always looking for employees. Positions range from wait staff to ski instructors. Perks include free or cheap skiing for employees and a chance to be at resorts and in resort towns that would otherwise be prohibitive in cost. Contact state tourism bureaus to obtain information on ski resorts and then apply to the ones you like best. These Web sites are a must see for people seeking skiing and snowboarding jobs and information: www.skiingthenet.com (resumes can be posted online and site also list seasonal jobs at guest ranches, rafting companies, outfitters, national parks, and resorts) or www.fresh-tracks.com (ski jobs in Europe and links to useful resources.

Gogebic Community College offers a Ski Area Management Program if you're interested in making a career out of being a ski bum! Seriously, the school has placed people at every major ski area in the country. For more information, contact the school at 906-932-4231. www.gogebic.cc.mi.us.

50. Travelsearch.com is a directory filled with travel-related data. This reference is also full of hundreds of Web sites that collectively provide information on every conceivable aspect of travel. Use and enjoy!

TIP: 10 Ways to Get the Best Deals at Ski Resorts for Skiing,
Snow-tubing, and/or Snowboarding

1. Early or late in the season merits best prices. Mid-November to mid-December and the fourth week of March until the season ends. Some resorts even toss in free lift tickets. Inquire about seasonal specials, dining discounts, and talk to locals upon arrival. Residents know where to find good food at good prices. Bargains can be found—even in Aspen!

2. Think "packages." Buying airfare, lift tickets, transfers, meals, accommodations, and equipment rental, as a package as opposed to individually will equate to significant savings. Check for packages offered by companies, airlines, and ski lodges by looking at brochures and magazines, travel agencies, on the Internet (including airline Web sites), and resorts' central reservations service. Two good companies to consider are Ski Vacation Planners (800-822-6754) and Moguls Ski & Snowboard Tours (800-666-4857.

3. Shy away from lodging on the slopes. You'll pay less by staying in a hotel or resort that offers shuttle services to the slopes. If you rent a condo, you often get a better weekly rate than a hotel or resort. Also, a condo has a kitchen so you can save money on meals, and many have laundry facilities. AMI News has a Web site that reveals hot deals, ski packages, lodging, ski reports, and prizes, such as free trips and lift tickets. www.aminews.com. The best deals are at hostels, such as Mount Mansfield Hostel in Stowe, Vermont (802-253-4010), Glenwood Springs Hostel at Aspen, Colorado (800-946-7835), Fireside Inn in Breckenridge, Colorado (970-453-6456, www.firesideinn. com), Davison St. Guest House in Mamoth Mountain, California (619-544-9093), and Crested Butte International Hostel in Crested Butte, Colorado (888-389-0588). See Chapter Six for more information on hostels and condo rentals). Also, buy lift tickets at a ski shop or on the Internet instead of waiting to buy them at the ski resort. They will cost quite a bit more at the resort.

4. Get a group together to save big bucks. Most ski resorts offer 10–20 percent group discounts on life tickets, rentals, and lessons. Group rates are also cheaper at hotels, or share a condo with friends or family reduces costs greatly. If you can't get a group together, join a ski club (average cost $30 annually). It's a great way to meet fellow skiers and save big money. To find ski clubs in your area, contact the National Ski Council Federation. www.skifederation.org.

5. Young and old skiers are entitled to the biggest savings. Children 12 and under can usually ski or snowboard for well under $20 a day. Anyone over 65 skis free at most resorts, including Telluride, Beaver Creek, and Winter Park.

6. Look for Internet promotions and specials, including last minute deals. Good sites include www.skimag.com, www.skitown.com, and www.ski-guide.com.

7. If you do much skiing, a season pass is definitely the way to go. If you're new to skiing, don't buy a pass until you know that you will go often enough to justify the cost.

8. You'll need skiing attire to stay warm on the slopes. If you're new to the sport, borrow ski clothes rather than buy them—at least until you decide how much skiing you intend to do. Always buy off-season when the prices are better.

9. Pick cheaper resorts. Upscale skiing "hotspots" like Vail and Aspen cost significantly more than other places. Top Ten Bargain Ski Resorts:

Brighton Ski Resort, Utah (800-873-5512) www.skibrighton.com.

Ski Santa Fe, New Mexico (800-776-7669) www.skisantafe.com.

Snowbasin, Utah (801-399-1135) www.snowbasin.com.

Silver Creek Resort, Colorado (888-283-7458) www.silvercreek-resort.com.

Targhee, Wyoming (800-827-4433) www.grandtarghee.com.
Alta Ski Area, Utah (801-359-1078) www.altaskiarea.com.
Solitude Mountain Resort, Utah (800-748-4754) www.skisolitude.com.
Bridger Bowl, Montana (800-223-9609) www.bridgerbowl.com.
Schweitzer Mountain Resort, Idaho (800-831-8810) www.schweitzer.com.
Purgatory Resort, Colorado (800-525-0892) www.ski-purg.com.

10. If you're planning on taking your family on a skiing vacation, look for family-friendly resorts. Some of the biggest resorts in Utah offer "Kids Fly, Stay and Ski Free" packages (usually ages 2-11). Southwest Airlines often offers packages. 800-SKI-8365. www.swavacations.com.

◆   ◆   ◆

Chapter Eight--Helpful Travel Resources

Chapter Eight--Helpful Travel Resources

The use of traveling is to regulate imagination by reality, and instead of thinking how things may be, to see them as they are.
Samuel Johnson

Money-Saving Travel Clubs And Resources

Most travel clubs charge annual fees, but members receive substantial discounts on everything from travel insurance to tour packages. Should you join? The answer depends on *your* needs. Joining to save money on hotel rooms or car rental fees is only worthwhile if you will save significantly more than you pay for membership. It doesn't matter if the club promises 50 percent off car rentals if you rarely rent a car while traveling. It's possible that you may save more by joining an organization, such as AAA or AARP. If enrolled in a frequent traveler or points reward program, be sure the hotel participates in the travel club you may be joining. Review what is offered and then decide if membership is right for you.

Adventures On Call is a last-minute travel club that offers discounts on airlines, cruises, tours, restaurants, hotels (up to 50 percent off or second night free), car rentals, and theme parks. 800-638-8976.

Insider Secrets Travel Club offers discounts on airlines, car rentals, cruises, and vacation packages. Free 30-day membership. 888-598-8214. www.insidersecrets.com.

International Travel Club provides savings on airlines, car rentals, vacation packages, dining, hotels, inns, and resorts. www.mytravelclub.com.

Last Minute Travel Club provides savings on worldwide lodging, airlines, cruises, and car rentals. No membership fee. 1249 Boylston Street, #2, Boston, MA 02215. 800-527-8646(LASTMIN) or 617-267-9800. http://Lastminutetravel.com.

Leisureplus offers 50 percent off rooms at more than 3,000 hotels, up to 30 percent off car rental rates, up to 70 percent off condo rates, up to 40 percent off cruises, up to 50 percent off theme park admissions, dining, park guides, flights, and vacation packages. Members receive 5 percent cash back on all travel booked on the LeisurePlus Web site. Free 30-day membership. 800-527-9833. www.leisureplus.com.

TIP: For true golf lovers the Golf Card is a must! This program was created for senior golfers (single or couple membership available). It entitles the bearer to two free 18-hole rounds at any of its 3,500 member golf courses worldwide. Save up to 50 percent on player's fees at additional courses. Also, you are entitled to substantial discounts at 300 international golf resorts and subscription to *Golf Traveler*, which has articles on America's best golf courses. Participants also receive the Quest International Card, which gives significant savings on participating hotels and restaurants, as well as a free Gold Card International Pocket Directory of U.S. and International Courses. 64 Inverness Drive East, P.O. Box 7021, Englewood, CO 80155-7021. 800-321-8269. www.golfcard.com.

Another option is John Jacobs Golf Schools. For about $1,000 a week, golf enthusiasts can stay in one of 32 lovely U.S. resorts and receive five hours per day of golf instruction. Meals included. 7825 E. Redfield Road, Scottsdale, AZ 85260-6977. 800-472-5007 or 602-991-8587. www.jacobsgolf.com.

Liberty Travel Preferred Club grants discounts and upgrades with participating airlines, resorts, cruise lines, hotels, car rental agencies, and more. Membership benefits include deals on limousine service, airport parking, passport photos, and sightseeing admissions. 800-887-1006. www.libertytravel.com.

Moment's Notice Discount Travel Club affords members substantial savings on cruises, car rentals, hotel rooms, airfares, and condo rentals. May book using Web site or 24-hour hotline: 718-621-4548 or 888-241-3366. www.moments-notice.com.

National Travel Club (also called **The Travel Holiday Gold Club**) offers members a one-year subscription to *Travel Holiday* and discounts on cruises, hotels, rental cars, airfares, restaurants, and travel books, as well as some accident insurance. 1633 Broadway, 43rd floor, New York, NY 10019. 888-682-2582 or 212-767-6000.

Prestige Travel Club offers a Discount Dining Card with cash rebates, coupon book, newsletter and e-mail alerts, special offers, and huge savings on hotel rooms, cruises, car rentals, theme parks, tours, and airfare. Free limited one-year membership. www.american-unlimited.com/travelclub.

Sam's Club Travel Services provides members with discounts on hotels/motels, car rentals, cruises, vacation/golf/ski/resort packages, and travel insurance. Sample participators include: Avid, Alamo, Budget, Days Inn, Hyatt, Baymont Inn and Suites, Red Roof Inns, Ramada, Wyndham Hotels & Resorts, Disney Cruise Line, Royal Caribbean, and Princess Cruises. 3901 SE Adams Road, Suite A, Bartlesville, OK 74006. 800-955-SAMS. www.samsclub.com.

Spur Of The Moment Tours And Cruises is for those who can utilize last minute bargains. It offers free newsletters twice a month. 411 N. Harbor Blvd., Suite 302, San Pedro, CA 90230. 800-4-CRUISE or 800-343-1991 or 310-521-1060. e-mail: Spur of@aol.com.

Travel And Leisure offers a travel club that discounts airfares, cruises, and hotels. 1120 Avenue of the Americas, New York, NY 10036. 800-888-8728. www.travelandleisure.com

Worldwide Discount Travel Club provides savings on cruises and all-inclusive tours. 1674 Meridian Avenue, Miami Beach, FL 33139. 305-895-2082.

◆　　◆　　◆

100 Travel-Planning Web Sites

According to a survey conducted by the Travel Industry Association of America, 59 million people use the Internet to research travel and of those, 25 million purchased travel products or services on-line: 84 percent buy airline tickets, 78 percent accommodations, 59 percent rent a car, 51 percent buy admission tickets, 17 percent buy vacation packages, and 8 percent purchase cruises. The Internet is a wonderful tool for researching travel, but it's also one of the biggest sources of fraud in the travel industry fraud. Be sure the company is reputable before giving out credit card information. You may accomplish this by following the advice given in Chapter One: Planning Your Trip.

You should also be aware that if you book airline tickets online and need to change them or get a refund, the problem usually cannot be handled online. You will have to call during business hours and speak to a representative. Additionally, the penalty fee to change a ticket can be considerably higher when purchased through some Internet companies than what the airlines charge. Be sure to inquire before purchasing. Sometimes an Internet company will require a credit card number or free membership enrollment before they will grant access to their Web site because they only want serious inquiries. This is accomplished by filling out an electronic profile and receiving a password. If providing your credit card number makes you apprehensive, don't do it.

For those of you who rely solely on the Internet for travel bargains and information—don't! In case I haven't said it enough, it is a wonderful tool but travel planning should include perusing brochures at a travel agency, talking to friends and co-workers, looking through travel magazines, and calling the airlines to find out what hotel and air packages and discount programs are currently being offered.

There are thousands of travel-related Web sites. I have included the ones listed below because they are user-friendly and they have "stood the test of time." As anyone who has dealt much with the Internet can attest, URLs frequently move, are inaccessible for who knows why, or simply disappear. The sites provided here have been around for a long time so I feel confident they will be useful *and* available. In addition to these sites, you may also use the search engines below and enter keywords such as travel, cruises, or tour operators. Additionally, browsers can sign up for free e-mailers and electronic newsletters, even catalogs and brochures, at many of these Web sites.

America Online	www.aol.com
Excite	www.excite.com
GeoCities	www.geocities.com
Go Network	www.go.com
Hot Mail	www.hotmail.com
Lycos	www.lycos.com
Microsoft	www.microsoft.com
Microsoft Network	www.msn.com
Netscape	www.netscape.com
Yahoo!	www.yahoo.com

♦ FYI: Internet usage doubles nearly every 100 days and the number of people using the Internet to make travel plans has tripled in the last three years to 85 million. Online travel, which is the biggest Internet business category, will reach $30 billion by 2003, according to the Travel Industry Association.

For travel guidebooks, go to a local bookstore or use online booksellers **Amazon.com, Barnesandnoble.com** or **www.Borders.com.** Sign up for free e-mailers announcing new travel books. It is even possible to request specific types of books, such as "notify me about adventure travel essays written by women."

www.travelocity.com is owned by BTI Americas, one of the three largest travel agencies in the United States, and it recently merged with Preview Travel). Winner of the Webby Award for best Internet travel site. It is one of the biggest general travel information sites, It lists discounts, last-minute deals, airfares, destination guides, and maps of airplanes so passengers can choose their seat.

www.expedia.com offers trip planning research and booking for many vendors, including airlines. It offers Hotel Price Matcher service. Input the price you're willing to pay, dates, and type of hotel, and you'll soon be notified if a match has been found. One caveat, Expedia relies on the hotel's own rating and listing of its amenities for the overall rating. Refunds are not given once rooms are booked.

www.galileo.com provides information on airlines, hotels, car rental agencies. TRIP.com has been bought by Galileo and is part of this Web site.

www.tripadvisor.com provides invaluable planning information. Select destinations and get information on hotels, attractions, and more.

www.yahoo.com/recreation/travel is a good place to start if you don't know where to go on the Internet. It offers general travel tips and information on everything from backpacking to vacation contest giveaways.

www.travelroads.com has information on cruises, specials, and tour operators. Browsers may input destination, activity, and special interest, and a list of suitable operators will be presented.

www.1travel.com has extensive offerings and an easy-to-navigate Web site. This company has something for every traveler, from Europe for independent travelers to vacation packages in the South Pacific.

www.fodors.com can be used to gather information or to reserve cars, hotels, and airline tickets.

www.americanexpress.com lists last-minute travel bargains, as well as vacation specials, travel resources, and offers online booking for car rentals, airfare, and hotel rooms.

www.frommers.com is brought to you by travel expert Arthur Frommer. It offers information on everything from vacation ideas to road trips.

www.things4travel.com is a good source for affordable travel books, maps, luggage, and accessories.

www.spafinder.com is for those looking for a spa vacation. Its site reveals specials and discounts. Spafinder also offers a free magazine published four times a year, and a directory.

www.ResortVacationsToGo.com is a clearinghouse that reveals great deals on all-inclusive resort vacations worldwide, including Club Med, SuperClubs, Breezes, Allegro, SweptAway, and Sandals.

www/travelweb.com is an online booking service for flights and accommodations.

www.izon.com is mainly for independent travelers seeking information on hostels and other types of low-cost lodging. There's also advice, tips, and links for backpackers.

www.travelscape.com provides general travel information, specials, airline and hotel bookings, and free travel contests. Travelscape also provides a "No Risk" reservation guarantee.

www.priceline.com allows consumers to input how much they are willing to spend and soon Priceline will let you know if they have found a hotel room, rental car, or airfare for that price. This free service also includes specials.

www.Travelagentspecials.com has worldwide trips and cruises for singles to adventure travelers. It discloses good deals on sports-oriented travel, Disney vacations, beach and sun resorts, and more.

www.LastMinuteTravel.com reveals last minute airfares, car rentals, lodging, cruises, and tour packages. The best part is that you can enter what you're looking for and an e-mail will be sent to you when the request is met. LastMinute also has information on exchange rates, weather, maps, city guide, maps, and FAQs.

www.go4less.com specializes in last-minute deals, from all-inclusive vacations to airline specials. Go4less even has a free on-line travel club anyone can join. Participation in this club entitles members to free travel if they make referrals.

www.lastminute.com offers everything from train trips to tour packages. Most depart from London, but many of the deals are worth the added airfare. Speaking of airfare, the company has an auction area of their Web site that includes low airfares and hotels. Also, Lastminute promises a "lowest price guarantee." This means they match the price, assuming you find a better deal.

http://www.11thhourvacations.com is for travelers who can go on short notice. Lead times on vacation package and cruises vary, from less than 15 days to more than a month. 11th-Hour Vacations says their fares are 40–70 percent off brochure rates. The site also has information on travel warnings, insurance, passport, and currencies.

www.site59.com has last-minute weekend deals, fly and drive, sports adventures, resorts, and cultural excursions, from major U.S. cities.

www.tourscan.com is a clearinghouse for all-inclusive deals to the Caribbean.
www.wtg-online.com is a great Web site that provides facts and overviews of a country, its passport and visa requirements, public holidays, accessibility, travel insurance, and more. World Trade Guide also has city guides and information on skiing, airports, attractions, weather, tours, events, and vacation packages.

www.travel.state.gov/passport_services.html takes a passport applicant through the process required to acquire/renew a passport. Applications can be downloaded.

www.senior.com has information on travel for seniors.

www.studyabroad.com is a commercial directory with lists of language, study and work programs.

www.freedomtrek.com offers maps, facts, tips, hostel information, rail passes, travel advisories, weather forecasts, and work/study programs.

www.longitudebooks.com specializes in adventure travel books.

www.crazydogtravel.com has information for backpackers on hostels, gear, destinations, packing, planning, money, and passports and visas.

www.lonelyplanet.com produces many travel guides and their Web site has photos, message boards, resources, and advice.

www.Hadami.com is an eBookstore that carries travel-related publications, ranging from travel essays to niche guidebooks.

www.citysearch.com has specifics on restaurants, events, and entertainment for most major U.S. and international cities.

www.whatsgoingon.com list events that are happening wherever you are going in the world.

www.icruise.com is a cruise consolidator.

www.bid1travel.com is a cruise consolidator.

www.cruises-n-more.com is a cruise consolidator.

www.cruise411.com is a cruise consolidator.

www.cruise.com is another Internet cruise consolidator.

www.flightarrivals.com lets browsers know if a flight is arriving or departing on time. On commercial flights within the U.S. and Canada. Information is updated every four minutes. If you don't have the flight number handy, enter the city/airport and a list of all flights within two hours of the time you enter will appear.

www.farechase.com searches all major travel sites and comes up with the best fares for the destinations, dates, and departure cities that were requested.

http://flight.thetrip.com allows travelers to enter a flight number (or city and time) and the airline, and Flight Tracker will reveal how far the flight is from the airport and its estimated arrival time.

www.ITAsoftware.com can be used to enter the airport you wish to depart from and the dates and this site will almost instantly provide you with numerous flight options for United States and Canada.

www.safewaytravel.com is an airline ticket consolidator for U.S. and international destinations.

www.Orbitz.com is owned by five airlines (American, Continental, Delta, Northwest, and United), but carries fares and information for roughly 25 airlines.

www.Hotwire.com is owned by several airlines (American, America West, Continental, Northwest, United, and US Airways). Travelers enter where and when they want to travel and the airlines respond with their best deals. The only drawback is that you will not know the airline until booking.

www.bestfares.com can be used to find airfare specials, hotels, and rental cars.

www.Lowestfare.com provides low airfares, car rentals, and cruises.

www.webflyer.com is for people seeking find airfare specials, hotels, and rental cars.

www.1800airtravel.com promises low airfares.

www.bedandbreakfast.com has photos and descriptions, as well as links to nearly 25,000 bed-and-breakfasts worldwide. It notes establishments that offer special rates and packages.

www.hostels.com has everything you ever wanted to know about hostelling, including a directory of 5,000 worldwide hostels.

www.FreeCampgrounds.com reveals places where campers can legally park and stay, free of charge. These are not campgrounds, despite what the name implies.

www.cyberrentals.com can be used to find houses and apartment rentals in the U.S. and worldwide.

www.vacationspot.com is another Web site that has 25,000 rental properties at 4,000 worldwide destinations.

www.roadsideamerica.com is the site for those looking for something out-of-the-ordinary to see and do in America. Just type in the state and watch with amazement at what comes up!

www.geocities.com/TheTropics/2442/database.html is offered by The Database of Travel Helpers. If you would like to talk to someone who resides in the area you'll be visiting, log on to this site for a database of volunteer travel helpers. This is a free service that provides names and e-mail addresses of persons willing to answer questions and talk about what to expect where you'll be traveling. The database is categorized by region, country, and town. Anyone with helpful information is permitted to join at no charge.

www.medicineplanet.com allows you to type in your zip code and destinations to find the nearest health clinic where you can receive inoculations for upcoming travel. MedicinePlanet also informs travelers which inoculations are needed for where they are going, as well as risk and diseases.

www.travlang.com reveals important phrases for most countries, even pronunciations, gadgets, and resources.

www.experienceispa.com is affiliated with International Spa Association and shows 1,400+ facilities in 48 countries, ranging from day spas to resorts. Nifty feature is the "FAQs," which is a must see for people who are unfamiliar with spa retreats.

www.travelroads.com is a huge adventure travel directory that lists over 6,000 tours from 400 companies.

www.outahere.com lists travel and events for the intrepid and environmentally friendly, such as ecotourism, adventure tours, activities and organizations.

www.playbill.com provides theater listings for New York (Broadway and off-Broadway), London, Canada, Brazil, and summer stock across U.S. It can also be used to purchase tickets to the posted shows.

www.oanda.com shows 164 daily exchange rates. Input codes shown for money conversions you are interested in, and within seconds it will show you the most up-to-date money conversion.

www.xe.net/currency/ tells what the dollar is currently worth where you'll be traveling to, so you'll know how far your money will go.

wwwmapsonus.com allows users to obtain customized maps, Yellow Pages, routes, and weather information.

www.delorme.com created free customized maps. Browsers will be asked some questions, such as if the shortest route is desired and what speed (average) you'll be going. Directions will appear on the screen after this information has been entered, as well as maps and drive-time estimates.

www.mapquest.com gives travelers door-to-door or city-to-city directions. Users can find anything from restaurants to ATMs.

www.mapblast.com provides door-to-door instructions to U.S. and Canadian destinations.

maps.yahoo.com gives travelers directions for requested restaurants in most major U.S. cities.

www.subwaynavigator.com has information and directions for subways around the world.

www.zagat.com has guides to 20,000 major U.S. and international restaurants.

www.weather.com is the official Web site of The Weather Channel. Type in the city name and get a weather report.

www.intellicast.com offers up-to-the-minute reports on driving, skiing, and golf conditions, worldwide.

TIP: From Mid-July to August, bargains can be found in New York City. Travelers can get hotel rooms and theater tickets (www.playbill.com) to most Broadway shows for half price, as well as discounts on attractions (including city tours) and shopping. For more information on cheap lodging, contact 1-800-NY-Hotels (694-6835) or www.1800nyhotels.com. The company has more than 100 listings and discounts up to 70 percent.. Or, check out Urban Ventures. The company rents nearly 800 apartments. 212-594-5650. www.nyurbanadventures.com. A Hospitality Company offers more than 250 apartments and provides continental breakfast for stays of a week or less. 212-965-1102. www.hospitalityco.com. All of these companies offer apartments throughout the city, including Manhattan and rates start as low as $99 per night.

For one week every summer, the restaurant association offers big discounts. Dine at places you normally wouldn't be able to afford! For $20.01, patrons can enjoy three-course meals (lunches) at one of approximately 100 participating restaurants. Many of these same restaurants will continue this special deal throughout August. Additionally, Big Apple Greeters, a volunteer organization of true New Yorkers, gives visitors free information and tours of the city, if contacted two weeks prior to visit. 212-669-8159. For more information, or to order the official NYC Guide, contact the New York City Visitor Information Center. 800-692-8474.

www.gosolotravelclub.com is a good resource for solo travelers. Private rooms guaranteed. Small groups.

www.Priceline.com offers unsold inventory from North American and European airlines, hotels, and car rental agencies, which is why they are able to offer such good fares. According to Jens Jurgen at Travel Companions, it is best to avoid using Priceline for airfares because frequent flyer miles are not awarded and participants do not know on the front end whether a flight departs in the morning or evening. However, Priceline offers exceptional hotel (particularly upscale) and car rental rates, once you learn how to best use the system.

These are good **Web sites** (self-explanatory):

> www.rec.bicycles.off-road.com
> www.outdoors.national-park.com
> www.rec.travel.misc.com
> www.rec.skiing.nordic.com
> www.rec.bicycles.com
> www.travel.cruises.com
> www.cruises-n-more.com
> www.boats.cruising.com
> www.rec.travel.europe.com
> www.rec.travel.asia.com
> www.rec.travel.usa-canada.com
> www.travelwithkids.about.com
> www.familytravelguides.com
> www.family.go.com/Categories/Travel
> www.doitcaribbean.com

◆   ◆   ◆

Appendix

HANDY AND IMPORTANT INFORMATION

Name of travel agency and your agent's name_____

Address_____

Phone number_____Emergency toll-free number_____

Credit card account number_____ exp. date_____

Credit card phone number_____
   *Since this information is just in case you have to report a lost or stolen card, include the toll-free
                    phone number located on the back side of a credit card.
Credit card account number_____ exp. date_____

Credit card phone number_____

Credit card account number_____ exp. date_____

Credit card phone number_____

Name as it appears on your Passport_____
Passport number_____ exp. date_____

Airline flight information _____

Airline flight information _____

Airline flight information _____

Airline flight information _____

Hotel/Hostel/Rental information--name/address/phone number/dates of visit:

Tour company information _____

_____

Contact person phone and address_____
*This should be a family member or trusted friend whom you can call day or night in case of an
emergency, such as needing money).
Back-up contact person_____

Names and addresses of people you want to send postcards to:

_____

_____

_____

_____

_____

Additional information _____

_____

_____

_____

Tip: Keep one copy and give a copy to your spouse or traveling companion. Even if one of you loses the sheet or you get separated, the other will have the information. This should be kept on your person so you can fill out immigration forms, present an address to a cab driver, or dash off a postcard.

HANDY "FAVORITE" ADDRESSES

FAVORITE TOUR OPERATORS

_____
_____
_____
_____

FAVORITE AIRLINES

_____
_____
_____
_____

FAVORITE CRUISE LINES

_____
_____
_____
_____

FAVORITE CONSOLIDATORS

_____
_____
_____
_____

FAVORITE ACCOMMODATIONS

_____
_____
_____
_____

FAVORITE UNTOURS AND INDEPENDENT TRAVEL RESOURCES

_____
_____
_____
_____

FAVORITE CAR BROKERS AND RENTAL AGENCIES

_____
_____
_____
_____

FAVORITE RESOURCES

_____
_____
_____
_____

FAVORITE WEB SITES

_____
_____
_____
_____

FAVORITE MONEY-SAVING TIPS

_____
_____
_____
_____

Miscellaneous Phone Numbers

Company/organization_____

Company/organization_____

Company/organization_____

Company/organization_____

Company/organization_____

Company/organization_____

Company/organization_____

Company/organization_____

Company/organization_____

Company/organization_____

WHERE I WANT TO GO IN THE NEXT 1–5 YEARS

Examples:

destination:<u>Costa Rica</u>, <u>adventure (MUST visit Arenal Volcano)</u>, <u><$2,000pp</u> destination:

<u>Mediterranean</u>, <u>cruise</u>, <u><$3,000pp (including air from Chicago)</u>

1. destination_____type of travel_____cost_____
2. destination_____type of travel_____cost_____
3. destination_____type of travel_____cost_____
4. destination_____type of travel_____cost_____
5. destination_____type of travel_____cost_____
6. destination_____type of travel_____cost_____
7. destination_____type of travel_____cost_____
8. destination_____type of travel_____cost_____
9. destination_____type of travel_____cost_____
10. destination_____type of travel_____cost_____

Note: Give this list to your travel agent so she can notify you about good deals to those places

TRIP PLANNING CHECKLIST

√Decide where and how you want to travel, such as sightseeing tour, adventure vacation, or cruise.

√Talk to your travel agent. Find out what she suggests, and get all brochures the agency has on hand.

√Call appropriate tour companies or cruise lines and get their brochures.

√Call consolidators and obtain their best rates.

√Determine which trip is best for you by comparing costs, itineraries, and taking How to Pick the Right Itinerary for Your Interests and Pocketbook Quiz (Chapter One). Get a guidebook on the destination to make sure you know what there is to see and do (most especially what *you* want to see and do) so that you get the most out of the trip. Check with your local library or bookstore for guidebooks and/or videos. Also, many travel agents and AAA offices have videos available for loan.

√Make sure the company you selected is reputable by reviewing Chapter One.

√Ask about discounts for booking early, paying in full ahead of required time, last minute/stand-by fares, reduced rates for membership in organizations such as AAA or AARP, senior fares, government rates, etc.

√Book your fun-filled vacation! Make sure you understand cancellation and refund policies. Find out if any visas are needed for entry [into a country].

√Make sure all your travel documents are up-to-date and won't expire *during* travel, such as credit cards and passports.

√Obtain any necessary immunizations (check with the local Health Department to ensure you get all required *and* recommended inoculations) and visas.

√Buy airline tickets necessary to get to where the trip originates. Check with airlines, consolidators, Internet companies, and your travel agent for the best fare. Refer to Chapter Four for more information.

√Start packing early so you can get anything you need, such as travelers cheques, good walking socks or camera batteries. If you need shoes for the trip, buy them as soon as possible and "break them in." Never start out on a trip with shoes you haven't worn before! Put half your clothing in your spouse's or traveling companion's suitcase, and vice versa. That way, if one suitcase gets lost or delayed, you still have clothes in the other bag. Pack tickets, medications, eyeglasses, cameras, and any other "irreplaceable" items in your carry-on bag, along with a change of clothes and underwear.

√Make any necessary arrangements for your absence, such as boarding pets, stopping newspaper and mail, or getting a house-sitter. Lock the garage and outbuildings, such as storage sheds. Put your lights on a timer so it looks like someone is home. Let a trusted neighbor know that you'll be gone and ask to keep an eye on your house.

If you haven't received all your travel documents by 10 days before departure, call your travel agent or tour operator and make sure they are sending soon and verify they have your correct address. If possible, pick up tickets personally.

√Fill out "Handy Information" Sheet and make a copy.

√Verify flight departure time on the day of your flight.

√Water plants, turn off water, turn down thermostat, turn on answering message, and fill the gas tank of the car you are taking to the airport. Put aside enough money to pay airport parking.

√Consult this checklist ONE LAST TIME before heading out the front door, and have a wonderful adventure!

COMPANY COMPARISON GUIDE

Insert the names of all companies you are considering, and trip cost of each, in the blanks below. Be sure to include "hidden costs," such as port charges, airfare, airport tax, tips, and meals and sightseeing fees NOT included, as well as any discounts afforded. The idea is to get a full picture of what each trip *really* costs.

Example:
Company X   Happy Tours $1,025pp x 2 = $2,050
*includes air from Baltimore, which is only an hour's drive but $110 gas and airport parking, all meals, +$25pp x 2 = $50 for half day XYZ excursion we want = $2,210 total

Company Y   Fun Tours x 2 = $2,050 total
*includes air from New York so have to add another $150pp x 2 = $300 to get to NY and two dinners and lunch on own so factor in at least $50pp x 2 = $100. Total = $2,450.

Company A_____ $_____Trip

_____

Company B_____ $_____Trip

_____

Company C_____ $_____Trip

_____

Company D_____ $_____Trip

_____

Company E_____ $_____Trip

_____

Company F_____ $_____Trip

_____

Company G_____ $_____Trip

_____

Now, compare what's included (such as more tours/better tours, or special deals, such as welcome dinner and party or lecture by noted speaker) that might make one company better than another.

Example:
Company X   <u>Happy Tours</u>   *same sightseeing package as Fun Tours. No extras.*
Company Y   <u>Fun Tours</u>   *farewell party, day trip to castle with wine-tasting, medieval banquet, and private tour of XYZ.*

Company A _____

_____

Company B _____

_____

Company C _____

_____

Company D _____

_____

Company E _____

_____

Company F_____

_____

Company G _____

_____

Now, make your decision based on these comparisons.

Example:
Even though Company X (Happy Tours) costs $240 less than Company Y (Fun Tours), choose Company Y (Fun Tours) because it offered many extras we really wanted.

Company Chosen_____

NOTES

NOTES

NOTES

American Institute for Foreign Study, 144
American Orient Express, 62
American Society Of Travel Agents, 46
American Society of Travel Agents (ASTA), 5, 6
American Trans Air (ATA), 86
American Wilderness Experience (AWE), 25, 33
American-International Homestays (AIH), 124
Amerisuites, 112
Amtrak, 62, 63, 137
An Advisory on Ticket Consolidators, 80
Annette's Adventures, 37
Apple Vacations, 25
Archaeological Digs, 130
Archaeological Institute Of America, 130
Around-the-World Air Consolidators, 81
Asia-Hotels.com, 111
At Home Abroad, 122
Atelier Bez, 25, 33
ATS Tours, 58
au pair, 143
Austrail Flexi-Pass, 65
Austrian Airlines, 18, 87
Austrian Railpass, 65
AutoEurope, 69
Avis, 70, 71

Background Notes, 73
Backroads, 25, 33, 42, 144
Bar H Dude & Guest Ranch, 26, 33
Barclay International Group, 122
Barge Cruises, 101, 105
Baymont Inn and Suites, 112, 152
Baz Bus, 68
Beaches, 26, 34
Benelux Tourail Pass, 65
Best Inns, 112

Best Western, 112
Better Business Bureau, 7, 13, 124
Better Business Bureau(BBB), 7
Big Five Tours And Expeditions, 42
Breakaway Adventures, 26
Breezes, 30, 35, 154
Brendan Tours, 20, 58
Bridgestreet Accommodations, 122
Britireland Pass, 65
British Airways, 54, 83, 87, 88, 138
British Universities North America Club (BUNAC), 144
Britrail Pass And Britrail Flexipass, 65
Britrail Southeast Pass, 65
BTI Americas, 4, 153
BTI Americas/Executive BTI Travel, 4
Budget, 40, 58, 70, 71, 112, 120, 152
Budgethotels.Com, 110
Bulgaria, 65
Bus passes, 67
Busabout, 67
Buses, 62, 67

CampAlaska Tours, 26
Camper Clubs of America, 118
campgrounds, 112, 118, 125, 157
Camping and RVing, 117, 124
Campus Lodgings Guide, 125
CanaBus Tours, 68
Canadian Airlines International, 88
car broker, 68, 82
car rental agencies, 3, 48, 68, 69, 70, 71, 115, 138, 139, 142, 152, 154
Carlson Wagonlit, 4, 20, 58
Carlson Wagonlit Travel, 4
Cathay Pacific Airways, 88
CBT Tours, 26
Central Holidays, 20, 58
Central Reservation Service, 111
charitable organizations, 130
charter flight, 80
Cheap Tickets, 80